A SOMERSET MISCELLANY

A SOMERSET MISCELLANY

Robert Dunning

With illustrations by Alan Boobyer

Somerset Books

First published in Great Britain in 2005

British Library Cataloguing-in-Publication Data
A CIP record for this title is available from the British Library

ISBN 0 86183 427 5

SOMERSET BOOKS
Somerset Books is a partnership between
DAA Halsgrove Ltd and Somerset County Council
(Directorate of Culture and Heritage)
www.somerset.gov.uk

Halsgrove House
Lower Moor Way
Tiverton, Devon EX16 6SS
Tel: 01884 243242
Fax: 01884 243325
email: sales@halsgrove.com
website: www.halsgrove.com

Printed and bound by
The Cromwell Press, Trowbridge

CONTENTS

Preface   5

1   Somerset titles   7
2   Three small discoveries   19
3   Civil servants   27
4   Rebels, rogues and traitors   37
5   Somerset men abroad   49
6   Inspiring religion   61
7   Doing deals   71
8   Their records are our history   83
9   Food, feasting and conviviality   95
10 Invasion threats   104
11 All about money   115
12 Leisure pursuits   125
13 Crossing the Atlantic   136
14 Travelling in Somerset   145
15 Three men of the cloth   157
16 Day school and night school   165
17 Modern war   173

Select Index   181

PREFACE

This collection of historical pieces began life as a series of articles commissioned by the late Jack Rayfield and Roy Smart, successively editors of the *Somerset Magazine*, between 1991 and 2001 and for Jenny Nicholls for the *Somerset Life* in 2001 and 2002. I am grateful to Roy Smart, and Anita Newcombe of *Somerset Life* for their ready agreement to publish versions of those articles which appeared first in their magazines. They have been now grouped into chapters sharing a common theme but without their original titles. The articles came into being sometimes as a result of questions asked by correspondents, at other times from unusual sources found by colleagues or by myself in the course of normal duties, from family documents, from current events and, on one occasion through the discovery of an item of R.A.F. cutlery found in a garden. Their common theme is Somerset and its rich history, the many curious people who have come within its borders, the stirring events which have taken place here over the centuries. The illustrations, by Alan Boobyer, are one man's reaction to phrases used or situations portrayed in words, and go to prove that history is not boring but entertaining.

1

SOMERSET TITLES

"Edmund... marching through Glastonbury, breaking open the prison at Wells..."

The earldom of Wessex in the years before the Norman Conquest was an acknowledgement of political power, but in the course of time titles came to be conferred by kings and queens as rewards for support, political, military and sometimes personal. With them went membership of the upper House of Parliament, the House of Lords, land, government, influence. Curiously, Somerset was one of the least aristocratic of counties in that its main landowners were not peers but instead highly respectable and persistent families without titles, but still over the last thousand years or so heiresses of its fertile soil have attracted noble suitors, royal properties have been given, if only temporarily, to members of the family, and in one case Somerset provided a safe haven for a short while for a royal duke trying desperately to escape his creditors.

The earldom of Wessex, conferred in 1999 on Prince Edward, the Queen's youngest son, is an ancient title by any reckoning, so ancient that the compilers of that great work *The Complete Peerage* decided not to include it. It was an Anglo-Saxon concept rather than a Norman one, and in the sense that it had been used at that time it was rather a political post than a title of honour.

That is not to say that the revived title is either an anachronism or meaningless. The people of Wessex, if no others, were duly delighted about such regional recognition after so long a silence. Sussex and Kent of the ancient Saxon kingdoms have had their dukes, two of them royal, the sons of George III. Essex has had many earls, one of whom was a favourite of Queen Elizabeth I. So why not Wessex?

Partly, perhaps, because the kings of the West Saxons, who traced their ancestry back to Cerdic in the early sixth century, came to be kings of England, an achievement acknowledged when Edgar was crowned in Bath Abbey in 973. Wessex, it may be argued, was the silent jewel in the English Crown.

Edgar's two sons, Edward the Martyr and Ethelred the Unready, were less successful than their father, the first assassinated while still a teenager, the second temporarily exiled when King Sweyn of Denmark took control. Ethelred's son Edmund Ironside succeeded in 1016 to an already divided kingdom with Canute, Sweyn's son, already in charge in Wessex. Edmund was defeated by Canute at the battle of Ashingdon, but his ancestral Wessex was returned to him. His death soon afterwards and his burial at Glastonbury left Canute in total control. Three years later Canute became king of Denmark and nearly ten years after that king of Norway and of the southern Swedes.

Canute the Wise had some foolish warriors if the story every schoolboy used to know about him was anywhere near the truth; his wisdom included regional government. England was no longer threatened by Viking raids for a Viking was now in control. Canute chose to exercise that control in a continental way, not through local 'ealdormen' who might reflect local traditions, but through men with the Viking title of 'eorl', the creature of the king. Sixteen of those men are known from Canute's reign, more of them foreign than English, and of the English one was Godwin, known as earl of Wessex.

Godwin, who may have come from Sussex, owed everything to Canute – his wife, the sister of Canute's brother-in-law; his powerful position at court; and his title as earl, given before the end of 1018. When Canute died in 1035 Godwin and the recently widowed Queen Emma supported the king's youngest son Harthacnut as his successor, but he was too busy in Denmark to leave at once and another party in England were for a regency to be led by Canute's second son Harold Harefoot. Emma, and presumably Godwin, agreed to a compromise that gave the queen a foothold in Wessex and the royal treasury at Winchester.

The whole situation was desperately complicated, like most Anglo-Saxon history, because Emma had also been married to Ethelred the Unready and had two sons by him then in exile. One of them, Alfred, wanted to visit his mother in Winchester but was arrested by a party loyal to Harold Harefoot which now included the turncoat Godwin. Godwin was later blamed by everyone for his death.

But Godwin was a survivor as the sons of Canute were not. Neither Harold Harefoot nor Harthacnut reached their thirties and when the latter died in 1042 their English half-brother, Emma's elder son by Ethelred the Unready, became king, later to be known as Edward the Confessor. And when Edward married Godwin's daughter Eadgyth, her father's power increased.

The earldom of Wessex stretched from Cornwall to Kent, and Godwin's disreputable eldest son Sweyn was earl in the counties of Hereford, Gloucester, Oxford, Berkshire, and Somerset while his second son Harold controlled Essex, East Anglia and the Fens. Power they had but friends they lacked and in 1051 they were all forced into exile and Queen Eadgyth was sent to a nunnery.

But that was by no means the end of the family. Godwin and Harold invaded various parts of the coast, Harold fighting the Devon and Somerset militia at Porlock. With the particular support of seamen Godwin was restored to power and property and his enemies such as Norman courtiers, the archbishop of Canterbury and the bishop of Dorchester were dismissed. None would oppose him, not because they liked him but because a civil war would expose the whole country to yet another threat from Denmark. Better the devil you know.

But Godwin did not long enjoy his triumph. He died in April 1053 and his son Harold succeeded to his earldom of Wessex which now again included Somerset and Berkshire. Over the next few years Harold became supreme among the leaders of the realm under Edward the Confessor; only part of the Midlands was not under the influence of the great House of Wessex.

In face of threats from Denmark and Normandy the choice of Harold to be king on the death of Edward in January 1066 was both obvious and practical. He proved to be the one man who could fight for England, as the Danes found to their cost; but that unfortunate arrow at Hastings brought the Normans to power.

Strictly speaking that was not the end of Godwin's family, for Harold had at least seven children of whom one married the king of Novgorod and another became a nun at Wilton. It was, however, the end of the earldom. The Normans were not keen on regional government of that kind.

—*mm*—

Edward Seymour, 'Protector Somerset', was the first member of the fourth family to acquire the dukedom of Somerset. He presumably conferred the title on himself in 1547 in the name of his infant nephew Edward VI. Why he chose the title is not quite certain, but by that time he owned vast estates in the county, acquired by bullying and conniving and generally taking advantage after monks and bishops had been forced to surrender their estates to the Crown.

The third Somerset duke had been Henry Fitzroy, Henry VIII's only acknowledged illegitimate son, created duke in 1525. Before him came another royal prince, Edmund, the third son of Henry VII, who died as a child in 1500. And before him in 1443 was the first, already earl of Somerset and created duke by the authority of parliament. That was John Beaufort, grandson of John of Gaunt.

The Beauforts were illegitimate, for John of Gaunt and Catherine Swynford had not married before they were born, but the family hardly suffered. Duke John's father, also John, was high in favour with Richard II, who created him earl of Somerset and in 1397 both marquess of Somerset and marquess of Dorset, only the second marquess in the realm. Why he chose the Somerset title is again not certain, but he was lord of the manors of Martock, Curry Rivel and Langport Eastover, all properties that his descendants held until 1509.

John Beaufort was degraded to earl by Henry IV, who did not care for the foreign title of marquess, but he held many important posts at Court and was Constable of England and Lieutenant of South Wales. He married into the rich Holand family but died while still under 40 in 1410. Of three sons who in turn succeeded him as earl, Henry died a teenager in 1418. John the next son was a prisoner in France for seventeen years and on his release stayed there to fight his former captors. In 1443 he was rewarded with the dukedom of Somerset, but only for life.

His promotion was followed by military disaster. The war was going badly and he returned home in disgrace, which he suffered for a month or so and then died, barely forty years old, at the family home Corfe Castle. He lies buried in Wimborne Minster. Edmund, the third brother, could not succeed as duke but added to his brother's Somerset lands the manors of Stoke sub Hamdon and Milton Falconbridge.

Deeply involved in the disasters of the war with France, Edmund at least took Harfleur back and was rewarded with the earldom and marquessate of Dorset. For his attempts at making an honourable peace and for serving as the English commander in France he was made duke of Somerset in 1448, but in the following year he was forced to surrender the English capital, Rouen, and then lost both Caen and a vital battle.

At home he was blamed for the failure of Henry VI's government, was twice arrested, and was killed at the first battle of St Albans in 1455. His two sons, Henry and Edmund, both died violent deaths, the first at the battle of Hexham in 1464, the second after the battle of Tewkesbury in 1471. Shortly before the battle Edmund had recruited in Wiltshire and Somerset for the Lancastrian cause, marching through Glastonbury, breaking open the prison at Wells and frightening the Dean and Chapter into giving him £30. After Hexham Stoke and Milton had been lost to the family and Martock, Curry Rivel and Langport had passed to Duke John's daughter Margaret after his death in 1444. She also inherited land from her Holand grandmother.

Margaret, married at the age of six to John de la Pole, at twelve to Edmund Tudor, at fourteen to Sir Henry Stafford, and at twenty-nine to Thomas, Lord Stanley, might be thought of as an unfortunate pawn in the dynastic game, but Lady Margaret Beaufort was a formidable woman, devoted and influential mother of Henry VII and, as an adult, was certainly no pawn. As a typical landowner she was constantly on the move and came to Somerset several times. In 1467 she presided at a great court at Martock and visited Curry and Langport. She was at Curry again in 1472, at Queen Camel in 1474. Through her influence members of her staff like Bernard Oldham and Christopher Urswick found themselves appointed to such rich livings in the county as Chedzoy and Crewkerne.

Lady Margaret was well known for her piety as foundress of two colleges at Cambridge and of two professorships that still bear her name. That name was also included in the chantry founded in the chapel of the manor house at Martock. Both house and chapel have long disappeared but there are two reminders in Somerset of the great lady, her portcullis badge high up on the tower of Langport church and on the porch at Curry Rivel.

A tradition still current in the seventeenth century was that Langport church had been built by a distinguished Langport man, John Heron. That may be so, for Heron was a member of Lady Margaret's household. And Langport continued to remember her, using her badge on its seal. And John Heron went on to serve his mistress's son as treasurer of his household.

—*m*—

The dukes of Somerset from whom the present duke descends have never lived in Somerset. They trace what may be described as their peerage ancestry from Edward Seymour, 'Protector' Somerset, who was a Wiltshireman. The 'Protector' was condemned to death for high treason and was beheaded on Tower Hill in 1552, and his successors continued under different titles for some time as if there was some danger in the Somerset name. The earldom of Somerset was revived for a Scot who was a favourite of James I in 1613, but the Seymours, eventually recovered their influence and William, marquess of Hertford, was made duke of Somerset in 1660. By that time he was an old man, and more than once had sailed rather close to the wind like his ancestor. He had spent a year in the Tower of London for marrying Arabella Stuart, and later suffered huge fines for supporting Charles I in the Civil War. The dukedom was his reward but he lived only a few months to enjoy it.

Later dukes of Somerset died in their beds (one of a malignant fever), often at Maiden Bradley, just over the county boundary in Wiltshire, though they owned Witham Friary so counted as Somerset landowners. The first earl of Somerset, William Mohun, was lord of Dunster and much else in West Somerset, but others who held Somerset titles often had weaker connections. So Bath was the earldom given to Philibert de Chandée, a Breton follower of Henry VII, in 1486, but he presumably qualified by enjoying a pension paid by Somerset taxpayers. After his death without heirs the vacant title was given in 1536 to John Bourchier, a Devon man but with estates in Somerset, and when the Bourchiers died out it went in 1661 to John Granville, a Cornishman. And failing Granvilles, the title passed in 1742 to William Pulteney from Leicestershire, who in addition to being earl of Bath was also Viscount Pulteney of Wrington. And in 1789 the extinct Pulteneys gave place to a Wiltshireman, Thomas Thynne of Longleat, Viscount Weymouth. All were without doubt, proud to be named after the city.

Another famous local title came in an unlikely way. Philip Guedalla, the duke of Wellington's brilliant biographer, referred to 'some feudal ancestor' who, he believed, had held land near the town. The family name had been Wesley for many years but Richard Wesley about 1790 'discovered' that his family originated in the hamlet of Wellesley near Wells. In 1797 he was thus created Baron Wellesley of Wellesley, Somerset, in addition to the Irish earldom of

Mornington which he had inherited from his father. He was, of course, thoroughly Irish. When his brother Arthur achieved greater fame after forcing the passage of the Duoro river and defeating the French at Talavera in 1809 Richard is said to have consulted a gazetteer. Close to Wellesley on the printed page was the name Wellington. But which one to choose? Somerset's Wellington, of course, to keep the county in the family.

Wellington, Wellesley, Bath, Somerset; but why not earl of Chard or Viscount Crewkerne or marquess of Midsomer Norton? Is it chance which has taken some places into the House of Lords and left others out?

His birth there or else his fondness for the place must account for H.O. Wills's choice of Baron Dulverton in 1929 for he was born at Northmoor in the parish; and birth for the inclusion of South Petherton in Sir John Harding's title. And residence must be a consideration: Sir Robert Sanders lived at Bayford Lodge and so chose to be Baron Bayford of Stoke Trister in 1929. Sir William Mason was probably wise to opt for Blackford, where he owned land and went to church, rather than Compton Pauncefoot where he lived. Baron Taunton was entirely suitable for Henry Labouchere in 1859 for he had represented the borough in parliament for nearly thirty years, and in the late twentieth century Harptree, Weston-super-Mare and Yeovil have figured in barony titles conferred for political services.

Baron Radstock might not have been a felicitous choice for those who knew the place in its mining heyday, but his lordship was a Waldegrave and Waldegraves owned the mines. Ownership of property certainly accounts for the title of the first Baron Stawell of Somerton (1683) and for Lord Lovel and Holland, Baron Lovel and Holland of Enmore (1762) the consequence of the Irish earl of Egmont's conviction, shared with few others, that he had an illustrious medieval ancestor from there.

The prospect of influence in a parliamentary borough may be the origin of Stephen Fox's choice of Ilchester in 1741. From 1747 he was Baron Ilchester and Stavordale and baron of Redlynch and from 1756 earl of Ilchester. At least he lived at Redlynch, which is not too far from the other two. But why Charles Berkeley, Viscount FitzHardinge, was also created in 1664 Baron Botetourt of Langport is a mystery.

And what can one make of the title Baron Mendip taken in 1794 by Welbore Ellis, a loyal supporter of Lord North and later of the duke of Portland. Twice he was MP for Petersfield, a seat he owed to William

Jolliffe, owner of Ammerdown, the mansion with such splendid views towards Frome and Downside. Was his choice of title some acknowledgement of Jolliffe's friendship?

James Grenville of Butleigh Court had property within the parish when he was made Baron Glastonbury in 1797. Entirely appropriate. But earlier, in 1719, the title of Baroness of Glastonbury was bestowed with the earldom of Feversham and the duchy of Kendal on Ermengarde Melusina, Baroness von der Schulenberg, one of the two famous mistresses of George I. How proud Glastonbury must have been.

—*mm*—

Queen Elizabeth called her 'The Good Lady Marquess' and she knew her well, a Swedish aristocrat who had come to England in 1565 as a very beautiful teenager. Her rank as well as her friendship with the queen made her the entirely suitable chief mourner at Elizabeth's funeral in 1603. But what was her link with Somerset? One of her daughters was mistress of Ashton Court, another of Montacute; and she spent the last years of a long second widowhood living with one of her sons in the old manor house at Redlynch, near Bruton.

Such was Helena, daughter of Ulf or Wolfgang Henrikson von Snakenborg of East Gothland, Sweden, descendant of the jarls of Orkney. She came to England in the retinue of the Swedish margravine of Baden, a lady bent on arranging a marriage between Queen Elizabeth and her own brother King Eric XIV. When that scheme failed Helena was about to be packed off home but discovered that she rather liked England and that William Parr, marquess of Northampton and brother of old Queen Katherine Parr, rather liked her.

That was awkward: in the eyes of the prudish queen the marquess was little better than a bigamist since he had remarried after his first wife had eloped and their marriage had been annulled. His second lady was now dead but the first still lived and so the Swedish beauty was put out of harm's way, or rather under the queen's eye, by being appointed gentlewoman of the queen's privy chamber.

At last, after a wait of five years or more, the marquess's first lady died and the two were wed in February 1571. The bridegroom only survived the excitement until the end of the following October when he died 'very christianly' at the age of fifty-eight 'sore troubled with the gowte ... and so payned and feble'.

'His Integrity', Henry VIII had called him; 'Honest Uncle' was Edward VI's description; a man who delighted in music and poetry, an unsuccessful soldier, 'of a very gay and florid fancy and wit'. What the lady thought of him is not recorded.

The marquess proved too poor to pay for his own funeral, and the lady had little choice but to stay at Court in the queen's service. Some years later she attracted the attention of a fellow courtier, a groom of the privy chamber named Sir Thomas Gorges, a descendant of the Somerset family from Charlton in Wraxall. They married, unwisely without the queen's consent, for the lady was the widow of the senior marquess and thus the senior peeress in the land, by marriage related to Elizabeth herself. So the bridegroom was lodged in prison, the bride put under house arrest in Whitefriars, from where she wrote a pathetic letter to Elizabeth. The lovers were forgiven before the end of 1577 and the queen was godmother to their first child.

They remained at Court for the next thirty years, he serving as little more than a high grade messenger until he travelled as ambassador to the king of Sweden in 1582; and from 1587 he was vice-admiral of Devon, where he made vast sums of money in the distribution of prizes taken by Drake and others. He also made huge profits from issuing subpoenas in Chancery. Much of the money his wife persuaded him to spend on rebuilding his house, Longford Castle in Wiltshire.

She at Court remained a close friend and confidante of the ageing queen; and she was immortalised by the poet Spenser, who dedicated to her his poem Daphaida and called her Mansilia 'best known by bearing up great Cynthia's train ... the pattern of true womanhood and only mirror of femininity'.

Sir Thomas Gorges died in 1610 and was buried in Salisbury cathedral. The Lady Marquess, who had already lost her great friend and patroness, sensibly retired from the dubious pleasures of Court life under James I and came to live in Somerset. Her youngest son Sir Robert Gorges had bought the manor of Redlynch from the penurious FitzJames family in 1612 and there for many years she lived, keeping in touch with her daughter Smyth at Ashton Court and her daughter Phelips at Montacute.

Redlynch was her permanent home in the last years of her long life; she drew up her will there, and there she died in the spring of 1635, desiring to be buried 'without ripping, imbalming or spicery' in the night in the most reverent manner, beside her 'dear late husband' Sir Thomas Gorges. Under that same will a lady whose grandmother had nursed Sir Thomas was left £100, and her daughter Smyth held a sealed box with mementoes for all the family.

She remembered, too, the poor of Wraxall, her late husband's ancestral home, and left money to buy a field in Nailsea to provide a small endowment for them. Half a century later the new owner of the house at Redlynch still referred to one of the rooms as the Lady Marquess's Chamber. So was her memory still green in the house she came to love.

―――――

King Charles II had fourteen children, none of them legitimate. Six of the boys became dukes, one only an earl; four of the daughters married earls, two became nuns. Three of the dukes had Somerset connections. The first, and the eldest son, was James, created duke of Monmouth, whose first visit to the county in 1680 was made at the suggestion of the Whig leader the earl of Shaftesbury. The duke's 'Progress' began late in July at Bath, and after a visit to Longleat he rode through Ilchester and South Petherton where herbs and flowers were spread in his way and he was presented with a bottle of wine. A crowd estimated at 20,000 followed him along the Ilminster road as he approached Whitelackington, and watched him as he dined under a Spanish chestnut in the park.

Invitations to Brympton and Barrington followed, and then came a 'collation' at the public expense at Chard. A night at Forde Abbey was followed by another at Whitelackington and a church service at Ilminster before a longer journey to Exeter, where the popular greeting was much less enthusiastic. So he came back to Somerset and to the Spekes at Whitelackington, then on to Hinton St George, Brympton d'Evercy, Clifton Maybank and back to Longleat.

Five years later and the response was very different, for the stakes were higher and the risks greater, but still the memory of that first visit was clear in people's minds and what he stood for struck a chord in many hearts. Perhaps 3000 men were with him when he left Axminster en route for Chard, Ilminster and Taunton, and Taunton itself provided almost a complete new regiment. And at Taunton he became a traitor, for he allowed himself to be proclaimed king.

More men joined the duke at Bridgwater and they all were soaked in the rain at Glastonbury. Monmouth led them on almost to Bristol, into Keynsham, skirting Bath and came for a few days to Norton St Philip. There, having rested briefly, he was preparing to leave when the vanguard of the royal army attacked his outposts on the Bath road. A barricade manned by Captain John Vincent and fifty-nine musketeers was attacked by Captain Hawley's grenadiers, and very soon men of the First Regiment of Foot Guards found themselves outmanoeuvred and forced to retire. Some hours later the whole royal army withdrew.

The rest of Monmouth's second memorable visit to Somerset ended with his own hurried withdrawal from the battlefield at Sedgemoor a few days later, and his own life came to an abrupt end on the scaffold on 15 July 1685. In spite of all the sufferings they were to endure for months to come, many of those who followed him would not have denied that the cause was just nor that the duke had been right.

The duke of Monmouth was Charles II's first son by Lucy Walter. His third son Henry by his fourth mistress, the dreadful Barbara Villiers, was at the age of twelve created Duke of Grafton and in 1681 at the age of eighteen was appointed colonel of the First Regiment of Foot Guards – that very regiment which found itself in difficulty on the outskirts of Norton St Philip. Half-brother was pitted against half-brother at Sedgemoor, too, where the Guards were drawn up in the centre of the royal line. Resolution and bravery, so the *London Gazette* reported, characterised his behaviour.

But loyalty had its limits and blood (or rather half-blood) was no guarantee of friendship. The duke of Grafton was one of the first of the king's officers to desert King James's camp in face of the advance of the Prince of Orange through Devon and Somerset in November 1688. Thereafter Grafton was a loyal supporter of King William, playing a vital part in the battle of Beachy Head but being mortally wounded at the siege of Cork two years later.

And the third royal duke with Somerset connections was Grafton's elder brother Charles FitzRoy formerly Palmer. He was styled in his childhood Lord Limerick, later as earl of Southampton after his mother had been created duchess of Cleveland. On the day after brother Henry had been made a duke he himself was created baron of Newbury, earl of Chichester and duke of Southampton. He was not as bright as his brother but was sent to Oxford where the head of his college reported him to be 'very simple'. Lady Cowper thought him a 'natural fool'. No official post came his way and his heiress wife died of smallpox at the age of seventeen when he himself was barely nineteen. After that little has been known of him.

Some letters found among the archives of the earls of Ilchester help to fill the gap. They were written by Thomas Allen from Redlynch to his employer Sir Stephen Fox in London and begin in 1682 with the rumour that the duke had bought Redlynch and Kilmington from Fox. Between then and the end of 1688, years when half-brother James had rebelled and brother Henry had deserted, Charles had fallen into debt to Fox and was evidently living in Bruton. Whatever had been his political views during those years, Southampton was now in the Orange camp, was being financed by Fox, and in the middle of January left Bruton 'in a great rage' with Lord Fitzhardinge, a leading supporter of Dutch William.

And he left the town with his mistress Lady Mary Gerrard and with debts not only to Fox but to Edward Cheeke, a local innkeeper, and other townsmen to the tune of over £336. He owed Fox nearly £600, and the only goods his creditors were able to recover from the house he occupied at West End were twelve silver plates.

The duke found a second wife in 1694 and survived until 1730 when he was buried in Westminster Abbey. He is not known to have visited Somerset again after his rather ignominious departure, and historians have very little of credit to say about him. 'He was of weak intellect', says one, 'and voted with the Whigs'. He was at least consistent in his political opinions.

2
THREE SMALL DISCOVERIES

*"The monks of Glastonbury were the best diggers
and diverters in the business."*

*A letter of enquiry, a casual reference in a book on an obscure subject, or just a lucky
find in the course of more general research, all can be the beginning of a piece of
research which becomes a little story. Was it Coker or Creech or Crewkerne, asked a
scholar from the University of Hull; John Parker had licence for a chapel at his castle
at Nunney, wrote the author of a general book on domestic chaplains, but his name
had not appeared among the castle's owners in local histories; and what did Bristol
Corporation do with their newly-acquired estate at Hamp? The answer to the first
question is not absolutely clear, for the sources are few and far between, but a gap
has certainly been filled in Nunney's history, and another episode in the long history
of flood relief on the Levels can be told.*

―――――

What is the connection between Somerset and the Crown Jewels? Not
those magnificent jewels, crowns, sceptres, orbs and the like to be seen

in the Tower of London, for most of those are not all that ancient, but the much older ones dating from the eleventh century. The answer is, perhaps rather surprisingly, the Domesday manor of Coker. The source of the story is a medieval manuscript which itself could possibly be a forgery, and which has been known for at least a hundred years.

The story seems to have come to light in 1424 when the Vicomte de Caen – Caen being then a city under English rule after Henry V's victory at Agincourt – drew up a legal document declaring that he had seen a 'book or charter of ancient writing' which recorded that William the Conqueror had left his regalia at his death to his 'own' monastery of St Stephen at Caen. There is just a little doubt about the copy of the charter the Vicomte had made, if not about the original, for it gives the date 1088 for the Conqueror's death, when it should have been 1087. But that may be simply a copying mistake. What matters for Somerset is that the charter goes on to say that in order to redeem the jewels – crown, sceptre, rod, chalice and gold candlesticks – William Rufus gave the monks of Caen his manor of Cocre in Somerset.

Long ago John Batten of Yeovil in his *Historical Notes on Parts of South Somerset* told the story of the charter and the jewels but did not believe it. Dr Barbara English of Hull University told it again from a different angle at the end of the twentieth century, prompted by her interest in what actually happened after the death of the Conqueror and especially by the fact that the 1424 document has found its way into her university's library. It had come from the duke of Norfolk's collection of papers at Carlton Towers, brought there by the duke's ancestor, the antiquarian collector Thomas Stapleton, who had acquired it from the Abbé Gervais de la Rue of Caen.

Now, how had William the Conqueror disposed of his lands? It looks as if Normandy passed by hereditary right and with no difficulty to his eldest son Robert. England, which he had won by force, was a different matter. God had, in the Conqueror's view, given him this new kingdom and it was, in a sense, up to God to dispose of it – a very proper feeling. But disposal by Divine will was a serious matter and the Divine needed a little guidance if the Conqueror's second son, William Rufus, was to acquire it after him. So Divine will came to be the decision of Archbishop Lanfranc of Canterbury, who had been tutor to Rufus and who could so arrange that he was in England sooner than any other possible claimant.

That was, of course, the outcome. Rufus went to England and was crowned (probably with regalia given by Edward the Confessor to Westminster Abbey).

The Conqueror's regalia still had to be redeemed, for it represented something more than the rule Rufus's brother Robert held over the duchy of Normandy; the crown and other jewels at Caen stood for the fact that the Conqueror had entrusted his English lands to God and held them by Divine will. His successor in England had to get his hands on them.

John Batten, sober historian and solid Protestant, thought that death-bed gifts to monasteries were open to suspicion and he could not believe that the Conqueror would not have given the regalia to his son unless he had lost his mind! And, further, he could not believe the story about Coker because he found no other connection between Coker and Caen.

Other historians have tried to suggest that the Cocre of the charter is not Coker but either Creech or Crewkerne, but the monks of Caen already owned a large part of Crewkerne, represented by the rich church there, and the old spelling of Creech was Crice, and was not very long afterwards given to the monks of Montacute. The manor of Coker certainly belonged to the Conqueror at the time of Domesday and in 1066 had been one of the estates of the Countess Gytha and thus part of the lands of the Saxon royal house. It was larger than Creech but not so large as the great manor of Crewkerne. If it really was Coker that was exchanged with the monks of Caen it seems likely that they sold their interest in the estate not many years later, for nowhere has any later connection between the two been found.

It must surely be Coker, but East or West who will ever know? What is not in question is that a Somerset place played a significant part in the transfer of power from William the Conqueror to William Rufus in 1087. Those events ensured that England was not to be an offshore part of the duchy of Normandy but a sovereign state, sovereign under God's dispensation. Under Henry I, another of Rufus's brothers and his successor, England became the heart of the empire which began that Anglo-Saxon influence on the Continent through the Angevin empire that was continued in the conquests of Edward III and Henry V.

—*mm*—

There is more surviving of the fabric of Nunney castle than from its written history. There it stands beside the Nunney Brook and thus at the bottom of a valley at the centre of its village, not the most sensible place to build a castle as was later to be proved. Still, it is undoubtedly impressive, with its strong circular corner towers said to have been based on Paris's castle, the Bastille. It was undoubtedly more impressive still when its steeply-pitched roof was intact, but it was more of a moated and castellated manor house than a castle.

As for its history, it was probably built by Sir Peter de la Mare, but the date usually quoted, 1373, is only the date of the planning permission he received from the Crown. That might well have been obtained after the event. And who, in the family genealogy, was Sir Peter de la Mare? An American enthusiast has spent many hours trying to find out, with no certain success.

And who lived in it after his time? For years it was owned by that amazing Tudor civil servant William Paulet, successively Baron St John, earl of Wiltshire and marquess of Winchester. Amazing because he managed to hold high office throughout the reigns of Henry VIII, Edward VI and Mary, and for thirteen years under Queen Elizabeth, and in all that time spent but a month in the Tower of London for supporting Lady Jane Grey. He himself, with remarkable honesty, put his survival down to political pliability, likening himself to a willow rather than an oak. Others say he was simply a superb and incorruptible administrator. He was Lord High Treasurer from 1550 until his death in 1572.

Unusually for a Treasurer, Paulet was a personal spendthrift with a passion for building at his home at Basing in Hampshire. Just before his death he owed £647 11s 10 ¾d (£647.59p) to Queen Elizabeth, and she graciously allowed him to sell some of his ancestral estates to pay the debt. Among those were the ancient Paulet family land of Melcombe Poulett in North Petherton, the former Glastonbury abbey manor of West Monkton, the manor and borough of Milverton, and two estates at Nunney. One of those had also been a Glastonbury manor called Nunney Glaston, the other was sometimes called the manor of Nunney castle. That last had come from the de la Mares when Eleanor, the last of her line, married William Paulet in the early fifteenth century.

It seems that the old marquess, who must have been nearly ninety, died just before any sale could take place, for his son was still in possession of Nunney a year later. Exactly what happened in the next few years is not at present certain, but in 1577 a man named Swithun Thorpe sold the Nunney estates including the castle to one John Parker. Parker was said to have paid the large sum of £2000, but only a year later he sold them to Richard Prater. Prater's family lived in the castle for many years; in fact they were still inside in 1645 when Colonel Rainsborough trained his guns on the building under orders from Sir Thomas Fairfax and blew a large hole in one side. Colonel Prater wisely decided to surrender and the castle was torched.

It might reasonably be thought that John Parker never came near the place, but if he did not, he certainly intended to. That is known because, according to a book entitled *A social history of the Domestic Chaplain, 1530–1840* by William Gibson, a former resident of Taunton, his father gave him licence to have a chapel in the castle, for John Parker was none other than the elder of the two surviving sons of Archbishop Matthew Parker, archbishop of Canterbury from 1559 until his death in 1575. Like William Paulet, Matthew Parker had lived something of a charmed life, especially since he served as chaplain to Anne Boleyn, supported the ill-fated Lady Jane Grey, and as a married man was deprived of all his offices under Queen Mary. Roman Catholics late in Queen Elizabeth's reign told a scandalous story that his consecration as bishop in the Nag's Head in London had been neither lawful nor apostolic.

Matthew Parker's son John was only a young man when he was connected with Nunney. He had been born at Cambridge, where his father was Master of Corpus Christi college, in 1548. He had already served as an MP in 1571, elected through his father's influence as one of the first two members for Queenborough in Kent. How he came to have Nunney for a short time is a mystery, though it is likely that he was, like many of his kind, speculating in the land market. His later career had nothing whatever to do either with Somerset or with politics, but instead, again through his father's influence, he was an official in the Prerogative Court of Canterbury, the court which dealt with the probate of wills of prosperous folk all over the country. He later served his father's two successors and lived the life of a prosperous gentleman, either in a house at Lambeth inherited from his mother or at Bekesbourne near Canterbury in a house let to him by Archbishop Whitgift.

As a youth someone said that John Parker and his brother were 'very hopeful young men and adorned with all their father's and mother's manners'. Later in life John was thought to be shrewd if not unscrupulous as a businessman. Yet he is also known to have been generous to his relatives, and perhaps that generosity was misplaced. His son Richard proved a spendthrift and at the end of his life he himself was in financial difficulties. A knighthood no doubt cost him a pretty fee in 1603, and honorary admission to Gray's Inn in 1597 probably cost him something, if only for entertainment. After the end of Elizabeth's reign Parker seems to have retired to Cambridge. Corpus Christi, his father's old college, took pity on him, made him a grant of money, and paid the expenses of his funeral at Great St Mary's on 29 January 1619. Nunney, if it ever knew him, had long forgotten.

The problem of flooding on the Somerset Levels has been around ever since Somerset Man decided there was a living to be made there. Even before the time of the timber trackways now buried deep in the peat to the era of the most modern pumping gear there have been many attempts, largely unsuccessful, to control what makes the Levels wet. Thus is the countryside there divided by rhynes and ditches in an attempt to move water from one place to another; and banks to change the course of rivers, to keep them within bounds, or to divert the inevitable flood to neighbouring land. The monks of Glastonbury were the best diggers and diverters in the business.

After the dissolution of the monasteries the initiative passed to the new landowners, among whom were counted the Corporation of Bristol, owners of the manor of Hamp near Bridgwater in succession to the monks of Athelney. The Parrett meandered through the estate, forming a great loop, the narrow neck of which might be cut through. The Corporation was persuaded that such a cut would improve its flow and help to prevent flooding further upstream; but to do so dams had first to be built to protect the diggers of the new course; and there were questions as to who should pay and who would organise the work and the workers.

First a Decree was issued in 1567 with the full backing of the law of the land. If a cut were to be made, then places as far away as Somerton would feel the benefit, and therefore such places should contribute: North Petherton, of course, and Chedzoy and places near at hand, but also High Ham, Greinton and so on. The first list of potential partners might not produce the necessary labour or cash, so six more parishes were brought into the scheme by precept of a Commissioner for Sewers: Long Sutton, Pitney, Compton Dundon, Kingsdon and the Charltons, not all beside the Parrett but all in some way thought to benefit from the rich grasslands of the Levels. Still it was calculated that there would not be sufficient support, so North Curry, Curry Mallet and their neighbours were enlisted, for when the Parrett flooded, then so did the Isle and the Tone. They were all in it together.

Work began on one end of the proposed new cut on 5 April 1568 and on the other end on 21 April. Each village or town served for a week: one hundred and twenty men from Chedzoy came during the week of 26 April with twenty-five carts and consumed a modest thirty-eight gallons of drink. The next week a few more came from Westonzoyland who drank rather less, and about one hundred and forty from Middlezoy who downed forty-three gallons.

A weekly record was kept not only of the number of labourers and carts employed but also of other necessary works such as rooting up twenty-two elm trees in the middle of June and the cost of the ferryman, who charged 8s (40p) a week but saving the labourers two miles walk every day. There was almost a disaster at the end of July for the high Spring tide came over the temporary dam at the west end of the new cut; one hundred and twenty-nine labourers found themselves very wet, but there were no casualties. By the middle of August working in water had become normal for the labourers, but there were still eleven feet (3.3m) to go down. Someone had calculated that if that depth could not be achieved the slime would fill up the new channel in four years.

At some time during August there was something of a crisis meeting at Langport about how the river could be prevented from returning to its old channel, and during the last part of that month as many as one hundred and seventy-four labourers started the huge task of throwing earth reinforced by hurdles into the old channel. The work became more exciting and more men had to be employed: one hundred and ninety-seven in the first week, two hundred and eighty-eight in the second. More high tides nearly spelled disaster again and a boatman called Wylmotte almost lost his lighter when its rope broke under the strain.

Nearly five hundred men worked during the last two weeks of September, among them none harder than Michael Denning and his two men who between them produced four hundred and fifty wooden piles ranging between 12 feet (3.6m) and 18 feet (5.4m) long to make sure that the banks of the new cut were secure.

The total cost of the whole undertaking came to £446 12s 7d (£446.63p) and fourteen pages of the mayor of Bristol's audit book contain the details. It had been a great cooperative effort, no doubt not without difficulties not mentioned in the financial record. The man in charge of the whole operation must have been a remarkable man. Twenty-five times he rode from Bristol to Bridgwater and out to the site on the 'commons', as he called them. He was evidently not a horseman, for he declared in his claim for expenses that he 'many times felt such a heat in my back to my no small grief'. His clothes were spoiled, he worked and watched day and night when the dams were being made; and on the day the tide flowed over he, too, was drenched and went home 'like a drowned rat, my feet as though they had been sodden through and the wet earth that I trod in'. For all his reasonable complaining he served the mayor and corporation well, and they paid his claim for £10 without demur. But the name of this remarkable man was never mentioned.

When the next winter came, no doubt the floods came too, though probably in a different place. The people of Hamp could watch the river flow past as never before, and a semi-circular piece of North Petherton parish on the east side of the river is the only clue as to where all the work was done.

3
CIVIL SERVANTS

English kings governed on the cheap, and throughout the Middle Ages most of the work done by what we would now describe as the civil service and most of the offices of state now held by politicians was carried out by clerks, that is men in Holy Orders. They were the educated élite, for only a clerk could normally attend a university and a clerk could be found a benefice and the successful ones more than one benefice – to begin with a vicarage or rectory, later on a canonry in a cathedral, perhaps even a deanery or a bishopric. And thus the king would have no need to find a salary for his officials: they would be paid from Church endowments and the tithes and offerings of the people. Absence from parishes and other duties seems not to have troubled many consciences; curates and other deputies could usually be found. Four men among many were distinguished leaders of government, administrators of quality, diplomats and loyal servants: civil servants par excellence.

*"Richard of Ilchester...
'had the king's ear'."*

Richard of Ilchester was, by any standard, a remarkable man. He had become a government official by 1156, during the reign of King Henry II, and held the title of 'scribe of the court', probably a junior but still an influential post under that rather more famous civil servant Thomas Becket. A few years later he was approached by the abbot of St Albans in a dispute with the king about a church because he 'had the king's ear'. That approach cost the abbot two thirds of the value of the church by way of a fee. Richard was in the thick of the crisis between Henry and Becket and went on three missions to the pope on the king's behalf. Becket, or at least his friends, felt that Richard was sympathetic to their cause until, on the king's request, he went to meet the German emperor to declare support for the anti-pope. Becket thus had no choice but to excommunicate his former colleague.

The king, of course, continued to employ such a faithful servant and made him a judge. In that capacity he sat both in the Exchequer court in London and on circuit; and because he was an expert both in Exchequer methods of financial calculation and of the ways in which the business of government was recorded and communicated, he was given an official seat at the Exchequer between the treasurer and the justiciar – as we might say between the Chancellor of the Exchequer and the Prime Minister. There seem also to have been records of legal matters that were his entire responsibility. Here was a civil servant par excellence.

As the dispute with the exiled Thomas Becket worsened Richard was excommunicated again in May 1169, but he still remained in royal service, either in England or Normandy, working away as if nothing had happened. One of his duties was to escort the king's eldest son Henry, later Henry II, on his way to Westminster for his coronation. Early in December he went back to the old king in Normandy to tell of the quarrel Becket had picked with the bishops who had crowned the young king. That news among other led to the king's remark that in turn led to the murder of the archbishop at Canterbury at the end of the same month.

The murder tipped the balance in the dispute in favour of the Church but the loyal civil servant was still regarded by his fellow churchmen as the best arbiter in their own disputes. His reward was to be made Bishop of Winchester – and thus lord of Taunton and Rimpton – in 1173; and to be described as a devout lover and imitator of St Thomas – hardly the kind of description the unrepentant Henry II would have welcomed.

Yet he remained high in the king's favour, trusted on important diplomatic missions and in 1176–8 appointed in supreme control of the government in Normandy, from which he returned to take his honoured place at the Exchequer once again. He died in 1188.

The monks at Winchester once complained to the king that Bishop Richard had reduced the number of dishes at their dinners from thirteen to ten, but they remembered him favourably after his death. A contemporary writer declared that he had more common sense than scholarship and was more versed in worldly affairs than in the liberal arts. That is what made him such a supremely good civil servant.

But what of his Somerset origins? Contemporary writers say he was born in the diocese of Bath and that his surname was Hokelin. On his tomb at Winchester he is named Richard Toclyve. Now, in or around the year 1220 William le Deneys built a hospital for pilgrims at Whitehall in Ilchester and stated that he did so 'for the health of the soul of Richard, Bishop of Winchester, born at Sok'. A year or two later another member of the Deneys family went to court to claim some land at Sock which had formerly been held by his kinsman Richard, once Bishop of Winchester. So Sok and Sock must be Sock Dennis, now the name of a farm just outside Ilchester but once a parish in its own right.

And Dennis, Deneys, is in Latin Dacus, that is Dane. Anyone who attempts family history in the early Middle Ages is taking risks, but two American scholars have chanced their arms and have, as it were, wondered in print whether Richard was not descended directly or indirectly from either John the Dane or Turchil the Dane, both of whom held land in Somerset before the Conquest, or even possibly from Strang the Dane who held in Gloucestershire. They think he may also appear in government records as Richard of Bath and Richard le Deneys, and if so that he held a mill at Ilchester and land at Biddesham.

John, Turchil and Strang most likely came over to England during the reign of Canute after 1016 and their extended family survived in Somerset until the mid-thirteenth century. Apart from the name Sock Dennis there are two other traces of the family, an estate called Seavington Dennis in Seavington St Michael and a church in Ilchester, only mentioned in the twelfth and thirteenth centuries and dedicated to the Norwegian Saint Olaf.

Richard of Ilchester left more than a reputation as a distinguished civil servant. He also left two sons, Herbert and Richard le Poore, both of whom became bishops, one of Salisbury, the other successively of Chichester, Salisbury and Durham; the one who conceived the idea of removing his cathedral from the chilly site on Old Sarum, the other who carried it out.

—*MM*—

Edward Troteman of Wells also had two remarkable sons, born towards the end of the twelfth century. Both were civil servants in the government of King John, which might not have been something to be proud of; both became most distinguished bishops and astute politicians. Both were great builders, and both were known usually as 'of Wells' rather than Troteman.

Hugh, the elder, began his career at home as a clerk in Bishop Savaric's household but had joined the royal service by 1201, possibly through the influence of Simon, then archdeacon of Wells and himself a highly-placed government official. Jocelin's career also began at home with the bishop and perhaps with the prior of Bath, but he followed Hugh into royal service in 1202 and in 1203–4 had risen so swiftly he was presiding over powerful royal courts dealing with both law and taxation.

Both, naturally, were duly rewarded as medieval civil servants usually were, for both were in Holy Orders. Hugh was made archdeacon of Wells, a canon of Lincoln and rector of a Norfolk parish. Jocelin was made a canon of Wells and parson of Winsham and livings in Hampshire and Herefordshire. And Jocelin was soon to outdo his brother, for in 1206, after more than a year traipsing around the country with the king (and often with his brother, too), he was elected, of course with King John's approval, to succeed Bishop Savaric as bishop of Bath. Brother Hugh received his reward three years later, the rich bishopric of Lincoln, which he ruled with distinction until his death in 1235.

Jocelin inherited a problem at Wells, for in 1197 with the full approval of the pope and the canons of the cathedral Bishop Savaric had become abbot of Glastonbury, making the abbey church his co-cathedral with Bath and taking a quarter of its income for his share. Jocelin had played his own minor part in this drama in 1200 when he went to the abbey with other Wells canons and returned with five monks who had refused to obey Savaric's orders.

Glastonbury monks had from the beginning objected to the arrangement and the arrival of a new bishop gave them an opportunity to reverse what had once had the pope's approval. The pope himself clearly had second thoughts, but before any final decision could be made, king, pope and bishops became embroiled in the great row over the appointment of Stephen Langton as archbishop of Canterbury.

Before that business came to a crisis, in the late summer of 1207, King John was in Somerset with Jocelin, and at Wells granted him the right to create a deer park beyond his new house in the city and to divert the road from Wells to Dulcote around it. And despite the king's frantic attempts at avoiding confrontation, just before Easter 1208 three bishops in the name of the pope placed the whole country under Interdict. All churches were closed, work on the building of Wells cathedral stopped, and most of the bishops fled abroad, the king having threatened to cut off their noses and ears.

Hugh of Wells, not yet a bishop, was still transacting government business as usual, and when the king and court came to Wells again in September 1208 both brothers were in attendance. Both spent Christmas in the royal presence at Bristol, and later spoke up for the king when a threat of excommunication was made against him. In the following summer there was almost a reconciliation between the king and Langton in which both brothers were involved, but it came to nothing and the king himself was duly excommunicated.

Then the whole affair was complicated by Hugh who, having been elected bishop of Lincoln with the king's approval, went abroad to be consecrated by Langton against the express wishes of the king. John was no doubt furious and Jocelin could hardly remain in England, not just because of his brother's action but also because to serve an excommunicate king was to be excommunicate.

The two brothers remained in exile for three-and-a-half years but both returned to support their defeated and humiliated king. Both were named as his councillors in the preamble to Magna Carta, but while Jocelin continued to support the royal government of John's son and heir Henry III, Hugh gave more support at first to the disaffected barons.

While they were both in exile Hugh made a will in which he left huge sums of money for the building of his cathedral at Lincoln and for the cathedral of his birthplace. He also allocated another huge sum for the foundation of a hospital at Wells. Jocelin joined his brother in the hospital foundation, but is better remembered for his generous continuation of the building work on his cathedral. It was thus appropriate that he should have celebrated its completion when on St Romanus's Day (23 October) 1239 the great West Front was consecrated. It was not then quite finished and work still remained to be done when Jocelin himself died in November 1242.

He was buried, as was right for the man who could almost be described as the new founder of the cathedral, under a marble tomb in the middle of the quire, upon which lay a flat brass said to be one of the earliest of its kind in England. Brother Hugh had died seven years earlier and was similarly buried in his cathedral, remembered as a great organiser within his huge diocese and like Jocelin the principal creator of an episcopal palace in his see city.

—*m*—

Only two men have moved directly from the Bishop's Palace at Wells to the Lambeth home of the archbishops of Canterbury, since William Laud does not count, having never moved in. The second was George Carey in 1991, the first was John Stafford in 1443. Stafford was the illegitimate son of a Wiltshire squire, a lawyer, a diplomat, a successful politician and naturally a civil servant. And Stafford, like Archbishop Carey long afterwards, had been for a time rector of the church of St Nicholas, Durham.

There the similarity ends. George Carey in his book *The Church in the Market Place*, tells how he revived the church and parish. John Stafford probably never went near the place for he was still a law student at the time and used the income from the benefice, as many did in those days, as a student grant. In fact, because of his illegitimate birth he could not become a clergyman without the pope's permission and he did not get that for at least a year after he became rector.

But the son of Sir Humphrey Stafford of North Bradley had no difficulty in getting on in the world chosen for him. His training as a lawyer made him useful to all sorts of people and finally led to the top job in the government, Chancellor of England. Meanwhile the young clergyman had to live and he collected parishes all over the country with the best of his contemporaries.

The West Country was where his family had most influence so the young man became at one and the same time rector of Farmborough, vicar of Bathampton and prebendary of Wells, and when he resigned the first two he took on Crewkerne and the deanery of Wells. He became bishop of Bath and Wells in 1425. As if these were not enough to absorb his time, Stafford joined the government and became Keeper of the Privy Seal, an office very close to King Henry V, and then, on the king's tragic death in 1422, Treasurer of England.

Though no stranger to Wells, he was welcomed to the city in 1425 with a great feast, probably held in the banqueting hall in his own palace. Those guests privileged to sit at the high table enjoyed three courses, the rest only two; and what courses! Swan, heron, crane and venison were the basis of the first course, rabbit, peacock, teal, curlew and gulls of the second with pastries, dates and almonds; meat, eggs, poultry, cheesecake, brawn and fruit had to suffice for the third.

The bishop was, it is clear, a staunch supporter of the Crown in that difficult time when Henry VI was a small boy and various people tried to gain power and rule. Stafford's name meant stability and for nearly twenty years he held the senior government office of Chancellor of England. He kept the job for so long at least in part because he was a superb diplomat and somehow managed not to get mixed up with the unpopular policies of Cardinal Beaufort and William de la Pole, earl of Suffolk. He it was who crowned the young king in Paris in 1430 when the English Crown still held on to something of what Henry V had won at Agincourt, and he crowned Margaret of Anjou after her marriage to the king in 1445.

With all those duties Stafford still found time each summer to visit Somerset, and one of his enemies actually declared that he had several children by a Somerset nun. That same critic, perhaps soured because he was never promoted, attacked all bishops bitterly. 'As ecclesiastical governors', he wrote, 'they had been taught to combine the wisdom of the serpent with the innocence of a dove – a combination so difficult that many...found it desirable to specialise'. Whatever the attacks on Stafford, an account roll shows that he was not at all ashamed of his birth. The roll, still kept at Lambeth Palace, records that he spent the huge sum of £49 1s 4d (£49.6p) on his mother, Emma of North Bradley, in the last few months of his time at Wells. More than half went on a generous allowance, including an advance for Christmas, and the rest on wine shipped from Bristol to Southwick in Wiltshire where she evidently lived.

It was quite a task to settle all his debts in Wells before he left for Lambeth: £10 to the abbot of Cleeve, £40 to Gilbert Cammell, £10 to William Felyps of Bath, £20 to Sir William de Botreaux. And there was the whole cost of moving what was called 'hernes' but probably meaning all kinds of equipment – 43s 4d (£2.16p) for taking nine cartloads from Wells to London.

Bishop Stafford left more than memories behind him at Wells. While he was there the cathedral cloisters were being built and he permitted workmen to breach his wall, a gateway still there and used by today's cathedral masons. His coat of arms in the chapel at the end of the Vicars' Close suggests that he had something to do with that work too. And in a rather curious agreement made with the dean and chapter of the cathedral the bishop agreed to give ten books to the library, most of them legal works. But there was a condition: the bishop was to keep them for life. Whether they ever reached Wells after his death is not known, though the agreement is still kept safely among the cathedral's archives.

So in 1443 Stafford moved on to become archbishop of Canterbury, thus combining the top jobs in church and state, but historians have very little to say about him, good or bad. At a time of growing political unrest, perhaps that in itself is remarkable. He was, perhaps, fortunate to die in 1452 before the shambles of civil war when the king he had served so loyally was reduced to a nervous wreck. He had just one taste of the trouble to come when he was on a commission to deal with those in Kent who had followed the rebel Jack Cade in 1450.

mm

Among the players in the almost constant shuttle diplomacy during the Hundred Years War was a Somerset-born civil servant and scholar whose secretary left behind a detailed and very rare record of one of his missions. Thomas Bekynton, born as his name declares in the parish of Beckington, was no career diplomat, for the profession had not been invented. He had specialised in Civil Law at Oxford around the time of the battle of Agincourt and had later served on the staffs of the archbishop of Canterbury and of that strange scholar-politician Humphrey, Duke of Gloucester.

He was, naturally, a clergyman, and enjoyed a very substantial income from various sources without having the inconvenience of running a parish himself. And now in the 1430s the glory of the victory at Agincourt was a distant memory and the martyrdom of Joan of Arc had done wonders for French morale. So for the weakening English, negotiations for a peace or at least a truce were the order of the day, with the prospect of a royal marriage between the infant Henry VI with a French princess part of the equation.

Thus between September and December 1432 Bekynton was absent from his other posts on a mission to the French Dauphin for a truce and apparently travelled on to attend a Church Council at Basel. In 1439, by which time he was King's Secretary, he was second-in-command of a high level embassy to Calais to meet French ambassadors. His third and last international mission, which he led, was to negotiate a marriage between the king and a daughter of the Count of Armagnac. That last journey proved a failure, but a journal kept by one of his staff must be one of the earliest accounts of travel through Somerset.

The party set out from Windsor on Tuesday 5 June 1442 and spent the first night at Henley-on-Thames. Next day they rode to Sutton Courtenay where Bekynton had a house, for he had been rector of the parish since 1420. They stayed at Sutton until Saturday, but on the Thursday went over to Abingdon for lunch with the abbot and the bishop of Salisbury. Saturday, Sunday and Monday nights were spent at Great Bedwyn where Bekynton had another house attached to his prebend in Salisbury cathedral. From there on Tuesday the party rode over to Devizes to meet Lord Hungerford, no doubt to discuss politics and the state of the army in France; there they had supper and slept at the house of the town's mayor.

On Wednesday two of the party returned via Bedwyn to Windsor while Bekynton and the rest rode on to his birthplace at Beckington. Lunch, perhaps with childhood friends, was accompanied by two gallons of wine sent by Lord Hungerford. That was what diplomacy was all about. Then they went on to Wells where he had another house assigned to him as prebendary of Dultingcote in the cathedral. Actually he could not go there immediately, so he had an early meal with Canon John Bernard and then a drink with the precentor of the cathedral before being formally installed in the cathedral quire. Then he went on to Glastonbury to have supper with the abbot, with whom he exchanged a horse.

The party must have stayed in the abbey overnight and had lunch there but slept at Taunton. Next day was spent at the home of Sir Edward Hull, then constable of Bordeaux, at Enmore, where the state of that part of England's diminishing empire was no doubt discussed. They stayed overnight and some of the next day, but then rode on to Tiverton, where they lodged at the Earl of Devon's castle.

The party continued its rather stately way through Devon via Columjohn, Exeter, Chudleigh and Ashburton. They seem to have stayed at an inn in Exeter but several of the cathedral canons gave them meals and the Earl of Devon sent some venison. The bishop of Exeter was their host at Chudleigh. Ashburton was mentioned only because it was there that Bekynton's servant Little John was taken ill and left the party.

At Plymouth they put up at Thomas Hill's inn but had one meal with the prior of Plympton and received a present of a large quantity of white wine. They also received two letters from the king telling them that Sir Edwards Hull's report on the safety of Bordeaux was not encouraging (which would hardly have been news), but that they were still to proceed.

Diplomacy is said to be the art which cannot be hurried and the journey from Windsor to Plymouth had taken over three weeks. The return was much more speedy, for the party no doubt wanted to explain their failure as soon as possible. After what was evidently an uncomfortable voyage they finally reached land at Penryn on the Fal river on Sunday 10 February 1443. In ten days they were back with the king, having travelled through Truro, St Austell, Lostwithiel, Liskeard, Exeter, Honiton, Crewkerne, Sherborne, Shaftesbury, Salisbury and Collingbourne to Bekynton's house at Bedwyn. There the parishioners welcomed their rector with bread and poultry. Then on, of course, to Sutton Courtenay, Henley, Maidenhead, Eton and Colnbrook.

The whole expedition had been a failure, and a year later the king married another lady, still French but from a different family. Bekynton was at first promoted for his efforts, becoming Keeper of the Privy Seal, but the new alliance was against all he had worked for and it was better to leave the government. So he became bishop of his native see and gave up being a civil servant. And, as Sir Edward Hull had told him, Bordeaux was not to be English for much longer; it was lost when Sir Edward himself fell at the battle of Chastillon, when the French finally avenged the disaster of Agincourt.

4

REBELS, ROGUES AND TRAITORS

*"... romance was hardly in the blood of a family
better known for piracy and treachery."*

*Rogues, lawbreakers and tax evaders are the stuff of history, far better recorded and
often more entertaining than the loyal and the legal. Rebels and traitors are also easy
enough to find, though in England in the Later Middle Ages the definition of the
crime rather depended on which king or which kingmaker happened to be in power
at the time.*

The name Marisco has a rather romantic ring about it, but romance was
hardly in the blood of a family better known for piracy and treachery. Were
they not the thugs who lurked on Lundy Island and laid violent hands on
anything that moved in the Bristol Channel? And if so, then surely they
belonged to Devon rather than Somerset? Well, yes and no.

Jordan de Marisco, the first of the family to be officially noticed, lived during the reigns of Stephen and Henry II, and having offended the latter was declared to have forfeited Lundy, which was promptly given to the Knights Templar. Lundy was not Jordan's only possession; he also owned Alstone in Huntspill, which passed to his son William. Another member of the family, Geoffrey, owned other land in Huntspill. William was in trouble in 1199 when he rebelled against King John, who gave Lundy to the Templars again. William raised money on his estates at Huntspill and Cameley and held out on Lundy against the king's forces from Devon and Cornwall. The king replied by giving his Somerset estates to the Templars, too. La Cloud in Cameley was never returned to him and it was known thereafter as Temple Cloud.

Somehow William managed to talk his way out of trouble in 1217 when King John needed all the friends he could get, however dubious, and his outlawry was cancelled. He must have had influence in high places for another member of the family, probably his brother, was that Geoffrey de Marisco whose power in Ireland caused him to be the king's justiciar there for three terms between 1215 and 1232, though he was not entirely trusted either by John or by Henry III and the latter held one of his sons hostage for his father's good behaviour.

And they were right to mistrust, for in 1234 in a private Irish war Geoffrey brought about the death of the famous Richard Marshall, for which the whole family seems to have been rounded up. Geoffrey's son John proved his father was in England at the time, but Geoffrey's brother Jordan's land at Huntspill was confiscated and later handed over to Jordan's son William. Geoffrey somehow escaped serious trouble but in 1238 he was accused of plotting to assassinate Henry III and fled to Scotland. In 1244, after his son had been executed, the Scots lost patience and expelled him and he died in poverty in France a year later.

That son William, not to be confused with his brother William but just as bad, had naturally been involved in Geoffrey's private Irish war but his interest was focussed on Lundy. By 1238 he was creating trouble for the government and in 1242 three of his cronies, one named Geoffrey de Marisco, were ordered to be kept in Winchester gaol.

Matthew Paris, the national chronicler, takes up the story by describing how William de Marisco held Lundy with some 300 men but how he was cleverly captured by the king's forces. He and his men were first taken to Bristol castle and later he and most of them were lodged in the Tower of London and the rest in Newgate and the Fleet prisons. William's wife and others arrested by men of Bristol were sent to Gloucester castle, and a ship owned by William son of Jordan de Marisco, that is one of his cousins and which was tied up in the pill which gave Huntspill its name, was handed over to the sheriff of Somerset. The government was clearly taking no chances.

William the pirate was drawn behind a horse from his trial in Westminster through the City to the Tower where he was hanged, drawn and hacked to pieces, his four limbs being sent to the four principal cities of the land – probably the first recorded hanging, drawing and quartering. Sixteen of his henchmen were hanged too; and, disgrace upon disgrace, his shield of arms, for he had been dubbed a knight, was degraded, that is cut in half and his arms reversed.

In the crisis of the moment government clerks became confused and referred to Lundy Island as in Somerset, probably because they, quite rightly, thought of the family as Somerset people. That is truly what they were, for Marisco is Latin for marsh and they took their name from the low-lying ground on the western side of Huntspill beside the River Parrett. William son of Jordan who lost his boat in 1242 may have been entirely innocent: his son or grandson, another William, still lived in Huntspill at the time of his death in 1284 and still owned Lundy and most of the estate at Cameley and was entirely law-abiding. And after him came in succession John and Herbert and Stephen. Stephen was the last of his line when he died in 1381 but the estate still bore the name Huntspill Mareys, the French version of Marisco, until the end of the eighteenth century.

⟶⟵

The will of Richard Bruton is a model of generosity. He was a native of Bruton, from which he obviously took his name, though his family name was Frere, and he was a senior clergyman when he died in 1417. The will runs to more than ten pages of modern printed text and many folios of the will register Marche, where it was entered by a clerk of the Prerogative Court of Canterbury after probate.

Richard went to university in the 1380s and became a civil lawyer. He collected benefices like many of his kind: Buscot in Berkshire, St Endellion in Cornwall, Olveston in Worcestershire, Chulmleigh in Devon, and in his home diocese St Michael's in Ilchester, Minehead and High Ham. From 1393 he was a residentiary canon of Wells and later chancellor of the cathedral, and from 1410 he was also a canon of St Paul's and archdeacon of Middlesex. He held high administrative offices both in his home diocese and in the diocese of London.

So in his will it is perhaps not surprising that he remembered many of those churches and left money to them: to Buscot 33s 4d (£1.66p) for mending books and the chancel (both the responsibility of the rector which he, perhaps, had neglected) and 20s (£1) to its fabric fund; to St Endellion another 20s for the fabric, 20s for the chancel, and a pair of vestments; to Minehead 10s (50p) to mend the glass windows; to High Ham and Chulmleigh each a pair of vestments.

And he remembered people, too; not just friends of his own social and clerical class as might be expected, like Richard, who had been his curate at High Ham, and Robert of Lechlade, nicknamed Long Sir Robert, whom he had known since his Buscot days. He also remembered his servant Robert, his cooks Hugh and John Olum, and William Olym, formerly servant to his father.

But was all this generosity not just a trifle overdone? Was it all to secure the safety of his soul, and if so might the past just possibly conceal actions that required such extensive insurance? So comprehensive are the medieval records of this country that Richard Burton's murky past is not entirely lost. In 1392 he found himself brought before the justices of the peace in Gloucestershire accused of breaking and entering the house of Thomas Berkeley of Coberley, not far from Gloucester, and stealing goods to the value of 20s (£1). Fortunately for him he had influential friends, one of whom, Nicholas Slake, arranged for him a royal pardon.

In 1395 he was in trouble again, this time for refusing to pay taxes – not his own but those of the man for whom he stood proxy, the archdeacon of Wells. It is not clear why he refused, but he remained obstinate in his refusal and was excommunicated, and remaining stubborn for forty days was reported to the king. He obviously owed much to the man he was shielding, for the archdeacon was Nicholas Slake. Nine years later he was in court again, this time at Ilchester before the king's justices of assize, accused (as Richard Frere alias Bruton, canon) with Thomas Russell of Templecombe and Nicholas Younge of assaulting and attempting to murder Thomas atte Lee, the vicar of Templecombe. Lee and Bruton had quarrelled and had each put up a bond in the enormous sums of £400 to abide by arbitration, but presumably after the assault Lee had taken Russell and Younge to the ecclesiastical court at Wells, and Bruton had used his position at Wells to damage Lee's cause against them. The case cost Lee £100 and for nine months he dared not leave the protection of the abbot of Glastonbury.

The man who could do all this and still pursue a successful clerical career came in 1408 to be the most powerful man in the diocese of Bath and Wells, for the new bishop, Nicholas Bubwith, appointed him his chief legal and administrative officer. After that no-one in the diocese evidently dared to report any of his misdemeanours; but he dabbled in politics and was overheard in the house of a cardmaker in Wells speaking what turned out to be unwise words. On 14 October 1415 Bruton and others were obviously discussing the recent execution of Richard, earl of Cambridge, and Sir Thomas Scrope at Southampton for plotting against Henry V. Bruton let it be known (so John Williams of Cardiff reported to the Bristol sheriff and coroners) that in his opinion neither Henry IV nor Henry V were rightfully kings of England. Now that the latter was safely in France and might well remain so (the victory at Agincourt was just over a week away) he, Bruton, was prepared to spend £6000 to depose him.

No action seems to have been taken, for who would take the word of a Welshman against that of the senior church lawyer in the diocese? Someone who had evidently suffered at his hands wrote in an ancient book known as the Red Book of Bath (now kept at Longleat) that Bruton's charges for proving wills in his court at Wells were extortionate. The sum of £6000 was enormous too, but we have there the source of his wealth; no wonder when his death approached he had a heavy conscience.

There is nothing civil about a civil war and some of the events during the Wars of the Roses in the fifteenth century were very nasty indeed. One of the nastiest, and also one of the most puzzling, was the execution of Humphrey Stafford, Baron Stafford of Southwick and earl of Devon, in Bridgwater on 17 August 1469. He was not, it is true, a very nice man; in fact he was greedy and ambitious according to one historian. But he had fought for Edward of York at the battle of Towton against the Lancastrians in 1461 which gave Edward the throne. In return for this loyalty Humphrey was summoned to Parliament as Baron Stafford and he was a firm favourite of the king, one of the new men whom Warwick the Kingmaker did not much care for. So he was in the thick of trouble when in the summer of 1468 Edward's government began to see a Lancastrian conspirator around every corner.

Among those then accused of opposition were Henry Courtenay, heir of a former earl of Devon, and Thomas Hungerford. Both were arrested and taken to Salisbury for trial and Humphrey Stafford was one of the judges who condemned them both to a nasty death. He was later accused of arranging their downfall. That was not entirely true for the king himself was clearly much involved, but it was remembered later that Humphrey became earl of Devon just a few months after the trial in which the heir to the title had been condemned.

Now there really was opposition to the king, especially in the North, led by a man calling himself Robin of Redesdale, and Edward summoned troops from the West Country and Wales to meet him at Nottingham. Those from Wales were led by William Herbert, earl of Pembroke, those from the West by Humphrey, the very new earl of Devon.

The real opposition came from Warwick the Kingmaker, who declared that Pembroke and Devon were 'seducious persones' who were misleading the king. Warwick himself was powerful, far more so than the king imagined. One part of his forces moved from Kent to London and then north towards Coventry where another was in possession. Meanwhile Pembroke and Devon seem to have quarrelled and on 25 July 1469 camped separately. The rebel forces fell on Pembroke at Edgecote near Banbury on the following day and the Welshmen were overwhelmed. Pembroke himself was captured and soon summarily executed; Devon escaped. Very soon afterwards the king was a prisoner and Warwick was in complete control, executing all the former favourites he could lay his hands on, and they included, of course, Humphrey Stafford, earl of Devon.

Now this is where the problem arises. Stafford fled towards home and friends in the West Country. The route he took we do not know, but it is certain that he came at last to Bridgwater where, according to the historian John Warkworth, the only reliable source for many events at the time, he was executed 'by the common people'. That phrase sounds very much like some kind of summary execution by a mob, hardly the sort of behaviour to expect from a law-abiding Somerset town.

And the idea is inherently unlikely for he was well known in Bridgwater. He had property in Enmore and in 1465 Edward IV had appointed him constable and keeper of Bridgwater castle, steward of the lordship and manor, and keeper of Petherton forest. He may, perhaps, have been unpopular locally, but the corporation of Bridgwater entertained him more than once and the town's bailiff once went over the Wells to speak with him. He was a powerful figure in the West whose real enemies were Warwick and his Neville cronies who resented his influence with the king. But now, after the defeat at Edgecote, Edward IV was no longer in charge. Probably a Neville force had followed Stafford to Bridgwater and Nevilles were later at pains to blame others for his death.

And there is confirmation from Stafford's remarkable will. It is a very long document, begun in 1463, with additions in English in 1467 written in his own hand and which he had lodged with the abbot of Glastonbury for safe keeping. There followed a further letter, written at Cirencester on 21 July 1469 when he was evidently on his way to Edgecote, 'written in haste' to one of his trusted friends. In it he declared that he was sending some sealed legal documents that were not to be opened unless 'ye hire (hear) of me other tidings of me than goode'. It was as well to settle affairs before a battle, and with such a treacherous enemy. And that is not all. The very last part of his will was made at Bridgwater in very trying circumstances. The game was now up and in that final codicil he arranged for his burial at Glastonbury Abbey and for sermons to be preached in every church in Somerset, Dorset, Devon, Cornwall and Wiltshire. He asked forgiveness of all those whom he had wronged and had not in his will already given due recompense; and he freely forgave 'alle the worlde and biseche Jesu to forgyf me'.

Stafford's will is a touching document, and the most poignant phrase comes at the end: 'Writen (by) my hande the day of my dethe'. Here was no summary execution; Stafford knew he was to die and faced his end bravely. Here was no mob, as the Nevilles wanted to imply. The will is clearly not the work of one who had been taken suddenly ill; the headsman was waiting, but in no great hurry. And when it was all over there was apparently no disgrace. Stafford could hardly have been attainted for treason, for there was no-one more loyal to the king; but Warwick was now in power and for the moment Warwick's word was law. There was no sort of appeal against such justice.

Humphrey Stafford left no children but his wishes were carried out by his executors, led by John Kendall, a prominent Bridgwater merchant. He was buried, as he had wished, in the abbey church at Glastonbury, and there John Leland saw his tomb in the 1530s under an arch on the south side of the nave.

Among the archives of Bridgwater corporation now lodged in the Somerset Archives office are several documents in which the faithful John Kendall carried out Stafford's wishes: a receipt in 1474 for a debt of £10 to the man who married the late earl's widow, and another in 1476 for £15. Still in 1483 the executors were acting, making an agreement with an Exeter tailor.

And Bridgwater, which had never until that time taken a more active role in politics than to send men to represent it in parliament, was for just a few days at the centre of national affairs. Kendall, perhaps Stafford's closest friend in the town, continued to play a leading part in the affairs of the port, serving in parliament, negotiating a new charter, becoming the town's first mayor, doing business with men in London, Bristol, Exeter and Bordeaux, and possibly regretting that he had ever agreed to be Stafford's executor.

—*wm*—

It was not the first nor the last rebellion against heavy taxes, but it was more than that; tantamount, one observer said, to another civil war and the last hardly over. And Somerset felt the full force of it.

The year was 1497. About the middle of May trouble began in west Cornwall and by the end of the month there were enough angry Cornishmen under the leadership of Michael Joseph an Gof (the Smith) and Thomas Flamank to frighten the citizens of Exeter into opening their gates. By the time the rebels reached Taunton there were risings in their support in Devizes, Dorchester and Winchester, and by that time some gentry had joined them and a noble leader. James Tuchet, Lord Audley, whose home was at Nether Stowey, had been a strong supporter of Edward IV but had never been entirely trusted either by Edward's brother Richard III nor by Henry Tudor, Henry VII. Among the gentry were Roger Twynyho of Keyford near Frome, a former henchman of the late and untrustworthy duke of Clarence, and John Verney who had been enthusiastic for Richard III. Those men were not just against paying too much tax, they were political malcontents ready to support a York against a Tudor, this time a (pretended) Richard, duke of York, not done to death in the Tower. The Richard in question turned out to be Perkin Warbeck.

So when the rebels arrived in Wells early in June 1497 they sent for Warbeck, then in Scotland, and offered their support for his cause. By then east and central Somerset was in arms – estimates vary between 15,000 and 40,000 – but Bristol was prepared to resist them and the rebel leaders decided instead to press on for London. Joseph took the route to Winchester and Guildford while Audley went through North Wiltshire to the Thames valley.

At Blackheath, south-east of London, the rebel army was defeated by the king's forces led by his chamberlain Giles, Lord Daubeney – a Somerset man with homes at Barrington and South Petherton. Just possibly he had been a little equivocal in his action at an earlier skirmish near Guildford, for many of the rebels were neighbours, friends or tenants. But now, although Daubeney himself was wounded, there was no holding back. In order that the troubles which were the Wars of the Roses were not repeated, decisive action was taken, for the rebels had come too near London for comfort.

Audley, Joseph and Flamank were soon dead, the rebels in flight back to the West. The other player, Perkin Warbeck *alias* Richard duke of York, *alias* Richard IV, left Scotland in August and made for rebellious Cornwall. He landed on 7 September near Land's End among friends but actually a virtual prisoner of John Taylor, an Exeter man and a fanatical Yorkist. About 3000 men mustered at Bodmin and forced the earl of Devon to withdraw before them, but Henry Tudor was now prepared. Lord Daubeney, recovered from his wounds, mustered a vanguard probably between Bath and Bristol from Somerset, Gloucestershire, Wiltshire and South Wales. Robert, Lord Willoughby de Broke, led marines based at Portsmouth.

The rebels failed to take Exeter and marched eastwards, reaching Taunton on 19 September. Desertions from a muster of perhaps 8000 men were not stemmed by Taylor's claim that he had a papal bull declaring that Richard IV (Warbeck) was a true son of Edward IV and thus the rightful king.

On 20 September the rebels, camping in the fields around Taunton, were told that 'certain lords' were preparing to help them, but men began to disappear in greater numbers 'providing theyr aune saveguard', for Lord Daubeney was at Glastonbury and his scouts were several miles nearer, offering amnesty to all who would surrender. That night Taylor and Warbeck fled.

The rebels, leaderless, either fled next morning or became violent. One James the Rover, with several hundred thugs had captured the local tax collector who had been at the centre of the rebellion in Cornwall in May. The poor man, John Oby, a clergyman who held the office of provost of the college at Glasney near Falmouth, was 'tyrannously dysmembrid' in Taunton market place. Next day Daubeney entered the town.

Meanwhile Warbeck, Taylor and some 60 mounted men went to Minehead and then split up. Taylor somehow returned to France; some went to London to continue plotting. Warbeck and three friends took refuge in Beaulieu Abbey but soon surrendered to the king on the promise of his life.

The West was thus secure, but the king came to see for himself. On 29 September with 10,000 men he came to Bath and on the next day to Wells where, according to tradition, he stayed at the Deanery. On 2 October he moved to Glastonbury and the building called the King's Lodgings at the abbey was probably so named after his visit. He spent the next night at Bridgwater, the next two (4 and 5 October) at Taunton where one night, probably at the priory, he lost money at cards. Also at Taunton Warbeck appeared before the king, wearing the finery of Richard IV, and claimed he had been forced into treason. He then composed a full confession, saying he was not the duke of York at all but a native of Tournai.

Henry Tudor resumed his progress to Exeter on 6 October, taking Warbeck with him, and on his return to London made the erstwhile prince an object of general ridicule. For a time he was kept under ward at Court but escaped and was imprisoned in the Tower. The whole sorry affair ended in November 1499 when Warbeck was hanged.

On the day after his arrival at Exeter the king wrote that the people of Devon appeared before him in huge numbers with halters round their necks and that he had pardoned all but 'the chief stirrers and doers'. A year later (after the taxes which had begun the trouble had been paid in full) a commission began to inquire into those implicated in the rebellion. The whole of Devon paid about £500 in fines. A similar inquiry implicated over 3000 people, mostly from Somerset but nearly 200 from Dorset, Wiltshire and Hampshire. Somerset folk, for 'favouring and assisting' the rebellion, were fined nearly £8000. Sir John Speke of Whitelackington and Sir Hugh Luttrell of Dunster each had to find the huge sum of £200, John Tose and Richard Warre of Taunton and John Hervy of Congresbury £100. Whatever the real truth of the matter, the king evidently thought Somerset folk were more rebellious than the rest, and so they paid.

—*mm*—

Edward Stafford, duke of Buckingham, was an aristocrat and he knew it. He was also very vain and foolish and he fell out with Cardinal Wolsey, together a fatal combination. Of his birth he clearly boasted, for he was a descendant of Edward III through Edward's youngest son Thomas of Woodstock, and his nearer ancestors had been dukes since 1444 when his great-grandfather had acquired the title to add to his earldoms of Buckingham, Hereford, Stafford, Northampton and Perche and his lordships of Brecknock and Holderness.

And though he inherited all but the dukedom, his great grandfather certainly earned that for his loyal service to the Crown in France as Lieutenant-General in Normandy, Captain of Calais, Lieutenant of the Marches and Ambassador. And for that loyalty he paid the extreme price, killed fighting for his king, Henry VI, at the battle of Northampton in 1460. His son and namesake was already dead, killed fighting for the same cause at the first battle of St Albans in 1455.

So enter the second duke, born after the death of his father and before his fifth birthday both constable of Nottingham castle and duke of Buckingham. Still aged only nine he was made a knight of the Bath at the coronation of Queen Elizabeth, wife of Edward IV, in 1465 and was evidently soon committed to the cause of the Yorkists for his wife was the new queen's sister. Indeed, he played an important part in the dubious moves which gave Richard III the throne, and for his support was created Lord High Constable of England.

But Staffords were evidently not natural Yorkists and within a few months of Richard's accession the duke was incompetently plotting to place the earl of Richmond, Henry Tudor, on the throne. He was arrested and executed without trial at Salisbury, leaving Edward his son and heir aged just over five.

Richmond's victory over Richard III at Bosworth in 1485 changed the young duke's fortunes again and at the coronation of Henry VIII he was Lord High Constable, Lord High Steward and Bearer of the Crown. And loyally he followed his new sovereign to France, commanding in the right wing at the battle of Thérouenne in 1513. But he was so evidently proud of his ancestry, so fond of showing off and so rash in speech that his words were soon being noted and even taken seriously, however light-heartedly they were uttered.

Somebody remembered hearing him say, no doubt in his cups, words that suggested he was interested in the deposition and death of the king, and when visitors looked over the wall of the churchyard at Thornbury they no doubt marvelled at the almost fantastic castle being built there, some of its windows almost direct copies of windows at Windsor castle. And the new parts of the church itself included carvings of the family badges, the Stafford knot and the broom pod of the Plantagenets. In April 1512 Stafford sent his chaplain from Thornbury to the priory at Hinton Charterhouse near Bath, to speak with a monk there who had a reputation for prophecy.

Nicholas Hopkins, the monk, soon became an embarrassment to his fellows and eventually found himself a prisoner in the Tower of London; his cryptic words, promising the duke 'that he should have all' were received by Buckingham as a clear foretelling of his own succession to the throne. Letters or visits to Hopkins at Hinton Charterhouse continued and the duke was so entirely satisfied that he gave the monks an annuity of £6 to buy a tun of wine and the promise of a lump sum of £20 to provide a better water supply for the monastery. In fact only £16 was ever paid; Buckingham was more free with promises than with cash.

Late in March 1521 the duke set out from Thornbury for another trip into Somerset. Just before he left, his treasurer paid John Spanyerd of North Petherton 2s (10p) for a present of two live foxes. The duke's no doubt impressive cavalcade – his chancellor had spent large sums on cloth of gold and silver and silks in London – went via Keynsham abbey to Farleigh Hungerford castle, where Hungerford's servant showed the party round. The treasurer in his accounts noted that the castle was 'beside the charterhouse at Henton' because he knew the priory so well.

At the end of April the duke was shown round the bishop's palace at Wells by its keeper and moved on the same day to Glastonbury, where he lodged with Abbot Bere. The treasurer recorded payments over the next three days to the shrine of St Joseph, to 'an idiot of the abbey' and to the holy relics there, and made gifts to two of the abbot's servants, a French poet and a harper, and to another servant whose longbow had been broken by one of the duke's own men. Perhaps he admired some of the woven hangings in the abbot's lodging for on 20 May the treasurer made a small gift to the abbot's 'arasman'.

But by that time the duke had been dead for three days, executed on Tower Hill for high treason. Probably at the instigation of Wolsey, but on behalf of a king who was sensitive to any opposition and whose ancestry was much more modest than that of Buckingham, all those foolish words were taken literally and written down; so, too, were the words (according to Shakespeare) of the 'Chartreux friar ... who fed him every minute with words of sovereignty ... that devil-monk ... that made this mischief'.

Buckingham's honours were forfeited, his possessions taken into the hands of the Crown. With them went papers, and especially the accounts of his treasurer, from which the details of the duke's visit to Glastonbury have been reconstructed. He had no legitimate children, though a younger branch of the family continued to live at Thornbury until the mid twentieth century. The last Stafford owner knew far more about ancestry than the last duke: Sir Algar Howard was for six years Garter Principal King of Arms.

One final mystery. On 9 April 1608 it was recorded in the register of St Botolph's church, Bishopsgate, that 'the Lady Mary Bohun *alias* Stafford [was] buried out of Bethlehem House, aged 140'. Bohun was the name of the duke's maternal ancestor. Was Mary, perhaps, his elder sister?

5
SOMERSET MEN ABROAD

*"Should your falcon suffer from the frounce, fungus or rheumatiz,
the best cure was to make pills of salt and pepper in butter
and insert them in the bird's nostrils"*

*Few people nowadays have not been abroad; air travel has made even the
most exotic destination almost a commonplace. Military and naval service took
men from the county to places they might well not have chosen from the time
medieval kings laid claims to France to the time when Poland and the Empire had
to be defended from invasion; and before then religious and economic pressures
encouraged folk to seek their fortunes across the Atlantic. Other travellers went
as ambassadors for their king or as wandering scholars. The achievements of a
distinguished few were truly amazing.*

The man who composed treatises on the care of falcons and the use of the astrolabe and was the translator of Arabic scientific texts has a good claim to be Somerset's most distinguished son. Yet he was born so long ago that what he studied might not in modern terms be called science at all; and his native English and the Latin he was taught at a typical monastic school would hardly have taken him very far. But he was clearly a bright lad who had soon advanced beyond rudimentary mathematics and may even have started astronomy as a boy. As a man he travelled widely in Europe and the Mediterranean, and through his translations of Arabic manuscripts made the mathematics of Euclid the key to huge scientific advances in the Western world.

Why was the achievement so remarkable, and who was this Somerset prodigy? Simply that the date is the end of the eleventh century, not long after the Norman Conquest; and the young man was Adelard of Bath. Inevitably, very little is known about Adelard and most of it comes from his own writings. He was born in Bath about 1080 and was proud of it. To know so much about falconry as he did implies he was from a wealthy or well connected family: he knew a good deal about fishing and music as well. His father Fastrad seems to have been a substantial tenant of Bishop Giso of Wells in Wells, Yatton and Banwell; and to judge by his name he may well have been a native of Lorraine, Bishop Giso's home.

From son of bishop's tenant to member of bishop's household was no great step, and by 1106 Adelard was working for Giso's successor, Bishop John of Tours, the man who removed his *cathedra* from Wells to Bath and who, as a doctor, knew a thing or two about mineral waters.

Bishop John sent Adelard to his own home city of Tours where, as a student, he played the cithara to entertain Henry I's queen. After Tours he went to Laon, not far from Rheims, then very popular with English students, several of whom later had distinguished careers as bishops and financial advisers after learning how to use the abacus there. Adelard himself later wrote a book about the abacus and probably worked with his former fellow students in government finance back in England.

From Laon Adelard went, probably via southern Italy and Greece, to the Middle East. His goal was Antioch where he experienced a violent earthquake known to have affected much of modern Turkey in 1114. The successes of the Crusaders at the time brought Arabic manuscripts into Western hands, and during his seven years of travel Adelard acquired the thirteen books of Euclid which had earlier been translated from Greek (which Westerners did not know) into Arabic (which Adelard did). He might even have come across the mathematical and astronomical work of Omar Khayyam, better known then than his poetry.

Scientists at the time were not always popular and were often accused of dabbling in the occult. For that reason one book well known both in Europe and beyond was once called *A Little Key to Drawing*, intended to disguise the fact that it dealt with alchemy and magic. But at least one version of that book, which is now lost, had additions, probably by Adelard. They reveal not just a man incurably curious, but one with very personal tastes: directions on how to measure heights using an instrument based on a right-angled triangle, how to make alcohol, how to make sugar candy or toffee from sugar cane, how to make yellow and green dye.

Returning to England after such remarkable travels, Adelard seems to have entered the royal court, cast at least one horoscope for the king, and worked in the royal Exchequer. His greatest work, however, was a book on natural science that was read throughout the Middle Ages and was even translated into Hebrew. At about the same time he wrote his book on falconry, concentrating on the cure of ailments. Accidents to the chest, for instance, might be cured with iron filings mixed with dove's heart or radish and May butter. Should your falcon suffer from the frounce, fungus or rheumatiz, the best cure was to make pills of salt and pepper in butter and insert them in the bird's nostrils. And should your bird become feverish it should be given duckweed or bathed in water in which a crane had been cooked.

One other great contribution to rank with Adelard's translation of Euclid's works on mathematics was a translation of the Zij, astronomical tables that originated in a Sanskrit text brought from India to Baghdad. That may sound remarkably abstruse and even boring, but the work introduced trigonometry and sine to Europe.

Adelard, the lad from Somerset, ended his distinguished career as Court Astrologer and surviving royal horoscopes now in the British Library may even be in his own hand. His skill was required especially during the civil war of Stephen's reign in which Robert, Bishop of Bath, and his city were very much involved. The great scientist lived, it seems, to see the victory of his pupil Henry of Anjou as King Henry II.

mm

Richard Bere has only a lane named after him in Glastonbury but after Dunstan he was probably the most distinguished of its abbots. His name suggests he may have come from the hamlet of Beer in High Ham, but that is only a guess. His early career is equally shadowy and mysterious; he held, so far as is known, no office within the abbey until, almost out of the blue, Bishop Fox nominated him as abbot in 1493 after the monks had chosen a man whom the bishop would not accept.

All rather curious, though he had been made sub-deacon in February 1478 and deacon in 1479, which means he had been born about 1455. He must have done something more: Oxford University made him a Doctor in Theology in 1503 and he had been priested before 1493, so another guess would be that he had studied abroad, perhaps at one of the universities in northern Italy which specialised in law. The humanist scholar Erasmus of Rotterdam regarded Bere with respect as a fellow scholar with like interests.

Study in Italy is perhaps more than a guess because in 1503 Bere was appointed to head a diplomatic mission to Rome, to congratulate the new pope, Pius III, on his election. Some knowledge of Italy and of Italian would surely have been useful. But who recommended him for the post? The king must have had the final decision, and Henry VII had met Bere when he had stayed at the abbey in 1497, but Bishop Oliver King would have had influence in the matter for he was the king's main adviser, Keeper of the Privy Seal, and he was Bere's diocesan as Bishop of Bath and Wells.

Bere's embassy started rather badly because the new pope died before they set out, so it was his successor, Pope Julius II, who had to be congratulated instead. Another duty for the diplomats was to confer the Order of the Garter on Duke Guidobaldo of Urbino, part of a delicate manoeuvre to seek the duke's support so that Henry, then Prince of Wales and later Henry VIII, could marry the duke's sister-in-law Katherine of Aragon. The whole journey cost the abbot and his abbey a huge sum, well over £800.

On his way home Bere evidently visited Loreto to see the popular shrine which was said to include the very room in which the Virgin Mary had been born in Nazareth and in which she had been saluted by the Angel Gabriel. On his return to Glastonbury he constructed a chapel named after Loreto in the abbey church.

That was but one of Bere's building schemes. In his time the central tower of the abbey church started to collapse and arches were quickly constructed, not unlike the inverted arches at Wells, to save it. He also began to build the Edgar Chapel and created the crypt under the Lady Chapel to become the focus of the popular cult of St Joseph of Arimathea. He also built some almshouses for women near the abbey entrance, the chapel of which still survives. Elsewhere his initials on buildings like the churches at Chedzoy, Westonzoyland, Bruton and St Benignus's, Glastonbury, and on the so-called leper hospital in Taunton are reminders of his generosity, or at any rate his willingness to lend money for good causes. He is known to have rebuilt the manor house at Sharpham as a summer retreat from the hurly-burly of Glastonbury, and there on the rebuilt house is the coat of arms of the abbey, a portcullis for the king, and a pelican, the badge adopted by the abbot himself.

Bere was a great champion of his abbey and its history. In his time all novices took new surnames on entering the abbey and those names recalled its (not always quite accurate) past – Arimathea, Edgar, Athelstan, Arthur, Benignus, Joseph, Patrick, Pantaleon and, of course, Dunstan.

The original Dunstan brought Abbot Bere some trouble. It was a Glastonbury tradition that, before the Conquest, some monks had gone to Canterbury and repatriated Dunstan's bones. Those bones were hidden until the great fire destroyed the abbey in 1184 and were then recovered, found in a box marked with the letters S and D for Saint Dunstan. A shrine for the saint's head was planned in the thirteenth century and made in the fourteenth.

Now in 1508 Abbot Bere upped the stakes by moving the shrine to a more prominent place, probably in his new Edgar Chapel. Archbishop Warham of Canterbury was incensed: so far as he and his monks were concerned Dunstan had never left Canterbury but, to make sure, a proper investigation was made at Canterbury which revealed a coffin and bones that proved the case. Bere was thereupon summoned to defend his claim, but replied that if the bones the archbishop had found were genuine, then Glastonbury had a better claim to them than Canterbury, and that Somerset folk had always venerated Dunstan more than the people of Kent. The archbishop was not amused.

Bere's name will always be associated with a 'Perambulation' or 'Survey' (it is really both) of the abbey estates, a detailed record of boundaries and tenants of the abbey at the beginning of the sixteenth century. This included the description of a journey, made over several years, around the boundary of that central part of the abbey's land called the Twelve Hides. The whole estate was extremely valuable and, inevitably, as head of one of the richest monasteries in the land Bere found himself involved in politics and high finance as well as diplomacy. He was by virtue of his office a member of the House of Lords and thus an obvious target when the cash-strapped king needed a loan – a little matter of £1000, for instance, in 1521.

Whether he liked it or not he was sometimes host to the mighty, like the king himself in 1497 and the Duke of Buckingham in 1521; and he was banker to neighbours, abbots, and bishops. At his death people owed him over £2800 and among the debtors were the archbishop of Dublin, the bishop of Winchester and the Lord Chief Justice of England.

What he was like personally is difficult to fathom. Somebody remembered him as 'just and upright in all his ways and for so accounted of amongst all sorts of people'. At a time when many had nothing good to say about monks, that must have been a compliment. His personal tastes ran to the employment of a harper, a French poet, and a maker of wall hangings.

～m～

When in the 1650s the earl of Berkshire found himself in financial difficulties he raised a mortgage on his land at West Pennard, borrowing money from a group of eminent and well-heeled people. Among them was Sir Charles Harbord whose financial acumen was almost legendary, a city businessman whose loyalty to Charles I and the Anglican Church forced him into exile in Holland in 1642 yet whose expertise was welcomed by Cromwell and whose genius with money helped to keep Charles II solvent.

But why should such a man, with addresses in Charing Cross, Westminster, and Staninghall in Norfolk, and a seat in Parliament for Launceston have a Somerset connection? Simply because he was a Somerset man, born in Wraxall and brought up in Welton, in Midsomer Norton.

His father William Harbord, who claimed family origins in Wales and a grandfather who came to England with Henry Tudor, died in 1616 while Charles was still young, holding a farm in Welton that was part of the Duchy of Cornwall. Evidently a careful man, he left instructions in his will that his son should have his plate, household goods and farm implements only at the age of twenty-five provided he behaved 'honestly and discreetly' and 'lived in good credit' with the approval of the executors and of his uncle John Tynte. On such conditions Charles could have his inheritance for half its real value.

Charles trained as a lawyer in London, married the daughter of a jeweller as his first wife and entered the service of the earl of Pembroke. He later described himself to his son as a self-made man, but clearly others helped. In 1631 he began a distinguished career in the service of the Crown as a surveyor-general and later as auditor, in the business of making as much money as possible from the royal estates. From 1636 he also worked for the Prince of Wales, from 1638 for Queen Henrietta Maria, and later still for Charles II's wife Catherine of Branganza. He was knighted in 1636.

All this work came to a temporary end in 1642 when he went into exile but began again at the Restoration and ended only with his death in 1679. As a loyal Crown servant, from 1661 to 1679 he served in the House of Commons as a Member for the Duchy of Cornwall seat of Launceston and was incredibly busy, appointed to 694 committees and delivering 65 reports, making at least 123 speeches and taking the chair many times.

That meant, of course, that he was involved in most of the excitements of the period: measures against Quakers and insolent popish priests, licentiousness, excessive expenditure, hackney coachmen, kidnapping, arrests on Sundays, popish recusants and butchers selling live cattle; and measures for the restoration of bishops to the House of Lords, for retrenchment of spending by the Royal household, for repair of highways, for a more relaxed attitude to religious tests. And, naturally, for or against any financial matter that ever was.

Someone described him as 'a very rich and covetous man who knew England well; and his parts were very quick about him in that great age, being past eighty'. Supposedly unrivalled as a surveyor, he calculated that the total area of England was 76 million acres and was wildly out; but he reckoned that he had saved the Crown £80,000 during his career and himself had made very little out of the business when most of his contemporaries had their hands in the till.

In his will he remembered his Somerset origins, leaving £10 a year to the inhabitants of Wraxall and another £10 to Midsomer Norton to bind out two fifteen-year-old lads as apprentices either to farmers, smiths or carpenters. But for one so rich, hardly over generous.

Sir Charles had three sons and three daughters. William, the second son, educated at Leyden and the Middle Temple, was also an MP and married a daughter of Dr Arthur Duck of North Cadbury, thus keeping up the Somerset connection. He was several times tax assessor for the county among many others, followed his father as surveyor-general of the Crown estates, and held several offices in Ireland. He was deeply involved with the business which brought William and Mary to the throne in 1689 and became a Privy Councillor. But his career, especially in Ireland, was a disaster. He was blamed for failing to send enough troops to defend it against James II after he had pointed out that the plan to spend £300,000 was inadequate. One of his opponents declared that 3000 men sent at the right time would have saved the island from Catholic invasion. 'I would ask that gentleman', Harbord retorted, what 3000 men he would have sent over. To send our own was not safe, and not fit to part with the Dutch'.

As paymaster he was expected to raise much more cash than he doled out in wages – every respectable paymaster did the same – but when he was set upon by some Enniskillen troopers after falling from his horse, without being recognised, he judged it was probably time to leave office. This he did without permission and much to the annoyance of the king. Soon afterwards he sat on a Commons committee to enquire into delay in relieving Londonderry – today he would surely have been ineligible to serve – and the committee exonerated him of any responsibility.

He had certainly lined his pockets as purveyor and paymaster of forces in Ireland. When he left his post there was a deficit of £406,000 on his accounts. With a parliamentary enquiry threatening he accepted the post of ambassador to the Sublime Porte, that is to the Turkish Empire, conveniently far from home. There he found safety of another kind for he died 'of a malignant fever' at Belgrade on his way to take up his duties.

*

Robert Clarke of Castle Cary decided in 1829 to write his memoirs but, unwilling to take too much financial risk, thought it better to publish in small paper-covered parts of 24 pages each. Only the first two parts have been discovered and are quite unknown to the British Library. The title page promised naval stories, anecdotes of the nobility, stagecoach accidents, matrimonial disappointments, occurrences in Brighton and the author's own reflections on life, but only the naval stories were reached by page 48 which ends in mid sentence. Perhaps the general public was not quite ready for Mr Clarke's outpourings.

The Clarke family pedigree at the beginning of the work is rather sketchy, but naturally includes Robert's remarkable father 'Painter' Clarke, schoolmaster, sign painter, bailiff and surveyor to Lord Holland. Still in his son's possession in 1829 was a deed by which Denys Rolle, for whom 'Painter' then worked, entered into agreement with some forty people, including women and children, who were to set sail from Greenwich in October 1768 as settlers in Mr Rolle's colony in Florida.

If only the deed had survived! The Rolle family papers at Exeter are silent on the whole affair and the story can only be pieced together from Denys's own account presented to the Board of Trade. Denys was the fourth son of John Rolle of Stevenstone in Devon and entered Parliament in 1761 as MP for Barnstaple. In May 1764 (Clarke says 1763) he obtained from the Crown a grant of 20,000 acres at St Mark's in East Florida with the intention of settling 200 white people there in ten years.

In June 1764 he left his constituents, his fellow MPs and his family and eventually landed at Charleston, South Carolina, in August, moving on down the coast to St Augustine. St Mark's was 240 miles further on through Indian country, so he decided to develop somewhere nearer at hand. The governor of the colony, James Grant, allowed him to go to Picola Fort from where his party moved along St John's river well into the swamps. There he got on splendidly with the natives who called him 'the Squire'.

The settlers were less happy 40 miles or so from government protection and the governor proved unfriendly to their leader. Rolle decided to return to England in 1765 to get a more certain grant of land and more recruits. By September 1766 he had nearly fifty new colonists and was armed with a recommendation from Lord Shelburne, but the governor was still unhelpful and thought in any event that negro labour would be more useful than white settlers. Clearly Rolle was getting on his nerves and he wrote to the Board of Trade saying that Rolle 'trifles away a great deal of money, and has nothing to show for it'. Rolle for his part, seems to have regarded anyone who disagreed with him as his enemy. But, as the governor pointed out, Rolle could be directed to land as far removed from him as possible.

Rolle returned to England in 1768, stood for election at Barnstaple again and despite his absence from the House during the previous session, was re-elected. Very soon afterwards he was off to Florida again. The researchers for the History of Parliament did not know of Robert Clarke's Memoirs and therefore of those articles of agreement between Rolle and the new group of settlers that left from Greenwich in October 1768. Possibly something may yet be found among the State Archives of Florida to tell more of their exploits.

Rolle was evidently not away for long, for he occasionally voted in the House of Commons with the Opposition although he never spoke there. He lost the 1774 election but not his taste for colonisation. In spite of losing, so he claimed, £28,488 'on the very lowest estimation' in Florida he asked in 1783 for a grant of land in the Bahamas in compensation and evidently succeeded. He died there in 1797.

What has all this to do with Somerset? 'Painter' Clarke lived in Castle Cary and Denys Rolle owned land in Wookey, where the Clarke family once lived, in High Ham and in Shapwick, all of which he sold, presumably to finance his Florida exploits. But were any of his settlers Somerset folk?

Without much more information we shall never know for certain, but it may just be significant that Robert Clarke built a house in Castle Cary that he called Florida House, and by 1818 he had built others adjacent and called the development Florida Place. Judging by his Memoirs Clarke was no better at business than Rolle, but did he choose the name as a recollection of his father's patron, or were there people in Castle Cary in the late eighteenth century who had actually set foot in Florida two centuries before its attractions had become so universally irresistible?

John Jacob was no ordinary boy; he was, after all, one of the five lively and intelligent sons of the Revd S.L. Jacob, vicar of Woolavington. His mother came from Kent and claimed the Dutch Admiral De Ruyter as an ancestor, so there was fighting in his blood. And the way he organised the local lads into some sort of fighting force – wooden swords, of course, nothing dangerous – was noticed by one of his older brothers, who nicknamed him The Warrior. That same brother, attacked by his sibling and company from the top of a hayrick, was later to defend him from the totally unfair accusation of a local farmer that John had done nothing less than tear the whole rick down.

John had been born at Woolavington Vicarage in 1812. Lessons at home were probably less formal than they ought to have been and John was apparently sent to a private school in Milverton. What he had learnt at home was to prove more useful in later life, for he was much happier either on the back of a horse or at the carpenter's bench. Yet when his turn came to choose a career the mathematics required in the formal examination for entry to the Honourable East India Company's Military Seminary at Addiscombe proved no problem. And this lad, only fourteen years old, was un-impressed by what he saw of

London when he was interviewed at East India House. It 'did not seem a bit odd to me...it seemed exactly like Bridgwater'.

So he was set for some kind of service abroad in the days when the East India Company was the colonial power in India and beyond. John Jacob was small in size and had a stammer; his fellow students were not all entirely friendly and discipline was tough and usually unfair. Although he passed out with remarkable results he was sent not, as he had much wished, to serve as an engineer but instead as a gunner. In 1828 at the age of sixteen he was appointed a Second Lieutenant in the Bombay Artillery.

There was not much to do, for the times were peaceful, though he nearly died by drowning and was for ever risking his neck and sometimes his horse at his favourite sport of hog hunting on the Deccan plateau. But there was some trouble brewing in the North West, that frontier which was to bring the British so much difficulty, so in 1839 the young John Jacob was sent in command of artillery into the barren hill country north of Cutchee, towards the modern boundary between India and Pakistan.

There he raised a regiment of horsemen, the Scinde Irregular Horse, who were anything but irregular, and proved himself to be one of the best officers his commander-in-chief had ever met in his life. At the battle of Meanee in 1843 his charge proved crucial to British success and at the battle of Shah-dad-poor Jacob and 800 men defeated Shere Mohamed with 8000.

But then he fell out with that same commander-in-chief for criticising his brother's published history of the campaign (he was right but foolish) and had to wait seven years even to be awarded the relevant campaign medals. He was, however, too useful to be entirely rejected (he once built a bridge which scientists said was impossible) and remained in what was called the Upper Sind, not simply recruiting a second cavalry regiment and keeping good order, but making roads and digging canals.

At the beginning of his rule in the Upper Sind his headquarters had been a village of some fifty inhabitants. By 1851 it had grown through his efforts to a trading city of some 12,000 people. Lord Dalhousie, Governor-General of India, was so impressed that he changed its name to Jacobabad and it is now, still bearing the name, one of the principal cities of Pakistan.

Over the next few years Jacob remained in his post far from his Somerset home, finally rewarded for his achievements by deserved promotion to

Brigadier General and Aide-de-Camp to the Queen. In 1857 he was, for a short time, in charge of the government of Persia – perhaps best kept from the centre of government, for he was for ever writing critical pamphlets about the poor organisation and discipline of the Bengal army (of course he was right, for it mutinied). He also invented an improved rifle and an explosive bullet (he was right about those, too).

John Jacob died in 1858 in the city that still bears his name. It was said that 10,000 of the city's 30,000 inhabitants were present at his funeral.

6
INSPIRING RELIGION

Religion played an important part in the lives of most people until the twentieth century. Before the Reformation there was less uniformity than is sometimes realised, notably after the followers of William Wycliffe, often known as Lollards, began a involvement that appealed to working people. Villages on Mendip were home to generations of men and women whose independence of mind led them to object to the authoritarianism of the Established Church and instead to listen with enthusiasm to the preaching of the Wesleys. Yet a majority in medieval England were content to follow the teachings and practice of the Church; and when the authority of that Church was called in question in the sixteenth century there were those, at first a brave minority, who were unwilling to change their adherence and suffered the harsh treatment meted out to Catholic recusants.

"And something worse befell another nun, Joan Trimelet, who found herself to be pregnant"

In the seventeenth century the country divided on lines partly based on religious differences and came to civil war; and the religious divide was not healed when the duke of Monmouth called for liberty to worship as a matter of conscience when the country was ruled by a king who was a declared Roman Catholic. The Roman Catholic Church was still subject to legal restraint at the beginning of the nineteenth century, but by that time the non-Anglican churches had become not only recognised but also divided; the Primitive Methodist Church was one of the more intriguing rebels.

One of the lecture rooms in Cannington Court, part of Cannington College, is rather different from the rest. It is named Clifford Hall and has the appearance of a chapel. That is exactly what it was, a chapel built by Lord Clifford at the end of the eighteenth century for his own family and for local Roman Catholics; it was later remodelled when, in 1807, nuns came to live in the house for the second time.

The first time was in the first half of the twelfth century, perhaps about 1138 when Robert de Curci founded a house for Benedictine nuns on the site. Lord Clifford's chapel was on or very near the place where the first nuns worshipped; next to it is still a large room under an arch-braced roof that may well have been the nuns' refectory. The rest of the building is difficult to interpret as a religious house, but one survival from the days before the house was dissolved in 1536 is the pair of wooden barred gates at the entrance. They may date from the middle of the fourteenth century when the bishop decreed that there had been too much contact between the nuns and the outside world. Specifically, two of the nuns, Matilda Pulham and Alice Northlode, had been in the habit of going into their chapel at night to have, so the bishop discovered, 'long and suspicious conversations' with two chaplains, Richard Sompnour and Hugh Willynge, from which nothing good could come. Something worse befell another nun, Joan Trimelet, who found herself to be pregnant.

The bishop's judgement was severe. Poor Joan was to be kept a virtual prisoner for a year on a diet of bread, water, soup and ale. The real culprits were the prioress and her deputy for failure of leadership and control. Henceforth the priory was to be governed entirely by two senior nuns and the former leaders were demoted. A gate was to be built to keep the nuns in and the world out.

In 1536 the then prioress and five nuns were turned out into that world. Cecily Verney perhaps went back to her home at Fairfield; Joan Towse and Alice Bisse went to the abbey at Shaftesbury to continue the religious life there, only to find themselves turned out again in 1539. Radigund Tilley, from a local Cannington family, may also have gone back home. She was still alive when Queen Elizabeth came to the throne and was generously looked after by members of the Coombe family: Bartholomew Coombe left her £20 and several gowns, Joan Coombe £30 and a silver goblet.

The nuns' former home was soon turned into a house for a courtier, Edward Rogers. The Rogers family stayed there until 1672 and then Cannington Court, or Court House as it was usually called, was given to Thomas Clifford, one of Charles II's ministers, the 'C' of the Cabal. Clifford became a Roman Catholic and so his family has remained. Their main home was always at Ugbrooke in Chudleigh, Devon, where a chapel had been built late in the seventeenth century for the private celebration of Catholic liturgy.

There was a Catholic chapel at Cannington by 1776 when Mass was celebrated monthly. Family accounts still kept at Ugbrooke record that Mr Pickrell, the chaplain, was paid £15 a year in salary and 2 guineas (£2.10p) to provide wine for the chapel. In 1805 a new chapel seems to have been begun and Lord Clifford paid £40 in 1807 to complete the roof. By that time some Benedictine nuns were in residence and every so often Lord Clifford or his wife sent them presents: two guineas (£2.10p) in 1807, £2 for peppermint drops in 1821, £5 for a treat in 1823, venison and salt fish in 1826, paté de Guimore and more venison in 1829.

Meanwhile the chapel had been rebuilt, much as it is today, by the architect John Peniston. It is octagonal, with a domed and coffered ceiling rising to a lantern, the former chancel flanked by two enormous Corinthian columns. The nuns moved from Cannington about 1835, leaving behind memorials in the quiet of their garden commemorating several of their sisters and also the head of the Catholic Church in the West of England, the Vicar Apostolic Bishop Collingridge (died 1829), whose home Cannington had been. One of Collingridge's successors, Bishop Bernard Ullathorne, also lodged there on his journeys westwards. After the nuns left the house returned to secular use for a time, but between 1863 and 1867 a third group of nuns lived there.

There then followed a remarkable change. Between 1868 and the end of the First World war the house was occupied by the West of England and South Wales Industrial School for Catholic boys, in 1881 including a total of 81 boarding pupils ranging in age between seven and fourteen years. No doubt for them attendance at the chapel was compulsory. Then in 1919 the final metamorphosis, what was then called the Somerset Farm Institute.

—*mm*—

A fair or revel was ever an excuse for lads to create a bit of a disturbance, but the fair at Huntspill on 29 June 1687 was really rather an exception, for it was only two years since the county had been more than a little disturbed by the events of the Monmouth Rebellion. Somerset folk had divided between those willing to accept the rule of the Catholic King James and those who advocated freedom of religious expression and a more liberal view of government. At Sedgemoor the decision had gone in favour of the king and people described the countryside as looking like a butcher's shop because parts of human bodies were, after judicial executions, displayed widely in towns and villages.

Such treatment and the transportation of many rebels to the Caribbean might be thought to have put paid to all traces of opposition, but nothing could be further from the truth. Religious and political feelings were held as strongly as ever. A gang from Burnham started the trouble on Revel Day in their own parish on 23 May 1687. William Wryde stood up and declared within the hearing of some hundred cudgel players that he and his friends Humphrey Beaton, Stephen Wryde, John Mulford the younger and John Hardidge were for the duke of Monmouth. They and several others from Burnham and else-where, as William Morris of Huntspill was later to tell the magistrate, 'in a distinct body' challenged the men of Huntspill to a fight. Thomas Roode of Huntspill heard Wryde's declaration and Wryde also had words with Thomas Leaker, demanding why he wore a particular kind of hat and why he rode about at such a rate.

And what was all that about Monmouth? The duke had surely been dead these two years, King James was still on his throne and such words were dangerous. Yet Morris later told the magistrate that he had been 'credibly informed' that Beaton and Stephen Wryde had enlisted under the rebel duke. What were such men doing at large instead of hanged or transported?

So Burnham challenged Huntspill; and at Huntspill fair on 29 June came the opportunity. John Tilley, a small farmer, called it a 'grievous riot' and blamed Burnham men. Humphrey Beaton assaulted Thomas Leaker, wounding him in the head 'very grievously', Jeremiah Tucker of Berrow and John Hardidge struck George Bird, John Lyte of Burnham hit William Martin, and Thomas West of South Brent struck him down. Tilley himself was also beaten by Thomas West.

But actually Ralph Howell of Huntspill struck the first blow in the riot against Thomas Varman of the same village, revealing the real cause of the affair; for Ralph was a genuine Monmouth rebel who in 1685 had been reported at Quarter Sessions as 'a rebel in arms'. It was a good fight, involving between forty and a hundred people on both sides, and a victory for Burnham; and to mark their triumph the Burnham men held up a bloody handkerchief that they declared to be Monmouth's colours, and sang songs about the duke: Holland, said John Hurford of Burnham, had defeated France.

Now that is all very curious. Only two years before, Lord Chief Justice Jeffreys and his fellows had been in those parts, meting out what passed for justice after a huge round-up of men absent from home at the time of Sedgemoor, whatever their excuse.

And yet here was Ralph Howell of Huntspill described as 'a listed soldier in Monmouth's army' and William Gould, known widely as a Monmouth soldier who 'was to be transported but that he broke prison', and Humphrey Beaton and Stephen Wryde, also, apparently, 'listed under Monmouth'.

Further research might possibly show what happened next and might reveal whether John Prowse, the magistrate, took matters further; copies of the depositions made to the magistrate were certainly sent to London. Some of the Burnham folk intended to do so at the next fair up the road at Edithmead. Was it a question of settling scores, for in the round-up after Sedgemoor neighbours were encouraged to report on the behaviour of neighbours and man-catchers could line their pockets? Now was perhaps the time to gain some sort of revenge against quislings.

Joseph Priest of Huntspill admitted as much to the magistrate. He said that he had assisted Thomas Keball and Thomas Hurman, two royal officers, and Spencer, father and son, in arresting several rebels at Burnham. Now he felt rather insecure. Burnham folk were out for revenge and felt it was now safe enough to do so.

Burnham itself, according to the roll-call of rebels, had been home to only two Monmouth men, Hugh Roper and Joseph Wickham. Roper, sentenced to be hanged, was later freed, Wickham died in Bristol under sentence of transportation. Huntspill, on the other hand, appears to have been much less loyal with fifteen rebels including Ralph Howell himself, Thomas Hurford and John Leaker the younger. But Hurford had been hanged at Yeovil and Leaker was in Barbados working on a sugar plantation. Their Burnham cousins evidently blamed Huntspill neighbours for their fate. And perhaps Humphrey Beaton had a similar motive; Nathaniel and Robert Beaton, both tried at Wells, were still languishing in the Caribbean and may well have been members of the same family.

It is clearly unwise to put political labels on a community simply by counting the number of rebels in the Monmouth roll-call. Monmouth still had ardent supporters in Burnham, Berrow, South Brent and Mark; men who no doubt cheered the news of the coming of William of Orange and cheered even louder when they heard of the flight of King James and the death of 'Judge' Jeffreys.

—*um*—

Richard Searl, His Majesty's collector of customs at Minehead, and W. Warren, his colleague the controller there, were responsible officials of the best, if perhaps of the least imaginative sort. They were assiduous in ensuring that the business of the ports under their control – Minehead itself, Watchet and Porlock Weir – was carried out with no detriment to the claims of His Majesty's Customs and Excise and the law of the land. Any activity they had not come across before was, by definition, a likely threat to their work and thus a breach of the law.

So they were not a little perturbed in the Autumn of 1822 when 'Mr. L.' took it into his head to intrude himself into their immediate notice by inducing the master of the sloop *The Fair Trader*, then lying in the harbour at Minehead, to raise what was known as the Bethel Flag at his mast head. Having given notice of his intention, the minister proceeded to preach to a 'concourse' of people both from the town and the quay.

The appearance of the minister seems to have given offence to some and the flag certainly alarmed Mr Searl and Mr Warren. Thus they duly gave notice in writing that if the flag were to appear on any vessel within their jurisdiction, such vessel would be seized and its captain prosecuted and fined up to £500 as the relevant Act required. That, of course, was the question. Was the Act under which they proceeded relevant? Unfortunately for Messrs Seward and Warren the minister had done his homework. He had, in fact, been associated with what was called the Bethel Movement for several years, and while not so innocent as to expect no opposition, was on firm ground so far as the law was concerned and was not without powerful supporters far from Minehead. And he had, undoubtedly, been instrumental in the establishment of a branch of the Bethel Union in Watchet, which had invested in the flag that had so annoyed the Customs men.

The threat of punitive fines required action, and action was taken. Mr J.L., describing himself as Secretary to the Watchet Bethel Union, wrote from Minehead to the President of the national Bethel Union, none other than Admiral Lord Gambier, G.C.B., formerly a Lord of the Admiralty, an expert on naval signals, and President of the Church Missionary Society. His Lordship replied within a fortnight declaring with great force that the Bethel Flag was a signal flag, not any kind of flag envisaged in the Act that might be flown to mask identity or aid smuggling. Futhermore, the Bethel Flag was in use almost daily in the port of London and other ports, and appeared there without obstacle. His Lordship concluded that should there be further obstruction, he would personally solicit the Government for redress.

Lord Gambier's reply was handed to the officers at the Custom House at Watchet with some alacrity and a copy was sent to Minehead. Mr J.L. was informed that none of the officials would take notice of his Lordship's opinion, so he decided to act. One evening at the end of May 1823 it was proposed to hold a meeting on Watchet pier. The Bethel Flag was accordingly hoisted at the masthead of the sloop *Sociable Friends* with the full approval of Captain William Gimblett, both master and owner and a member of Watchet's Bethel Union Society.

Almost immediately Messrs Jenkin and Boswell, Watchet's customs officers, appeared and demanded its removal, first ascertaining that its appearance had not been ordered by the master of the sloop but by the secretary of the society. The flag duly came down from the masthead, but during the meeting the flag flew boldly from one of Captain Gimblett's oars lashed to one of the mooring posts of the pier.

Next day Mr J.L. sent a further letter to Lord Gambier, describing the most recent events and enclosing a letter he had just received from Messrs Searl and Warren, again quoting the law and saying that they proposed to send correspondence on the subject to the Honourable Board of Customs. Lord Gambier was as good as his word. On receipt of J.L.'s second letter of 30 May he wrote to the Customs Commissioners a letter of complaint and within a few days received a reply to the effect that what the Minehead officers were doing was very improper. On the same day, 9 June 1823, Searl and Warren informed Mr J.L. that it was the opinion of their Honours the Board of Customs that the Bethel Flag did not infringe the law, and that they, the said Richard Searl and W. Warren, were therefore directed to refrain from future interference and remained, Mr J.L.'s humble servants. There was no mention of any apology.

Such a pathetic end was something of a disappointment. A few civil servants had been made to look foolish, just the sort of story a modern tabloid would have offered money to expose. The equivalent in the 1820s was a pamphlet, nor written in pithy and exaggerated sentences but at length, occupying 36 closely-printed pages, printed, published and sold in Bristol by T.D. Clark and priced at 3d (1p) a copy. The author, and one senses the driving force behind the whole affair, was the Revd G.C. Smith of Penzance, demonstrably a Christian gentleman. His charity towards the Minehead customs officers was overflowing; he simply could not understand how, when the whole country knew about the Bethel Flag, Minehead did not. Was Minehead, he asked, 'the only dark spot in this distinguished land of religious liberty?' Searl and Warren would never be allowed to forget the episode. Before the story was told in such great detail the beginnings of it appeared in *The Sailors Magazine*. 'Few Officers of Customs', Mr Smith declared with more irony than charity, 'will be more distinguished in the profession'.

—*mm*—

Robert Williams, the author's great-grandfather, died at his home at Rodden near Abbotsbury in Dorset at the age of eighty-seven 'after sixty years and over of unbroken membership [of the Primitive Methodist Church] and nearly the same period as a local preacher. He will be long remembered as a true man, a genuine Christian and a most devoted and loyal member of our church. None can tabulate the long journeys and difficulties encountered by him in the discharge of his duties for God'. So ran an obituary, and a family tradition suggests that among the difficulties were his political opinions. One of his possessions was a portrait of Mr Gladstone, for besides being a farmer and preacher he was Liberal agent in the South Dorset constituency.

The 1860s, when Robert Williams was beginning his ministry, were probably the years when Primitive Methodism was at its most active, and every village – almost every hamlet – along the Somerset-Dorset border as well as in South Dorset bore evidence of the work of its missionary Teachers (ministers) and regular lay preachers. Not every visit of a Teacher resulted in a chapel, of course; meetings could as well be held in farmhouse kitchens and cottage parlours. A chapel was an expense far beyond the means of the labourers who made up much of the membership; 'Prims' were a social step or two down from the farmers and smallholders who belonged to the Wesleyan Connexion.

But with the 'Prims' there was enthusiasm; and enthusiasm meant, in the pioneering days of the 1830s and 1840s, 'rant and missile', informal, charismatic road-side preaching attracting stones and rotten eggs. In the more accepting times of the 1860s Sunday worship and hopefully a Sunday school, Missionary Meetings, Revival Meetings, and the curiously-named Protracted Meetings, meetings on up to six days in succession. And those meetings, there is no doubt, were not social gatherings. This was serious religion, this was about spreading the Gospel, about conversion. Leaders of each meeting received clear instructions: 'At the Revival and Protracted Meetings it is particularly requested that the discourses be very short, so that there may be more time for prayer'. Just possibly the brethren were talking too much.

And such enthusiam produced results. In 1847 the circuit of chapels and meeting-places based on Motcombe in Dorset included places like Semley, Hindon and Mere in Wiltshire. By 1861 a Sherborne branch stretched well into Somerset – Milborne Port, of course, and Yeovil, Tintinhull, the Chinnocks, Ash, Stoke, Montacute, even the little community at Ilchester Mead. A year later and there were Prims at Stoke Trister, Bayford and Charlton Musgrove.

It was a story of remarkable growth and Primitive Methodist bureaucracy has left us some splendid sources from which to follow it, the annual Circuit Reports comprising several pages of detailed questions and often very frank answers. The leaders of the connexion wanted minute statistics but also demanded to know whether the full-time Teachers carried out the required number of annual visits to members, whether they preached to excess, even whether they smoked. The remarkable results of the 1860s, of course, were only the results, the members would claim, of the prayers of the faithful and the Grace of God. And perhaps, too, a softening of approach: Tea Meetings and Camp Meetings introduced an almost frivolous social element so necessary in a more comfortable age.

The statistics are clear in their message of expansion. When the first, possibly open-air, meeting was held at Penselwood is not known, but a chapel was being built when the first surviving Circuit Report was made in 1860. By 1863 there were ten teachers and sixty-two children in a Sunday school. Two years later there were eighteen teachers and eighty-six pupils. Still in 1890 the school flourished with fifty-five children although the population of that and neighbouring villages had fallen seriously.

Not all was success. The group at Bayford lasted four years, at Stoke five, at Charlton seven. Such results are hardly surprising for many of those village congregations were very small and had to support themselves. In 1849 the largest in the Sherborne circuit was Sherborne itself with twenty-four members and two 'on trial'. Next came Preston with fifteen members followed by East Chinnock with fourteen and two on trial. Ten years later and Odcombe topped the list with thirty-two members and four on trial, followed by a chapel on Coker Hill with seventeen members. Sherborne was then down to nine members, Preston a total of eleven, Chinnock none at all. Revival in the

1860s had brought a total of 325 members in the circuit by 1863, but it was a total that could not be sustained.

The archive offices at Taunton and Dorchester have in their care a whole range of records of the 'Prims' and other branches of Methodism that played such a significant part in village communities. They are not always easy to use, and the little groups like those at Stoke Trister or Bayford will probably always remain an enigma, but the faithful men and women who preached or taught or prayed or made those vital urns of tea deserve to be remembered even if a few also merited the rebuke implied by the quotation printed on one of the circuit plans: 'Slow singing, long praying in public and late attendance on the means of Grace, are indubitable marks of a low state of piety'.

7

DOING DEALS

"... among many young men found to be drunk and disorderly at the fair was one called Thomas Wolsey, a young clergyman from foreign parts – so to the stocks for him!"

The market and the fair, whether in town or village, made the world go around. They were not just where the farmer drove his surplus stock and carried his grain or his cloth for sale and where his wife brought butter, cheese, eggs, cider and perhaps vegetables for those who could not produce them. They were, like the town emporium and the village shop, social centres. To market and fair came butchers and millers and clothiers, dealers in salt and kitchen wares without which life on a remote farm might be even more difficult. And, in the hope that a penny or two might be made before anyone noticed, a fortune teller, a tooth-drawer, a quack doctor, even a seller of spurious pardons. And when a sale had been agreed it had to be sealed over a pot or two of ale at an inn that was sure to be conveniently nearby where, perhaps, the clothier or the more respectable dealer was staying for a night or two. Inns were thus at the heart of Somerset business.

The title of the oldest inn in the county is impossible to prove though occasionally claimed: so much depends on the chance survival of records. Surely one of the earliest must be the tavern at Aley on the Quantocks, from which Geoffrey de Malecomb was returning in 1201 when William the cobbler killed him and stole his cap. Inns were essential, for water supplies were often polluted and convivial drinking was one of the pleasures of life. Glastonbury, often full of pilgrims, was also full of alehouses, and in 1314 the proprietors of sixty-eight of those were in trouble in court for selling watered ale. Wells, the county's largest town in the Middle Ages, had wine cellars and taverns, and one of the cathedral canons, Thomas de Haselschawe, was accused by the bishop in 1335 of too frequently drinking in the town. His excuse was that it only happened three times at breakfast because 'great lords' had invited him.

Bridgwater's records mention a tavern in 1367, probably in High Street, and by 1392 the *George* was in business in St Mary Street. By about 1500 there were also the *Bell*, the *Saracen's Head*, and the *Ship*, all three owned by the Church, the second by Athelney abbey. About the same time Wells cathedral owned the *Hart's Head* in Sadler Street, let for eight years to two cathedral canons from 1501 on condition they immediately rebuilt it. The canons of Bruton owned the *Crown* at Glastonbury, rival to the *George and Pilgrim* just up the road which had been built for abbey pilgrims by the 1450s. The medieval inn was obviously a good investment, and churchmen would have justified their financial outlay with the explanation that it was their duty to provide hospitality.

But, despite such respectable ownership, the tavern often attracted the unruly and the dishonest. The innkeeper of the *Ship* at Glastonbury in 1656 almost lost his licence because his customers made so much noise 'ranting, drinking and beating a drum that nobody could sleep'. Two cathedral vicars in 1683–4 confessed to the bishop that they had assaulted a man in the *Mitre* at Wells. Mary, wife of Edward Knight, was refused a licence renewal in 1673 because her house at Over Stowey was open during time of Divine Service, card games were allowed, and no lodging for travellers was provided.

Charles Matthews was similarly prevented from keeping any sort of establishment for three years from 1676 because he had permitted unlawful drinking and had harboured, so the magistrates discovered, 'other disorderly and idle persons, particularly Bartholomew Romane, who has been convicted ... as a common vagrant and wandering rogue ... who carried about with him several picklock instruments'. Inns were thus often to be found in obscure places, like the promontory of Stert Point and the island of Steepholm, well away from the eyes of the justices – though rather far, too, from regular customers and diffi- cult to reach without a boat.

The *Unicorn* at Bruton, the *Ship* at Bridgwater, the *Crown* at Wells, the *Red Lion* at Ilchester and the Hart at Bath all came highly recommended in the 1620s but, by the end of the century, the county justices were reluctant to meet in session at Ilchester because of the poor accommodation.

At least two travellers left behind impressions that were most uncomplimen- tary. John Taylor, the London poet and protégé of Ben Jonson, stayed at the Rose and Crown at Nether Stowey in the early seventeenth century. He sat there for three hours waiting for beef and carrots, and for another two hours having ordered egg and parsley as substitutes. He ended up with bread and butter, went to bed in a rage and could not sleep.

Thomas Baskerville had little better fortune later in the century at Kingston Seymour. He did not complain of the food but of his bedfellows:
> 'after I was abed I never but once before met with such tormen-
> tors, and that was in an inn ... at Kingston Seymour [where] the
> stings of fleas were so sharp as if so many needles had stuck in
> my flesh. This paine I did endure till towards day, when their
> bellyes being full there was a Cessation. Sure it shuld seeme ye
> Sun and Aire from ye Severn Sea do make fleas more venomous
> here than in other places'.

Has the English traveller always been so philosophical? Perhaps the regal names of many English inns in some way made up for their deficiencies, and the religious symbols on many inn signs might be thought to offer a modicum of respectability. One of the thousands called the *King's Head* was in business in the late 1820s in Milborne Port, a place where, at election time, beer flowed very freely. Either the owner or the licensee seems to have had a great sense of humour. It made no claims to high standards or religious fervour, but changed its name to stand for its typical customer: it was thereafter called the *Tippling Philosopher*.

Our traditions are as much part of our history as kings and dates; they stand for what cannot always be proved but has been believed for so long it must be true. The fascination of our past would not be so strong if the Giant of Grabbist or Jack the Treacle Eater were to be left out, or if the story of the Devil moving hills or digging valleys or shifting churches were forgotten. And the fact is that many of those, just because they are so deeply embedded in our history, are worth examination, for many of them have more than a grain of truth and most are the result of man's attempts to explain events or buildings he did not quite understand.

It is when those stories contain more than their fair share of real historical figures that they become most difficult to unravel. One of the most intriguing is the tradition of the young Thomas Wolsey at Lopen fair. There is no doubt at all about the fair. Exactly when it started is not known, but it was in existence by 1201 when Hugh de Westover and Richard de Esland paid the sum of ten marks (£6.66p) to King John to buy pardon for the deaths of three men that had occurred at the fair. It was probably then owned by the Meriet family, lords of Merriott and Lopen, who received rent from all those traders who set up stalls for business. The Meriets seem to have lost control of the fair by 1280, probably because they could not prove legal title, and the Crown took over.

According to official records, the stall rents were not worth very much, but if the Crown considered it was worthwhile to take over, it is likely that the official record is wrong. In the fourteenth century the right to hold the fair was let for £2 10s (£2.50p) a year, but then it was said to be worth only just over half that sum from rents and from fines levied on people who had misbehaved while attending. There is more than a suspicion that, with the help of what would now be called creative accounting, those figures do not bear too much relation to the truth.

Two things suggest some under-valuation. The first is that the fair clearly continued to be held for many years, and the second is that one group of buyers came each year between 1299 and 1330. They came on behalf of the little army of craftsmen who were then rebuilding Exeter cathedral. Sometimes the 'warden of the work' came with one or two assistants and pack horses; in 1302 it was Martin Roger the mason, in 1329 Peter de Castro, a boy and two horses.

In 1300 they spent 15s (75p) on 250 horseshoes, 3s 6d (17p) on 1,500 nails for the same, 10s (50p) on 1,000 lath nails for the plasterers, 2s (10p) on 1,000 large board nails for the carpenters, and 7s (35p) for a pair of iron cart bands. Thirty years later and the shopping list was not much different: 300 horseshoes, 300 'tachnails', 42 tacks for the carts and a pair of wheels. In the years between, quantities of nails, locks and hinges. Some of those Lopen nails may well still be in the roof above the choir and presbytery in the cathedral.

How long the trade in ironwork at this rather surprising spot continued is not possible to say, though the recent discovery that metal kitchen ware – skillets, pans and even cauldrons – were made in nearby South Petherton and Montacute in the seventeenth century suggests a source of iron still to be discovered. The Crown was still letting stalls at the fair in Charles I's reign and the fair was still being held in the early nineteenth century. In fact, business improved when the Western Stage Coach plying between London and Exeter adopted a new route via Ilchester and Ilminster through White Cross, the old name for Lopen Head, along the line of what became the A303.

So an inn was built at Lopen Head and stabling for changing horses, and someone very sensibly decided to move the village fair to the main road. The date was then also changed from the whole week after Pentecost to Trinity Monday. By that date the fair was more an entertainment than an occasion for serious business: it was called the Lopen Play and local talent spent its energies in wrestling and single-stick and cudgel playing. Even that sort of thing palled after a while and by the 1880s fair day had been changed to Trinity Wednesday in order not to clash with Somerton fair, and all that remained at Lopen was a gingerbread stall in the village street and the stone cross shaft of the medieval cross under the Cross Tree.

And still associated with the fair is the tradition that among many young men found to be drunk and disorderly at the fair over the years was one called Thomas Wolsey, a young clergyman from up country. To the stocks with him!

Whatever was Wolsey doing at Lopen, and could the tale possibly be true? George Cavendish, the cardinal's servant and first biographer, gives some of the information. He records that Wolsey, having successfully taught the two sons of the marquess of Dorset, was rewarded with a living in his employer's gift. Further, when he went to take possession of the living, he declares that Sir Amias Poulett 'dwelling in the country thereabout, took occasion of displeasure against him' and 'set the schoolmaster by the feet during his pleasure'. No mention of when and exactly where, but still an event.

Sir Amias Poulett of Hinton St George was a man of influence in and around Lopen, was an active Justice of the Peace, and quite rightly put drunks in the stocks. And Wolsey's home was certainly not far away from Lopen for a while, for in 1500 Lord Dorset had appointed him rector of Limington near Ilchester.

He held the rectory until 1509. And in 1500 Sir Amias had been honoured by being appointed to attend the future Queen Katherine of Aragon when she slept a night at Crewkerne on her way from Plymouth to London to be betrothed to Arthur, Prince of Wales. A young parson showing disrespect to such a man might be expected to be severely dealt with.

The end of the story is that Wolsey, having risen to great power, took revenge on Sir Amias by putting him under house arrest in the Middle Temple in London for five or six years. Poulett secured his release only by building a new gatehouse there, resplendent with Wolsey's coat of arms. Certainly, if true, it was a nice way to repay by striking at both liberty and pocket and at the same time by appearing to be a generous donor to a college of lawyers.

The story has not yet been corroborated by formal records, but there is a suspicious gap in the career of Sir Amias which could be neatly accounted for by a spell in London, though Wolsey's latest modern biographer, Peter Gwyn, points out that Poulett was for a time Treasurer of Middle Temple. George Cavendish, his first biographer, certainly took the whole episode seriously, writing it up as a moral tale in which Fortune's Wheel keeps turning and that power without some humility might soon be lost. After all, Wolsey could easily have engineered Poulett's appointment, and the pressure to build the gatehouse could be a form of imprisonment. Surely the only source of the story of a drunken frolic and the harsh punishment can only have been Wolsey himself.

In 1999 there were a total of 33,308 bed spaces available for visitors to Somerset, of which 11,005 were described as serviced and were to be found in hotels of varying sizes, self-catering chalets and holiday homes. Caravans and tents were not considered to have beds within the meaning of the regulations and were not counted; they were known instead as pitches.

In that same year the occupants of beds or pitches were estimated to have spent £509.6 million, and tourism-related jobs accounted for some ten per cent of all employment in the county. Such information is crucial for future planning.

Almost exactly the same considerations obtained when Somerset was overwhelmed with people, many of them visitors but many local folk staying away from home, something over three hundred years ago. Those visitors were not entirely unexpected but did not book in advance and were somewhat unclear as to how long they might stay. Too many came with empty purses and with little intention of paying bills even by offering to do the washing up.

Those visitors were, first of all, the folk from Dorset and Devon who marched in increasing numbers behind the duke of Monmouth and arriving at Taunton were joined by Somerset men from the town and the villages around. Their route to Bridgwater, Glastonbury, Frome, Keynsham and Norton St Philip involved many short stays and snack meals and their progress might have been traced in empty larders and vegetable plots. One bed the royal troops found in Keynsham when Monmouth had left in a hurry for Norton had fifteen pairs of boots under it. The *George* at Norton, ancient then and first built by the monks of Hinton Charterhouse to store cloth prior to sale at the village fairs, housed the duke and his officers.

The next visitors were the royal troops sent to confront and defeat the rebels and they, too, were none too generous in payment for beds and services. After the defeat of the rebels at Sedgemoor they were rounded up and housed until trial first in Westonzoyland church and later in St Cuthbert's at Wells and elsewhere where Chief Justice Jeffreys and his fellow judges sat on the Bloody Assize. Bridgwater was home to royalist wounded, for which the government paid the princely sum of £60 'for meat, drink and other necessaries by them furnished', but they had to wait two years for recompense.

But very soon after the rebel defeat the government realised that accommodation for its troops need to be organised should such trouble occur again, so a nationwide survey of beds and stabling was undertaken which is preserved among the records of the War Office. It is a bound volume arranged by counties and then alphabetically by towns and villages. Whoever wrote up the record was strong neither on geography nor on spelling. Hinstrick, Hinstrick Ash and Milbourn were all thought to be in Dorset, though, of course, Henstridge, Henstridge Ash and Milborne (Port) are not far from the county boundary.

There are many places said to be in Somerset which at present defy identification: Forrest, Patsone, Gosarnhall or West Quental will probably be recognised by those knowledgeable on other counties, though judging by the other information about them they were small places. That other information was crucial: beside each place in the list were two columns headed 'Guest Beds' and 'Stabling for Horses'.

It is no surprise that the four places with the greatest capacity for people and horses were then the county's largest towns, Wells, Bath, Taunton and

Bridgwater. Wells was found to have 492 beds (what might that mean in terms of occupants?) and stabling for 599 horses; Bath had 324 beds and room for 451 horses; Taunton had 262 beds and could take 293 horses, Bridgwater 143 beds and stabling for 246.

There are some curiosities in the record, not least that Yeovil is not mentioned either in Somerset or in Dorset. Wincanton could offer only 50 beds but stabling for 254, no reflection on local hospitality but recognition that the town was on the London road and changes of horses were more often required than an overnight stay. The same sort of balance in favour of the beast was obvious at Chard (91 beds, 342 horses), Crewkerne, Ilminster, Bruton, Shepton Mallet and Pensford – all places on busy main roads; but why Keynsham, with 28 beds, could put up only one horse is a puzzle.

If only the survey had asked for the names of the inns! For some places, reasonably accurate guesses can be made. Where else could most of the 35 beds at Norton St Philip be but at the *George*; and some of the 38 at Ilchester must have been at the *Red Dragon*. The 72 at Bruton were presumably shared between the *Unicorn*, the *Green Dragon*, the *George*, the *Swan*, the *Three Goats' Heads*, the *White Hart*, the *King's Arms*, and the *Bull's Head*; the 91 at Glastonbury will have included the *Bell*, the *Pelican*, the *Crown*, the *Ship* and the *George*.

The *Three Cups* at Taunton, the *Ship* at Bridgwater, the *Crown* at Wells and the *Hart* at Bath were still in business; less well known were the *Red Lion* and the *White Lion* at Milborne Port, and among the ten inns in Wincanton were the *Angel* and the *Bear*. All those and many more were essential to the commercial life of the county but had nothing to do with tourism, an activity confined only to a very few. Minehead and Dunster, of course, were then still commercial centres; Porlock, rapidly losing ground to its neighbour, could only offer 9 beds and stabling for 5. Elsewhere along the coast Berrow offered only 2 beds and stabling for 4; Clevedon and Weston expected no visitors at all.

—*m*—

James Fontaine was a Huguenot minister in Western France but left his native country after the revocation of the Edict of Nantes in 1685 removed legal protection for Protestants. He landed in Appledore, settled for a while in Barnstaple, where he married his fiancée who had escaped with him. For a time they lived on charity, but eventually he found a post with Sir Halswell Tynte. His wife moved to Bridgwater and kept a small shop while he himself was involved, rather unsuccessfully, in trading with France. His failure to obtain much assistance from more prosperous Huguenots in London prompted him to make further commercial efforts and he began by giving French lessons in Taunton, where he subsequently settled and there kept a shop.

The shop dealt, he recorded rather vaguely in his memoirs, in 'one thing or other', but Fontaine soon became a manufacturer with two other exiled Frenchmen producing cloth from worsted, yarn and dyes he bought in Exeter. He was also ordained as a Presbyterian minister, but his practical skills were clearly his salvation. He quickly understood the production process, invented new patterns, and prospered so well that he hired 'the handsomest shop in Taunton, opposite the Cross in the Market Place'. There he manufactured 'stuffs' upstairs while his wife and two assistants sold a variety of linens, galloons, thread, needles, and tin and copper ware made in Holland by French refugees. There were also exclusive French-made beaver hats from Exeter, French brandy and vinegar, Spanish raisins, stockings from St Maixant, and dyed chamois leather for long-lasting breeches.

Fontaine succeeded because of his undoubted energy but also because he sold much of his stock at wholesale prices, but that was no way to endear himself to Taunton's established traders. Unsurprisingly he found himself summoned to appear before the mayor and aldermen. His judges were, in his opinion, ignorant, self-made men, woollen manufacturers and shopkeepers to a man, who were simply jealous of his success and accused him, when they could think of nothing else, of being a Jesuit and 'a French dog taking bread out of the mouths of the English'. At law his accusers had a point: Fontaine had not served an apprenticeship in the borough in any of the trades he practised.

He defended himself fluently and was ably supported by the town's Recorder, who pointed out that Charles II had invited persecuted French Protestants to take refuge in England. He declared that he was sure Fontaine would be glad to resume his work as a minister if the leaders of Taunton society would be prepared to support him financially. There was, of course, an embarrassed silence and the case was dismissed, but Fontaine was in no doubt that the corporation remained bitterly against him, taxing him as heavily as they were able.

When a small detachment of William of Orange's men took possession of the town in 1688 he was accused again of being a Jesuit. The officer in charge happened himself to be a French Protestant well known to Fontaine: another mistake by the corporation, but they managed to add to his burdens by ensuring that more troops were billeted on him than on anyone else. Still, the political outlook was more settled and the enterprising Fontaine first sold all his stock to pay his debts, tried schoolmastering again and, finding it did not pay too well, managed to imitate a Norwich product called calmanico, a double twisted and very fine worsted. This he sold in Exeter for double his costs and was able within a few months to employ up to fifteen weavers in Taunton.

Understandably, the Taunton serge weavers were intensely jealous and indulged in industrial espionage. One of his weavers was persuaded to explain the process, but the resulting cloth was covered in long hairs and quite unsaleable, for the weaver did not known that every piece had to be singed before washing and pressing. Eventually, in 1693, the secret was discovered by the now desperate serge weavers. They gave up making the old, unfashionable serge but soon flooded the market with calmanico.

Fontaine tried introducing patterns in his pieces but was soon imitated, and having made £1000 in three years decided to return to his first profession. But when he left Taunton for Cork in 1694 he took with him enough materials to start a cloth manufactory there for, as he observed, his congregation was too poor to pay him a stipend. The exile moved on to a more welcoming home; a descendant, John Fontaine III, lives in Jackson, Mississippi, more friendly towards England than his ancestor's experience in Taunton deserves.

—⁓⁓—

Some time between 1906 and 1910 the Somerset Ilex Stores in West Huntspill closed its doors for the last time, unable to compete with the new shops springing up in Highbridge, though the building still stands and for many years until recently was occupied by a shop with lesser pretensions. In the days of James Davis Burnett and Gilbert James Burnett it was almost a department store.

Grocer, draper, outfitter, ironmonger, retailer of china, glass and patent medicines, stationer, tobacconist, undertaker – what else could they possibly sell that might be needed by the villagers and farmers of Huntspill? Well, since the farmers made butter and cheese and cider in large quantities, then the Stores stocked Mitchell's butter colour, Hansen's patent cheese rennet, and Purrett's cider colouring; and also on the shelves were Thorley's Food Lactifier and Ovum, Cooper's Sheep Dipping and Fly Powder, and Curtis and Harvey's gunpowder, which would between them take care of most problems.

All was extremely business-like and enterprising. By 1889 the firm had its own Victorian e-mail telegraphic address, Jaydebee, Highbridge' (for J.D. Burnett) which had been changed by 1894 to the rather more sober 'Burnett, Huntspill'. The firm claimed to be sole proprietors of the 'renowned Ilex Somersetshire Relish' and it also declared it had been established for two centuries.

Not, probably, in Huntspill, but shops like this certainly go back two hundred years and more, precisely as Napoleon declared. There was one, for instance, at Stogumber in 1685 belonging to Hugh Sweeting. When he died in that year his neighbours valued the stock at nearly £277 and described him as both shopkeeper and haberdasher, but in truth he was more than that. Haberdasher, of course, for they found brown and coloured thread, tapes, lace, waistcoat buttons, ribbons, pins and trimmings; but draper, too, for there were pairs of stockings and trousers, even a pair of drawers, and quantities of fustian, calico, stuff, canvas, say, crepe, kersey, chamlett, shalloon and serge.

But as they proceeded the appraisers, who had no doubt patronised the shop as well as their wives, found packs of cards, tobacco, reams of paper, string, brimstone, sand, soap and glasses; spices including pepper, nutmeg, mace and cinnamon, sugar candy, brown sugar, currants and canary seed. The discerning housewives of Stogumber at the time of Monmouth's rebellion had tastes more sophisticated and pockets deeper than might have been expected.

Stogumber, of course, was almost a small town and served a wide area, but Dodington has never been more than a tiny village and yet two years after Hugh Sweeting died, Bartholomew Bartlett of Dodington died too. His shop was full of interesting items: linen cloth, stockings, facing for cloth, silk, buttons, ribbons, tapes, sugar, figs, spice, tobacco, soap, candles and yarn. Probably the shop was on the main road and not actually in the village, and Bartholomew kept a few cows and pigs to supplement his income.

The list of goods is only part of the story; who supplied them, and from where did they come? Thomas Pacy, a Bristol grocer, was certainly a supplier when William Skynner of Bridgwater decided to set up shop in the town in 1506. Skynner admitted to having no cash, so asked his friend and fellow businessman Thomas Saunders to stand surety. Thereupon Pacy sold Skynner what he described as groceries for the total sum of 46s 8d (£2.33p): pepper, saffron, ginger, nutmeg, cinnamon, treacle, 'graynes' and 'cornfeles', as one might expect, but also thread, pins (London, paper and coarse), needles, nails, beads, penny girdles, silk points, silk ribbons, small ribbons, halfpenny beads, penny combs, pennyware glasses and six gold balances.

All this and more came to light when Skynner did not pay and Saunders said it was not his responsibility. Pacy took them both to court before the Lord Chancellor where he also reported that Saunders had similarly stood surety when a man named Thomas Hewys had bought from him figs, raisins, almonds, and sugar worth 57s 8d (£2.88p) and had again not come up with the cash.

And where had all those exotic things come from? Bristol merchants were by then trading widely throughout the Mediterranean and Pacy's stock came directly from Italy and Spain and indirectly, if North African pirates allowed, from traders in the Levant who were supplied by caravans snaking their way from the Far East. Mr Burnett's cocoa and coffee and Mazawattee tea in 1880s Huntspill were not so exotic and unusual as he declared in his advertisements, but that is salesmanship.

8

THEIR RECORDS ARE OUR HISTORY

*"The clerk or sexton at Porlock had a double-sided board on a long handle,
each side bearing a text to encourage wakefulness"*

*The work of thousands of usually anonymous government clerks make England's
administrative records the finest sources any historian could wish for, and parsons,
churchwardens and parish clerks almost match them. The rush to consult the 1901
census when it was made available in 2001 caused a temporary breakdown in the
system on line, witness not to inadequate preparation but to an underestimate of
interest in the painstaking work of an army of enumerators a century ago. Many of
those who caused that breakdown were people in search of their forbears, hoping to*

discover them in places where family memory last recalled them; but censuses only record a day in a decade. They are invaluable hooks on which are to be hung all the ephemera that survive from grandfather's time.

~~~

If ever there was too much government, it was in the Middle Ages. No matter who you were (except, of course, the King), there was someone above you asking questions, giving orders, demanding money with menaces, or requiring your time and labour. For those below the situation was at best unpleasant, at worst downright medieval, of course. Even for the upper classes, government must at times have been irksome, but for the historian the records of such transactions tell us a lot about ordinary, everyday life five hundred years ago.

Take, for instance, the question of widows. The law demanded that they had one third share of the property of their late husbands, but eldest sons had a curious tendency to make difficulties, so a government official intervened to make sure that the sorrowing lady received that to which she was entitled. And sometimes the description of her share is very revealing. When the lord of Merriott manor died in 1369 his widow Joan was assigned her proper dower, which included buildings in the farmyard beside the manor house: the eastern barn, byre and pigsty by the high chamber, the right to use the open courtyard, together with the east part of the garden and, a rare example this, the northern half of the 'nursery'. That is a very early reference to such a feature of medieval gardening, and Dr John Harvey believed it to refer to a tree nursery. And it is, of course, a fine example of how medieval people were as clever as ourselves. Scotts were not the first to recognise the value of the soil at Merriott. But there was no mention of a house or chambers for the widow to live in.

Not so far away, another widow and another manor house. Anne, Lady de la Pole, was awarded her proper share of Norton sub Hamdon manor in 1421. She accepted a ground-floor chamber on the south of the courtyard, a hayhouse above the stable on the north side, and a third part of the great garden, namely the eastern garden whose boundary began at a certain ash tree growing in the great ditch by the garden entry and crossed the garden to a certain apple tree which leant over the ditch to the north. It is difficult enough to visualise now, but probably quite clear to the lady; and again not much of a dwelling house, so she must have assumed she was to live in the manor house with her son and daughter-in-law.

Often enough a man holding land directly of the Crown died leaving a child as heir and the widow in charge. Hopefully the time came when she must yield to the next generation, and then the government official intervened again to make the transfer legal. What proof was there that the strapping youth or winsome girl before him was, indeed, of an age to take possession? All would be well so long as enough people came forward with plausible reasons for remembering the birth. Parents with foresight sometimes gave presents to neighbours or made other gestures so that the event would easily be recalled. At other times disaster struck or something unusual happened at the same time, quite dramatic enough to be embedded in the folk memory of communities where such events were few and far between.

In 1362 William Welde remembered the baptism of little Joan, daughter of Thomas Chastelayne, lord of Dinnington, very well indeed, because he 'flatly refused' to stand as godfather since he frankly admitted to a crush on the infant's mother and hoped to marry her should her husband die. John Leddred was at Dinnington on the day after the birth on business and when he visited the mother she gave him a silk purse that he should remember. On the following Sunday Nicholas Caddebury, a carpenter, came to the manor house to draw up plan for a new hall, and the proud father gave him an axe and a piece of rope so that he, too, should remember. And John Bruyn went to Donyatt Park to hunt with Thomas on the day of the baptism, and Thomas gave him the skin of a doe.

There might, of course, be a direct witness. Henry St John, giving evidence at Dunster in June 1399, could remember the baptism of Thomas, son of Peter of Bratton on 1 February 1378 because he and Peter were at lunch at East Luccombe when a messenger came to announce Thomas's arrival. Immediately they both went to Minehead church and Henry saw Thomas's name written in the church missal. Oliver Huish, William Worthy and William Cloutesham also saw the name written in the missal; no doubt they had been summoned for the purpose. William Hamelyn, John Huwyssh and John Ryvers remembered because they were just setting out from Dunster on the journey of a lifetime, a pilgrimage to the shrine of St Thomas of Canterbury. Thomas Stratton, the child's godfather, told them the news.

Not all memories were good. Henry Hamme recalled that a certain hall had burnt down the same day, and at another such hearing a witness said the day in question was etched on his memory because he had that very day fallen off his horse and broken his leg. Three others at that Dunster hearing told how on the same day they had become lessees of some land from the lady of Minehead manor and the deed was sealed in Minehead church. John Sandhull had the best reason of all to remember; his daughter was born and baptised on the same day. Minehead church was evidently a busy place.

—*mm*—

There are people who manage to pick up information without leaving home. A classic example is the Venerable Bede who in the eighth century hardly ever set foot outside his monastery at Jarrow but managed to write a comprehensive history of England and the English people. After him came a succession of monk-chroniclers who, though confined to their cloisters, evidently had a network of informants who gave them tidings of the events of their own day miles from home. The results form the raw materials of historians.

The great monasteries of Durham, Worcester and St Albans in particular produced some of the best national histories. Nothing of the same kind, perhaps surprisingly, came from Glastonbury, which was much more concerned with telling the story of its glorious past, but Somerset has three claimants to be a national chronicler, one a bishop, one anonymous and one a friar.

The first is much the most important, for unlike those histories by men in the cloister it was the work of an eyewitness, though this man was a monk as well as a bishop, Robert of Lewes, bishop of Bath. He was evidently present when King Stephen was in the West Country and was able, for instance, to give graphic details of the attack on the castle at Castle Cary by the king in 1136 when fire and showers of stones were hurled from wooden siege engines.

The second local historian is the author of the so-called Axbridge chronicle, which belongs among the town's amazing collection of records. It was written in the fifteenth century and is not really a chronicle at all but a short history of boroughs from the time of King Athelstan. Like many such chronicles it tells us nothing that cannot be found elsewhere but has important local flavour because it includes the dramatic story from the Life of St Dunstan of the way King Edmund (939–46) was saved from falling to his death in Cheddar Gorge while out hunting, and thus recalled Dunstan from exile. It also recorded that from the time of Domesday the men of Axbridge had hunting and fishing rights from a place called 'Cottellisasch' to a rock called 'le Blakestone' in the western sea.

The third is a true chronicle written by a man as remarkable as he is elusive. He may or may not have been a Somerset man by birth, but he certainly lived in the county for a time and his chronicle, or rather one copy of it, was kept at Bridgwater. The man was John Somer, a member of the convent of Franciscan friars at Bridgwater. In the late 1370s or early 1380s he may have been Warden of the Franciscan house at Bodmin, and later moved to Oxford where he became so well known as an astronomer as to be mentioned by Chaucer in his Treatise on the Astrolabe. For twenty years and more he was known and favoured by the royal family; he took a degree in theology at Oxford but continued to work in the fields of astronomy and astrology until his death, either soon after October 1409 or possibly 1419.

So famous was Somer during his own lifetime that he acquired more wealth than a Franciscan had any business to possess; but the friars of Norwich recorded that he left the huge sum of 200 marks (£133.33p) to build a new church for the friars in Bridgwater and 40 marks (£26.66p) for books for the convent library there. Friar John Wells, a member of the Bridgwater convent in the 1480s, boasted that he had once been Somer's servant, and several writers in the fifteenth and sixteenth centuries copied or noted his work on horo-scopes and star catalogues.

The chronicle or *kalendarium* is of more interest for its astronomical tables than for the history it contains. Ostensibly beginning with tables from the year 1001, it mentions some earlier events including 'Merlin 476' or 'the English accepted the faith under Gregory, 581', but mostly national events such as coronations and deaths of kings and popes. In fact one or more other authors continued the chronicle after Somer's death until the year 1532.

What makes the chronicle interesting to Somerset readers is that it includes events only a local man or a man present at the time could have known: that after the death of his queen, Anne of Bohemia, Richard II left Haverfordwest for Ireland on 29 September 1392 and returned to Bristol on 9 May 1395; that on 2 May 1402 Taunton suffered heavy rains, thunder and hail. Another hand, evidently continuing the chronicle at Bridgwater, recorded the laying of the foundation stone of the Franciscan church there on 4 March 1412.

One other glimpse of John Somer was overlooked by the recent editor of his chronicle. On the eve of the feast of St Mark 1406 John Bacwell was sent from Dunster castle to Bridgwater to fetch 'John Somer, a friar' to preside at the wedding of Elizabeth, daughter of Sir Hugh Luttrell, with William Harleston. The information comes not from the chronicle but from the account of the household of Sir Hugh preserved among the Luttrell archives.

Friars were very popular in the Later Middle Ages. People often left money to them in their wills and their prayers were thought to be more efficacious than those of the ordinary parish priest. Sir Hugh must have felt that this particular friar's combination of theology, astronomy and astrology offered a better foundation for his daughter's future than the ministrations of the vicar of Dunster.

—*uu*—

Among the important members of the community two centuries ago, chroniclers in their way, were parish clerks, who sometimes doubled up as parish sexton. The clerk kept the parish registers, put water in the font, said the Amen at services; the sexton dug graves and tolled the bell at funerals. Amen was the name by which Parson Holland of Over Stowey knew all his clerks.

Each parish decided on the actual duties required to be carried out. At Halse in the 1740s the clerk cleaned the church and the communion vessels, washed the parson's surplice, wound the clock, tolled the bell at funerals and organised an Easter dinner for the parishioners. His colleague the sexton cut the churchyard grass, rang the 'knell-bell' at funerals and kept out dogs during service time.

The 'saxton' at Huish Champflower combined both jobs, which included patrolling both church and churchyard during services, digging four-foot graves and clapping miscreants into the stocks. The clerk or sexton at Porlock had a double-sided board on a long handle, each side bearing a text from Scripture to encourage wakefulness during the sermon.

Parson Skinner at Camerton had difficulties with his clerk as with all his parishioners, though he certainly defended Harris when the farmers accused him of pocketing the ringers' money, but began to suspect him when on Boxing Day 1818 he managed to share the plum puddings rather frugally between the boys of the Sunday school so that he and his friends could have a feast. Several times Harris avoided church and once Skinner found him up his plum tree on a Sunday. They had a great row in 1821 when Harris had failed to return the church keys to the Rectory, but he stayed on for several uneasy years. The problem, as Skinner knew, was that a bad clerk was better than no clerk at all. The last reference to Harris in Skinner's diary was the joke he played on the parson by opening the Bible at the wrong place to confuse Skinner and make him look foolish.

Leading the congregation at services was usually the duty of the clerk. The one at Aisholt in Parson Holland's day would either beat time on his neighbour's shoulder and 'squeak out the psalms in a curious manner' or he would beat time on his stomach and raise his eyebrows 'in admiration' but 'poor man, he could not be heard and if he was it was not worth hearing'.

Such enthusiasm did not suit all tastes. Joseph Leech, once the anonymous 'Churchgoer', remarked on the system which allowed the parish clerk to read the psalms 'to the discomfort of all present who do not like to hear the sublime and beautiful verse brawled through the ruddy nose of some licensed victualler'.

But the clergyman himself was not perfect. When 'Churchgoer' visited Long Ashton in March 1845 the vicar looked up during the psalm and lost his place; the clerk continued as if nothing had happened. At Bleadon the vicar at the time often complained in public that the clerk was reading too fast or too loud, and in return the clerk would often point out that the vicar was reading the wrong psalm.

No record of such discord is found at the very edge of the county in the tiny parish of Penselwood, though it is clear from the parish registers that a succession of clerks were proud of their office. The recorded list begins with John Ryall from Stoke Trister who began work in March 1723. After him came David Picke (1748), Robert Davidge (1763), and George Matthews, who held the post from 1793 until 1832 and was followed by his son Rezia from his father's death until his own in 1875. The list continues until the 1920s. George Matthews turned his hand to almost anything except cleaning, and his wife Dina did that. The wardens' accounts are full of payments for mops and long handled brushes for Dina, and for carpentry and building work done by George. Between them they earned quite a reasonable salary in the service of the church.

Another parish on the edge of the county was also grateful to its clerks. In St Laurence's, Rode Hill, are two remarkable memorials. One is to Josiah Frances who served for fifty-three years as clerk until his death in 1891 and attended during that time 664 funerals. The other is in memory of two clerks, William Roddaway, aged seventy-two, of Woolverton, and Jeremiah Cruse, aged seventy, of Rode who 'having lived in Habits of Friendship and Mutual Assistances in their Parochial Offices during a long series of years entered Immortality nearly together and were both Interred the 4th day of June 1799'.

$\sim$

Parish registers often at first glance look formidable, with unfamiliar hand-writing sometimes nearly illegible as the result of damage by vermin or water; more often than not the product of a semi-literate parish clerk, occasionally a means by which a parson with some Latin or Greek could make a comment on a parishioner in the knowledge that the rest of his parish, and even possibly his successor, would not understand. And occasionally too, of course, a gem of incidental information: two weddings, for instance, in October and November 1748 which were celebrated, unusually, at Rodden chapel near Frome instead of at the parish church at Berkley, the first 'when Berkley church was shut up in order to be repaired'. Presumably the problem was more serious than first envisaged, for a month later the church 'was pulling down in order to be rebuilt'. A note entered by the rector on 11 November 1750 recorded the fact that the first service in the new church was held on that day.

The happiness of christenings and weddings must usually be imagined, but there was no doubt great satisfaction in Berkley when the rector married Squire Newborough's second daughter in 1632. And certainly another rector was more than a little triumphant at the baptisms of nonconformists, such as the entry for 20 October 1811 of Elizabeth Adams aged fifteen years 'having been before baptised by the Presbyterian form, but not satisfied with it'.

Burials more often excited contemporary comments. Sorrow must be assumed; and particular sorrow when, on 18 September 1585, both Margaret and Hugh Warman were buried at Bridgwater. There was, apparently, almost a tradition of comment there. The town's curate or parish clerk was particularly careful about social niceties: 'Mr' John Newport, a prominent merchant, in December 1654 but Robert Cuff 'gent' earlier in the year for one of whose wealth was in land; and later on David Price, preacher, Edward Bridges, schoolmaster, and Mr Henry Tuttle, customer, for men whose public position in the town and port required suitable respect.

Bridgwater, a cosmopolitan place, produced its peculiarities which must needs be recorded: Thomas Stone of Calmore in Walsall parish in Staffordshire, lardman, in 1591; Nicholas 'one that died in Matthew's Field' and Robert Moone 'a plaier slayne', both in 1597; Mary Woode, wife of Peter Woode, in the writer's Latin 'Aethiopus' in 1612, Peter himself 'negro' in 1619, and Anthony 'a Tawny Moore' in 1621.

Tragedies came regularly. Alexander Jones, the mayor, died in office in 1609 and Thomas Warre, Esquire, Recorder of the Borough, had the misfortune to fall into the Severn in 1617 and was drowned. Another public tragedy was the loss of Joan Strete, the midwife, in 1613. But two summers of plague were obviously far more devastating. Exact numbers will never be known but in July 1591 there were 54 burials and in August 20; and in July 1597 there were 57 – numbers far larger than a normal summer would bring.

Whoever actually recorded burials from 1643 onwards might well have had an eye to history, for the town was garrisoned for the king and the writer, probably the curate George Wotton, was determined to record the fact. The troops evidently suffered a fair amount of ill-luck: five accidentally killed by cannon, five by sword, three drowned and one killed in a duel. The great disappointment for historians of Bridgwater comes when the record ceases almost on the day when Fairfax and Cromwell stormed the town. That, of course, is the reason for the silence. Of those who died during the time of the garrison, almost a hundred were named as soldiers and often given their rank: Humphrey Wharton, major; John Byam, standard bearer; Richard Drake, commander (dux); Henry Wescombe, under officer (*sub-centurio*); William Patten, marshal.

The 'battle' of Petherton, little more than a skirmish over some munition carts in mid August 1644, brought two dead and, later in the month, Major Henry Killigrew fell fighting. Nearly two months earlier Joseph Wotton, probably the curate's brother, lost his life at Lyme and was brought to Bridgwater for burial. A few were genuinely unknown soldiers.

After the Restoration there was a brave attempt to return to normality. Curate or vicar resumed the practice of commenting on the dead, either describing their former occupation, the circumstance of the event, or some other remark, and nearly always in Latin for general comment, in Greek for those which might prove dangerous for the writer, and in plain English if it was intended to give offence. John Quarle was noted as a fisherman, Nicholas Hooper a sailor lost overboard, Widow Amy Rison died in gaol, William and Richard Jones were Anglo-Welshmen, William Rosseter drowned at Town Mill, Elizabeth, wife of John Chappell of Mark, fell off a horse. And the sad tale continued, linked with the town's inns: Thomas Underhay of Kenton in Devon died at the *Lamb*, Philip Gerrard, 'an old soldier of Ireland', collapsed at the *Black Boy*, Joseph Verries at the *Noah's Ark*, Henry Chapman at the *Rose*.

The two parish clergy died in the same year, 1669, the one described as a learned priest, the other as most vigilant pastor of the parish. One of them was the faithful George Wotton who was thrown out of the living for a time as a Royalist and recorded approvingly but in Greek of John Roberts that he was 'a lover of God and the King'. A much less tolerant successor as vicar, entering the burial of Tobias Welles in 1692, described him as 'the Anabaptist Holder Forth'. That was after some serious gaps in the register, as a note records: 'From this year [1677] to 1680, one John Haddon, then parish clerk, had the names of the persons dead, and they are dead, and lost with him'. A fatal loss to genealogists, too.

—*mm*—

Censuses have many uses and are rightly popular with those involved in family history. Local historians prize them for their fascinating details of place and business, for social conditions, communications, the development of religious practice. Each book the census enumerators compiled presents a snapshot of the place at a particular time, recording some things that had changed little since the previous enquiry, and some things that would inevitably change within a day or two. Among the ephemeral snapshots was that of the visitors in the port of Bridgwater on census day 1881 when twenty-nine vessels were tied up overnight. The enumerator tabulated the details of all the sailors on board, but the information is far more than a snapshot of a single night.

The ships' names are fascinating, to begin with. Most were the common Christian names of the time – *William, Hannah, George,* or *Eliza.* A few, like *Emperor, Victory* or *Providence,* suggest some attempt at marketing. The names *Staunch, Active* and *Happy go Lucky* might have been designed to convince the customer of the quality and speed of the service offered, and the *Gloster Packet* was certainly suggestive of something faster than a Severn Trow. *George Canning* and *Garibaldi* clearly had political overtones: the owners were men of business.

The vessels were all quite local on that spring night in 1881. How far they had actually come is not known, though the furthest from their home ports were the *Burncoose* of Aberystwyth and the *George Canning* of Padstow. As many as fourteen were registered at Gloucester, two at Cardiff and the rest at Bridgwater. They were all small boats which could most easily navigate the difficult waters of the Parrett. Most had a crew of three or four and the largest was the Bridgwater schooner *Clara,* only 6 tons. Nearly half of them were under 5 tons and the smallest was the Gloucester trow *Ann,* 7 tons. Half of the boats in port were trows like the *Ann,* open-decked, flat-bottomed. One or two were ketches and others were schooners or sloops, the differences lying in the number of masts and the type of rig.

Mostly they brought coal from Wales and the Forest of Dean, although some of the answers given to the enumerator about lading seem to have been deliberately vague. The schooner *Thomas* was said to be in the 'Home Trade', and the trows *Esther* and *Victory*, working from Lydney and Cardiff respectively, perhaps brought other things besides coal, but did not admit as much. Coasters, able to reach the many little wharves in the Somerset Levels like Lympsham, could move grain, timber, fertilisers or even livestock, as well as the occasional passenger.

All this sounds so very parochial, far removed from the romantic stories of a port where exotic goods could be seen and foreign tongues heard. Census day 1881 was obviously a dull day in Bridgwater. At any other time the snapshot might have been very different.

The career of Henry Goodland of Bridgwater, traced through his discharge papers kept by his family, suggest that his home port was as exciting as most others, whatever the Census return suggested. He signed up there in April 1874 as an able seaman on the *Paragon* of Bridgwater, 404 tons, which was bound for Quebec, perhaps taking emigrants to a new life. He was back home again in August, but may not have found another job until the following year when he rejoined the *Paragon* and went again to Quebec. He was back in July, but evidently did not stay long, for in September he signed up in Troon in Scotland for a job that took him for a month to the Baltic, presumably for timber, which was brought back to Leith. That winter he worked between South Shields and St Malo.

He was back in Bridgwater in the summer of 1876 for the Quebec run on the *Paragon*, found himself in New York on 10 April and then on 11 June he joined his first ship with an engine, the 1015-ton *Perine* of London, which in five months went from Cardiff to Smyrna in Turkey, back to London, out to Patras in Greece and back again to London. In the next three years Henry Goodland was rarely out of work but never signed on or off in Bridgwater. He served in that time on three ships, the *Florence Nightingale* of Sunderland, the *Edgar* of Whitby, and the *Ebbw Vale* of Cardiff, all three motor vessels. Very likely he put in sometimes at his home port, for the *Ebbw Vale* worked in the Bristol Channel between Cardiff and Newport as well as going to Mostyn in North Wales and to South Shields. In the *Florence Nightingale* from Middlesbrough he went to Rouen and Bilbao and, in the slightly larger *Edgar*, brought a cargo from the Black Sea to Limerick. He was still only thirty when he was discharged at Mostyn in September 1884 and there the story told by his papers ends.

A year later the Severn Tunnel was opened and the railways, which had already put paid to canals, now proved that they could move coal and timber faster and cheaper than coasters and trows. There was still, of course, international trade and, until the First World War, Bridgwater's brick and tile industry depended heavily on water transport and Bridgwater ships took their products across the Atlantic and to the Antipodes. But the days of the port of Bridgwater were numbered and by the 1920s a trow was a rare sight where once had been a forest of masts both in the river and in the dock. The likes of Henry Goodland no doubt regretted their passing.

9

FOOD, FEASTING AND CONVIVIALITY

"... the cheese made from the milk of 730 cows and weighing 11cwt which was presented by the farmers of Pennard to Queen Victoria"

There was not much feasting for the medieval peasant except at Christmas, while the merchant did well and the gentlemen and noblemen very well indeed, but who could do better than Somerset cider and Somerset cheese? Bishops and abbots recognised the value of both, and a prior seems to have been something of a pioneer in making cider much stronger and more interesting. Cheese and cider continued to be of importance to the county's economy, though the peacock gave place to goose, especially on the grasslands of the Levels where cheese, too, was widely produced and most prized; and still, like the peacock, kept for feathers rather than for meat. And feasting still continued: in villages at the annual parish perambulation succeeded by the annual Club Walk of the local Friendly Society, in towns at another sort of club, where like-minded people, most of them male, spent an hour or two most weekdays taking refuge from domestic bliss.

To prepare a peacock for spit roasting, the skin and feathers from its back should be brought forward and with feathers of head and neck must be carefully kept from the heat. When cooked, feathers should then be replaced, the tail in full display. The result was undoubtedly spectacular but probably tough. Indeed, the Scottish poet Alexander Barclay, once of Ottery St Mary and later in succession a monk and a friar, wrote of 'the crane, the fesaunt, the peacocke and the curlew ... seasoned so well in licour redolent that the hall is full of pleasant smell and s[c]ent'. No mention of taste.

'Peacock roasted' regularly appeared on the menu at medieval feasts, and they were evidently kept at manor houses throughout the county. In the 1390s the Master of St Mark's hospital, Bristol, kept some at his house at Pawlett, and we know about them because a man from nearby Horsey was fined in 1397 for stealing their feathers. The Hospitallers kept some at Templecombe just over a century later.

Perhaps a more serious producer was the abbot of Glastonbury. His bailiff at Sowy, the manor which comprised Westonzoyland, Middlezoy and Othery, recorded a total of 22 birds, cocks and hens. In 1300–1 24 birds produced 21 chicks, a good year in comparison with 1311–12 when 28 produced only four chicks. Six birds evidently flew off in 1313–14.

Details for the year 1333–4 are unusually full. Only 11 birds were left at the end of the year of which four were chicks; as for the others three had died and one had been sent to Abbot John Breynton at Glastonbury. Nevertheless three feathers from the wings (note that) of three cocks had been sent by the abbot to Sir John Durborough. That was all, the bailiff is explaining rather apologetically, for one of the birds was a peahen and there were, of course, no tail feathers. Sir John was evidently not wanting feathers for some exotic display for his hat but rather some distinctive flights for his arrows.

Later owners of manor houses liked the idea of peacocks strutting on their spacious lawns, helping to add an air of grandeur to the scene. That was certain the reason why in the 1950s the headmaster of Crewkerne Grammar School bought a pair of peafowl from a Norfolk dealer for £20. It was a small price to pay if the sight of them persuaded the right kind of parents to place their offspring under his tutelage.

He certainly achieved some notoriety for his school: a notice in *Punch* drew forth an interesting variety of names for the pair, but he soon discovered that his birds had a tendency to choose their own roosts, usually in places where they were most unwelcome. The answer, of course, was to clip their wings; the consequence was they had little else to do but to multiply. The headmaster had finally to admit that Pride and Prejudice had to go, but the proud parents and their brood only fetched £10.

It was the same sort of situation in East Coker about the same time: Churchill and Sarah came to live at Slades Farm. Rarely did he display when visitors came, and rarely did they roost at home. They knew they were manor-house birds and slept in the trees up at Coker Court where they made more noise than the church chimes and almost as much as the bells.

—ᴍᴍ—

In 1230 the bishops of Bath and Lincoln, the brothers Jocelin and Hugh of Wells, received a royal charter granting permission that when each died their executors might begin their accounts not on the day each died but at Michaelmas afterwards, and among their possessions were cider presses. Here were two Somerset men who knew a valuable crop when they saw one. Indeed, when Jocelin died in 1242 his cider and apples were reckoned as a significant source of income. The bishop of Winchester's bailiff at Rimpton in 1265–6 bought 129 apple and pear trees for the new garden at the manor house, but accounts for the following years mention only the sale of a few apples, so the conclusion must be that most of the fruit was consumed locally, probably in the form of cider. At the end of the thirteenth century when Glastonbury abbey and its estates were in royal hands after the death of Abbot John of Taunton fifteen casks of cider had to be sold.

It is, of course, rather accidental that bishops and abbots should be found to be the county's earliest cider makers; it is simply that the records of bishops and monasteries have survived, not that they were great consumers. Yet among the leading office-holders at Glastonbury abbey was the chamberer or chamberlain. His main task in the early fourteenth century was to provide his fellow monks with clothes, shoes, table knives and other necessaries from a common store funded from, among other places, the manor of West Monkton. The account roll of Brother Robert of Lydeard, chamberer for the year 1309–10, records that he bought three pounds of ginger, honey, cloves, mace and rock sugar.

The chamberer also paid cash to Master Roger Fisico – that is Master Roger the doctor – and to a man called Pikebon for collecting herbs – does not the name suggest that picking herbs was his profession? Elsewhere in his account Brother Robert mentioned ale given as doles to the poor and as the supper drink of the monks, and wine when the monks underwent regular blood-letting.

Another abbey official at Glastonbury was the gardener; not the difficult fellow who allowed the lady of the house only those flowers that he was prepared to spare from his greenhouses, but another monk. Thomas of Keynsham, gardener in 1333–4, accounted for, among other items he produced, flax, hemp, madder and leek plants, onions, five quarters and two bushels of apples, and three tuns of cider, all of which were sold, and a pipe and 105 gallons of wine and 70 gallons of verjuice from the vineyard, probably at Pilton. Another 156 quarters of apples from Glastonbury were added to more from other abbey orchards, most (43 quarters) from Pilton and smaller amounts from Batcombe, Ditcheat, Meare, Shapwick and Godney in that order, making a total of 248 quarters allocated for cider, and producing 31 tuns 80 gallons.

Lay people, of course, drank cider, but direct evidence for them doing so is uncommon, presumably because so normal before the end of the 1600s. People left beds and tables, clothes and tapestries, even household goods to family and friends in their wills, but hardly ever mentioned food and drink. The will of William Garland of Dinnington made in 1557 is an exception, for it includes the bequest to Thomas Sweete of some grain and a hogshead of cider.

So cider had a long and, of course, respectable history in Somerset. It could surely not be otherwise. But what about anything stronger? The will of the last prior of Montacute may suggest that cider brandy may have a long history, too. Robert Gibbes, in his days as a monk also known as Robert Sherborne (probably his birthplace) and Robert Whitlocke, prior of Montacute from 1532, surrendered his house and community to the king's officials in March 1539 and was given a generous pension of £80 a year and the manor house at East Chinnock for the rest of his life. He survived until the summer of 1560 and at his death was still in touch with four of his former monastic brethren as well as with his own blood brother, three nephews and two great-nephews.

One of those nephews, Robert, was a parson and perhaps shared his uncle's special interests, for besides being left a feather bed and his uncle's clothes he was given a 'lymbeck', that is an alembic, a vessel used for distilling, and also a 'stillatorie', which was a similar vessel used in Yorkshire for making alcohol. James Kitto, another beneficiary of the former prior and described as his 'lad', also received a feather bed, a bolster, blankets, sheets and a coverlet, two stillatories, a brass pot to make alcohol in and, among other things, books of medicine and surgery. The alcohol might, of course, have been for medicinal uses only, were it not that Robert Gibbes was given twenty dozen glasses of varying sizes.

Ex-prior Gibbes just might have been another of the many fools who thought that gold might be made through chemical reactions, but is it wishful thinking that those glasses sound less like rows of test tubes and more like something convivial?

—*mm*—

'To whom it may concern: I have pleasure in recommending Miss Williams as a cheese-maker. I purchased of Mr Drake the cheese made by her in the 1924 season and have now two drafts of her make in stock, which are very even, clean flavoured and have improved by keeping'. So wrote William E. Leversedge, cheese factor of Evercreech. Miss Williams was one of many farmers' daughters who practised an ancient craft.

According to Domesday Book one Somerset manor, probably Charlton Horethorne, was valued not in cash but at 100 cheeses and ten bacon pigs. The farmers of that part of the county were already finding something useful to do with the large quantities of milk which the rich grass there was creating – making cheese and fattening pigs on the whey.

Twice in the twelfth century Somerset's sheriff accounted at the Exchequer for receipts of cheese: in 1170 for 40 weighs (whatever they were) supplied to the king and in 1184 for almost as much supplied to Prince John. The first consignment was worth the massive sum of £40. That was not the last time Somerset cheese was to be highly praised and appreciated in royal circles. Lord Poulett of Hinton St George apologised to Charles I's Secretary of State that he could only send one Cheddar cheese, because they were so popular they were bespoken even before they were made. Another royal connection was the cheese made from the milk of 730 cows and weighing eleven hundredweight which was presented by the farmers of Pennard to Queen Victoria. It measured nine feet four inches round and was twenty inches thick.

Farms all over the county produced cheese every spring and summer for centuries. It went to great households and was consumed by ordinary folk. A farm at Stogursey in 1276–7 produced 202 cheese and the dairies of the bishop of Winchester at Poundisford and Nailsbourne a few years later were regularly selling their product in Taunton market. Richard Arnold of Glastonbury supplied the Luttrells at Dunster in 1403 and a dish called Dulcet Ryal, a sort of cheesecake, was served to the superior guests when John Stafford was welcomed to Wells as bishop in 1425. Ordinary folk like the labourers working on Bridgwater church tower in 1366–7 and the parishioners of Croscombe going on perambulation in 1495–6 were given bread and cheese. And bread and cheese were mentioned in the will of John Witcombe of Martock, who wanted to make sure that the priests who attended his memorial mass were properly fed.

In Henry VIII's reign Thomas Brown of Bridgwater made his living by selling cheese in London, and the town had its own specially-built cheese hall in the 1760s. Yeovil's prosperity, too, rested on cheese at the same time. Then, too, several visitors to the county were fascinated by its cheese. Bishop Richard Pococke, an inveterate traveller on the Continent, thought Somerset cheese tasted like Parmesan. Daniel Defoe was more interested in the manufacturing process, finding a sort of cooperative at Cheddar where the dairymen pooled each day's milk to make a single cheese which could sometimes weigh up to 150 pounds and took more than one man to put on a table. Cheddar cheese was, he declared, 'the greatest and best of the kind in England'.

Later in the eighteenth century John Billingsley described how the products of Cheddar and Meare were sold at the great Hampshire and Berkshire fairs of Weyhill and Reading to dealers in the London market. Of that fact he was rightly proud, but he was rightly most annoyed that the jobbers sold it under the name of Double Gloucester.

By the late nineteenth century Somerset half-skimmed cheese was being sold in Bristol and Bath, and the Wincanton area was well known for its skimmed-milk cheese. Farmer Kinglake of North Petherton made what he called 'raw milk' cheese from 1786 which he sold in Bridgwater. Wells was a leading market, selling both prime and 'household' Cheddars called 'Skim Dicks' or 'Dundry Daps'.

Frome's Cheese Show was first held in 1861 and has been held continuously since 1877. By that time some order had been introduced in manufacture. The Harding family of Compton Dando and Marksbury founded the 'modern' method of slip scalding. George Gibbons of Tunley Farm, not far away and a relative of the Hardings, won prizes in New York in 1878 and later in Copenhagen, Amsterdam and Paris.

So Cheddar cheese had achieved international recognition, and the Bath and West Agricultural Society decided to keep it that way by sponsoring Cheddar cheese schools in 1890 that were later taken over by Somerset County Council. One of the most successful schools was at Glendale Farm, Wedmore. In recent years cottage, curd, cream and other soft cheeses have been factory-produced in Somerset but there is a strong demand for the farmhouse-made product which includes varieties such as Caerphilly, made in the county as much as a century ago when the main season was over and which could be ready to eat within a fortnight. Today Caerphilly, said to have been 'invented' by Welsh miners, is made in Wedmore. The Mendip area still produces fine cheeses, a maker in Timsbury now using milk from goats and ewes just as the medieval dairyman had done. Still, Cheddar remains the county's staple product, made in the way that Miss Williams had made it and cheese-makers before her for a thousand years.

~~~

Every self-respecting county town had its club where members could enjoy cheese after their luncheon dessert even if peacock and cider were not available nor to their taste. Taunton was no exception. The Somerset County Club was founded in 1882, initially for gentlemen but later also for ladies. There they could gather to lunch, dine or sup, talk politics (only the gentlemen, of course), read the daily and weekly journals, write letters, play cards, have a quiet smoke or nap.

The Somerset County Club first occupied premises in the heart of the town, in Fore Street, but in the early 1930s moved to the Crescent, soon much more convenient for members whose business was in the new County Hall, just opposite, for it had the inestimable benefit of a car park. However, in the 1950s membership declined, the premises began to seem much less attractive, the TV set proved temperamental, the selection of reading matter not quite what some members wanted (might *La Vie Parisienne* replace *London Life* which no longer mentioned the 'old haunts'?), so the building was sold and for a short time members were harboured in the George Hotel in High Street. A new home was found in Melville House, Middle Street and the club's plate was put up again, but that proved no solution. It had become too local, too parochial. The last visitor signed the book in 1986. Thus the life of a noble institution came to an end.

Two leather-spined books have survived among the club's records, subsequently joined by a third brought from Cornwall, which reveal something of the flavour of the club in its balmy days and of the social group that it served.

The 'Advertisement Book' was a far more discreet vehicle for disposing of property than the public columns of the local newspaper when a chap needed a little ready cash. Its opening pages, beginning in 1910, reflect the club's 'county' standing. One member offered a ten-year-old bay gelding hunter, once bad to shoe but now quite quiet and accustomed to carrying a lady over any country. Another wished to dispose of 'Clandon Lad', the winner of many steeplechases, and assumed that fellow members would know both his age and condition. Members of the sporting fraternity might be interested in a well-mannered liver and white spaniel, a wavy-coated black retriever, a white West Highland pup or pedigree 'Scottish terrier dogs'. Mr A.E. Newton was looking to let the shooting on his estate and Colonel Baldock wanted one or two partners for another shoot not far away. Two members, wintering abroad, offered to let their houses, one with the undoubted attraction of Pickeridge golf course nearby.

Hunting and shooting were the life-blood of the county, but it was a changing world. Club members seem to have been competing with each other in the rush to dispose of even the finest, hardly-used, immaculately maintained and attractively painted victorias, dog-carts and broughams, one with extra headroom for ladies' hats, in smart dark blue and black livery. One vehicle was described as a converted London four-wheel cab. All because the motor car now occupied the coach house, and men like M.W. Wadham (whose employer was evidently concerned for his future) was permitted to use the club's Advertisement Book to declare that after eleven years as coachman, groom and helper in the garden, he was without employment. He was, unfortunately, too late to answer the request for 'a thoroughly reliable chauffer honest, trustworthy and a sensible age about thirty-six married, total abstainer, workshop training, vulcanizer, good and careful driver' who was offered thirty shillings (£1.50p) a week and a house by the owner of a new motor car.

Members might even find a suitable vehicle through the club, such as a 14/20 hp Leon Bollee 1912 type two-seater (to hold four), 'the smartest car in London, every refinement, never been out, only just delivered, to be seen at 28 Long Acre, WC'. More plausible was a 16/20 hp Wolseley with 3500 miles on the clock, offered at £400 because the owner was going abroad.

Then came the Great War, and members who returned had less to offer: in 1919 a pair of horse clippers, a house to let, and even two cheap billiard cues. After that no more entries until after the Second World War and a return to the old spirit for a while: boxer bitches, a pair of Newmarket boots, a twelve-bore and a set of match golf clubs, a stalking rifle, a mile or two of trout fishing, an open sports Singer 9 with a price tag of £375. Then no more.

But members were not all dead if the entries in the club's 'Suggestions Book' are any guide. Diners in the '40s and '50s requested good ground coffee, numbered table napkin rings, better soup, and dahl to go with the good curry already served; drinkers missed the white port and demanded tomato and pineapple juice and Mackesons; readers wanted *Everybody's* (already taken, replied the Club Secretary), *The Countryman* (no action), the *Evening Standard* instead of the *Evening News*, and complained that some members were making off with newspapers.

Far more serious was the lack of a wireless, for how could a fellow discover the county cricket scores? Nearly as bad was the state of the card room one afternoon when half the fourteen occupants were smokers and the complainant clearly was not.

Not all the suggestions were entirely serious, but the final agonies of the club were marked by a nice dispute over the provision of hairbrushes in the gentlemen's lavatory, the chronic unreliability of the TV set, and the abuse of the car park. The member who requested an atlas to settle arguments and a copy of the *Thoughts of Chairman Mao* in English might just have been testing the metal of the Club Secretary. He was, of course, exercising his undoubted right as a fully paid-up member of a gentleman's club to voice a private opinion in the most polite way possible.

10

INVASION THREATS

*"The Press Gang was busy everywhere... to take away all the
'loose, disorderly persons' they could find."*

*Invasion is the inevitable hazard faced by an island race and in the past almost
invariably meant war. Romans, Saxons and Normans were invaders and made us
what we are, gave us our laws and our language, our social structures, our patterns
of settlement, our place-names. After them invasions have been small-scale, sometimes good, sometimes bad, more in the nature of attempted régime change, but no
less serious for that, especially when a change of king might involve a change in religious allegiance. Thus Catholic France proved a threat for centuries, even when
under Napoleon it was less Catholic and more Imperialist.*

<div align="center">~~~</div>

The army that Henry V took to France in 1415 was tiny, but the largest he
could get together; another in 1418 for a second attack proved not much

easier to recruit, not because possible fighters were scared but because they knew they might well not be paid, and the risks were still very great. The king, of course, in both years had a further worry. Who would defend our vulnerable shores should the treacherous French actually cross the Channel in the opposite direction against all the rules of decent warfare? The answer, perhaps surprisingly, was the Church.

The order went down from the king to every bishop and every diocese 'to assemble with all speed the able and fencible clergy ... causing and compelling them to be arrayed and furnished according to their estate and means'. They were not just to be recruited, they were to stand ready 'to resist the malice of the enemies of the realm and Church of England' and to stand up 'for safe guard and defence of the realm and church and of the faith'. An early version of the Home Guard.

Loyally (though they had little choice) the clergy of the diocese of Bath and Wells rose to the occasion. In 1415, while the English army staggered on its demoralised way to the amazing and undeserved victory at Agincourt, 830 Somerset clergymen turned out as archers, 60 as men 'adequately armed' (whatever that meant), and 10 as light horsemen. Three years later there were 57 'men-at-arms', 770 archers and 12 horsemen. How long they were away from their parishes and exactly what they did will probably never be known, though there were certainly a few fighting bishops to command them at the time including Henry Bowet, who had been at Wells until 1407 and who in 1417 when archbishop of York went with troops from his own estates to fight the Scots.

Laws made from Henry VIII's reign onwards required men of substance to keep horses ready for the king's use and as threats of attack from Catholic Europe grew, so did the demand for men with smaller incomes to find weapons and armour in readiness. Clergymen were not required to fight but the best paid, archbishops and bishops, were to find up to seven horses each, and other clergy were to pay in part or in full for an arquebusier, a sort of rifleman. As usual the laity both paid and were ready to fight: in 1569 the muster for the whole county totalled 6,040 men.

In a later Somerset battle one fighting bishop played a prominent part. He was Peter Mews, bishop of Bath and Wells 1673–84 and thereafter bishop of Winchester. As a young Oxford student he had fought for the king during the Civil War. As bishop of Winchester who ought to have known better, he accompanied James II's army at Sedgemoor and his signal service – lending his coach horses to pull the royal guns into the correct position – earned him a medal and no little disgust from true Somerset folk.

—*mm*—

In August 1686 King James II felt safer than he had a day or two earlier when he visited the battlefield at Sedgemoor, and on his way from Wells to Wilton invited himself to dine at Lord FitzHardinge's table at Bruton Abbey. Only just over two years later and the birth of a son and (Catholic) heir later that same Lord FitzHardinge was entertaining William of Orange and Prince George of Denmark. It was not exactly a foreign invasion: William and George were royal family, for each was married to one of King James's Protestant daughters. Yet that was precisely the point. James, the victor of Sedgemoor, could be tolerated with the prospect of a Protestant successor, but not with a Catholic one.

So William had landed at Torbay on 5 November 1688 (what a day to choose) and George had joined him; but at first not many others, for had not West Country folk suffered enough for following Monmouth? Would these rebels succeed where he had failed?

The answer was to be yes and without much bloodshed, but William's progress from Devon was deliberately slow. In fact his growing force did not arrive in the Bruton–Wincanton area for a fortnight. Just outside Wincanton a skirmish took place between Colonel Patrick Sarsfield (who had fought with Hamilton's Dragoons for the king at Sedgemoor) and a detachment from Salisbury and some twenty-five men under Lieutenant Campbell for the Prince. Exactly what happened is not clear but both Sarsfield and Campbell were evidently among the fifteen dead 'tumbled into one grave' and the remaining royalists, 70 horse and 50 dragoons, took to their heels after a miller had told them that more Orangemen were coming.

The king's troops were already losing their nerve. Captain Kerk (could he be related to the man who had wreaked such vengeance after Sedgemoor?) had been in Bruton with a royal troop in mid October but the high constable, responsible for public safety in the area, was already accepting orders from 'Captain' Campbell on the day before Campbell lost his life, and sent out orders for carts to serve the Prince. A week later and he was arranging quarters for former royal troops who had changed sides. A few days later still and he was putting a guard on the carts and paying guides to show the

Orangemen the way to Kilmington, Chilmark and Hindon, providing an advance guard should the king move west from his base in Salisbury.

But there was little chance of such initiative. The two princes seem to have travelled very near the bulk of their troops. After Crewkerne they stayed with Lord Bristol at Sherborne Castle, lodged with Mr Churchey at Wincanton and brought their army to Bruton on 1 or 2 December. They themselves were welcomed by that same Lord FitzHardinge who had played host to King James.

All this time the high constable was kept very busy, paying guides to show men to their quarters either at Mr Cheeke's inn or in houses in and around the town. Warrants were issued in the names of Somerset's sympathetic Deputy Lieutenants summoning the county militia and within a matter of days Colonel Berkeley and Captain FitzHardinge had men who needed billets. Come rent day at Michaelmas 1689 one of Sir Stephen Fox's tenants at South Brewham was allowed the sum of £2 6s 11d (£2.35p) for having quartered some of them.

Those were exciting times at Bruton. Some people 'refused to bring in their red coats and arms' in response to the militia summonses but generally the town was *en fête*. A report that some Irish had burned Basingstoke cost the high constable 7s 6d (37p) (for what he did not record) and he paid 4s (20p) to Joan Phelips 'for beer when the town was in arms' and £2 4s (£2.20) by Lord FitzHardinge's order 'at the dispersing of the late king's army'. Later William Palmer and Richard Chaffin claimed expenses for candles, beer and fuel for 'guard fires' at the same celebrations.

The military collapse of King James's government was followed by the stately progress of its political destruction. The parliamentary Convention was proclaimed in Bruton as elsewhere in the country and on 24 February 1689, the politicians having completed their work, William was proclaimed king and Mary queen. Wine and beer that day cost the hundred constable (and therefore the parish) £3 5s 6d (£3.27p).

But peace did not follow, for King James took an army to Ireland, and France was always willing to support his cause. During the spring and summer of 1689 Bruton's high constable pressed carts, billeted troops, provided guides and mounted a guard at the Town Hall as Ensign Roberts, Major Devenish, Lieutenant Freak, Captain Coward, Major Fox and Colonel Earle went about their business. In the middle of August another rumour about the burning Irish had to be quenched with beer.

Colonel Trelawney brought his regiment into the town for a short time a year or two later, but not until there was trouble in Scotland were troops once more in Bruton. Colonel Chudleigh's regiment of foot arrived early in October, and two foot companies stayed there from January until March. By that time the crisis had passed. James Francis Edward Stuart, that child who had caused such excitement by his birth in 1688, had landed in Scotland in December 1715 in support of the earl of Mar's rebellion. Six weeks later he had sneaked away again. No doubt the people of Bruton consumed beer as usual, but this time the high constable did not pay.

—*m*—

Burke's famous *Peerage, Baronetage and Knightage* has always relied a good deal on family traditions as well as on traditional historical research for its information, but when neither comes to its aid it has to admit itself beaten. So, in its account of the somewhat colourful Scots family of Ruthven, all it can say is that William, second son of James, Lord Ruthven, who was born on 16 February 1736 (no doubt a date entered in a register of baptisms and perhaps also in a family bible) died unmarried at an unknown date.

It is a long way from the Ruthvens' native Perthshire, but in the north aisle of Somerton church is a marble memorial recording the death of 'the Honourable William Ruthven, son of Lord Ruthven, Ensign in the Old Buffs', and the date of his death, 9 June 1756. In the parish register his burial was recorded on 12 June, and the vicar or the parish clerk described him as 'William Ruthvin Esquire, ensign of the Old [inserted] Buffs, son of Lord Ruthvin'.

So there is no doubt whatever about William's identity: he was the second son of James, Lord Ruthven in the peerage of Scotland, a man who according to strict peerage doctrine (but not, of course, to family tradition) had no right to call himself a baron at all, or even to use his family name. More than one of his ancestors had been opponents of James VI of Scotland and one, John Ruthven, had been that baron Ruthven and earl of Gowrie who with his brother had been condemned in 1600 for their (probably innocent) part in what was called the Gowrie Conspiracy. Both brothers were killed at the time and were declared by the Scottish parliament to have been guilty of high treason. All their honours were forfeit and the name Ruthven was declared abolished.

The rest of the family rather ignored the judgment. A very distant cousin, Sir Thomas Ruthven, a supporter of the English Parliamentarians, was persuaded to become a royalist in 1651 and accepted a barony from Charles II, one of nineteen peers created by the king-in-exile. Thomas's son died without male heirs and the so-called title of Lord Ruthven passed through the female line. The William who died at Somerton in 1756 was a rather distant cousin of Thomas several times removed.

The newspapers of the mid 1750s were full of wars and rumours of wars. In February 1756 the Cinque Ports were in a state of readiness, for a sea war was in prospect with France. On one side, so a French source declared, stood 'hatred and naughtiness', on the other 'vengeance and animosity' threatening 'horrible tragedies on the ocean and the coasts washed thereby'. Admirals were daily reported ready to sail, the earl of Effingham was anxious to join his 34th Foot in Minorca; noblemen were rapidly discharging any French servants in their employ; Admiral Byng was off to Port Mahon, but returned almost immediately.

At home military camps were being set up near the south coast, ready for invasion, and tents appeared in St James's Park. The Press Gang was busy everywhere and the Justices of the Peace in the City of Oxford encouraged them to take away all the 'loose, disorderly persons' they could find.

Excitement mounted. Admiral Hawke blockaded the French fleet in Brest, Admiral Byng finally left for Minorca to prepare for his own downfall, and 12,000 Russians were expected (no doubt with snow on their boots) in the Isle of Wight. The duke of Kingston, Lord Doune 'and several other persons of distinction' arranged to raise troops of horse, and ten noblemen and gentlemen declared they had taken ten newly-raised regiments under their protection. That kind of subsidy was to ensure that enlisting of new troops for service at home and overseas, including the American colonies, could be finished in three months. The troops themselves were to serve for three years. Ensign the Honourable William Ruthven, a young man with few prospects, must have wanted some action and the times provided it.

The regiment William belonged to, known as the Old Buffs or the Buff Howards, had seen service in Scotland in the early 1750s, and there no doubt he enlisted. In 1755 they came south into Sussex to guard the coast. Successful recruitment produced a new regiment in May in the West Midlands and the Welsh border. A report appearing in the *Western Flying Post*, dated at Worcester on 20 May, said that the new regiment was ordered to march out of Hereford for Exeter under the command of Colonel Anstruther.

The regimental history of The Buffs declares that the men spent some time in Devizes from where they sent detachments to Somerton, Glastonbury and

Langport. In July they moved through Blandford and Exeter to Plymouth. But the Honourable William Ruthven was not with them. There is no record of the cause of his death in Somerton, but it is unlikely to have been some military accident since the parish clerk would surely have recorded the fact. There was no plague in the town at the time, but the drains may not have been of the best nor the water the purest. He was not the only soldier of the regiment to die in Somerset, for John Bivern (according to the parish clerk of St John's, Glastonbury) 'soldier in Amstruther's regiment' was buried there on 17 May 1756. Marching from Hereford in ten days with full kit for a man who had taken the king's shilling without a medical examination might easily have been as effective as an enemy bullet.

The threat of French invasion remained ever present throughout the 18th century and someone thought that statistics were as good a weapon in the defence campaign as any other. The need to know about food and its supply was the impetus for the newly active Board of Agriculture, which published county reports on farming, and after various surveys of wheat supply and harvest results from 1795 onwards, the Home Secretary asked the bishops to arrange with their clergy to collect information from their parishes about crops grown and acreages under cultivation.

The same threat of invasion also produced the Census of 1801 and the first of the long series of Ordnance Survey maps of which this country is justly proud. So when Napoleon's vast army waited on the French coast, the British militiaman had behind him an organisation which was impressive in its thoroughness: nothing less than a plan to move people and property from one part of the country to another. And behind that again a great survey, almost comparable with Domesday, to assess dead and live stock. The original idea had been only to survey parishes within 12 miles of a coast, but in 1804 the whole of Somerset was included. If only more of the results had been preserved we should have an amazing picture of the county at a critical time. As it is we know a good deal about 25 parishes in the Frome area and a few more further west.

So, in the Frome subdivision of Frome hundred, including Frome and the villages of Rode, Berkley, East and West Woodlands and Woolverton, there were 465 oxen, 13 bulls, 3713 cows, 1939 young cattle and colts, 4646 sheep and goats, 1393 pigs, 261 riding horses and 860 draught horses. Sheep were kept in large numbers at Hemington, Hardington and Kilmersdon, and at Hardington also there were 130 deer in Sir Charles Bampfylde's park. The speciality at East Woodlands was a quantity of bark collected in the woods on the Longleat estate for the tanning industry.

There were cheeses and sides of bacon at Hemington and Kilmersdon; £450 worth of linen drapery at Kilmersdon and £200 worth of woollens and linens at Holcombe, presumably revealing small factories or very well-stocked shops. There were 156 spades, shovels, billhooks, hatchets and pickaxes at a small manufactory at West Woodlands. At two other places there were much larger businesses making the same types of implements. Those were at Mells, where physical remains of the works can still be seen. In 1804 James Fussell had in stock 1700 dozen scythes, 500 dozen reaphooks and the whole paraphernalia of means to make them: 9 water wheels, forges, hammers, bellows, anvils and grindstones. John Fussell had 160 dozen spades and shovels, 12 dozen hooks and axes in stock with similar machinery, fuel, steel and iron.

Anyone who knows the Frome area knows that it produced (and its people consumed) large quantities of beer. There were 200 hogsheads at Kilmersdon, 800 beer barrels owned by Joseph House at Ashwick, 330 hogsheads of beer at Woolverton (shared between John Collett and Roger Moger) and even larger quantities of beer and malt at Rode and Frome.

The survey was probably made throughout Somerset and one of the few other parishes whose returns survive is West Quantoxhead. There, it seems, the independence of the Somerset farmer was revealed. Farmer Samuel Tucker would not answer the questions of William Price, the superintendent of the parish survey, believing it was some sinister government ploy to discover his tax liability rather than in fact to afford him some insurance cover in the event of invasion. Without Farmer Tucker West Quantoxhead returned 16 oxen, 38 cows, 31 young cattle and colts, 562 sheep and goats, and 48 pigs. Between them the other farmers could muster just 7 carts and 5 waggons, and in their barns and bartons were 87 quarters of wheat, 75 quarters of barley, 6 quarters of beans and peas, 76 loads of hay, 20 loads of straw, and 6 quarters of malt. A typical Somerset parish.

And what of the great evacuation plan? In the parish church at Molland, just beyond the county boundary in Devon is a set of printed instructions which the parish received in 1803 which would enable it to carry out the government's scorched-earth policy should Napoleon's troops invade. All livestock was to be placed under the control of drivers answerable to a conductor, to be removed as speedily as possible. Dead stock was similarly to be moved, or in dire emergency live and dead stock destroyed, horses especially being mentioned because of their value to the enemy. The sick and infirm were to be taken in carts and waggons whose drivers were to take food for two days, spare horseshoes and nails, and tools to breach hedges and fences where necessary along the roads, for it was vital that evacuation should not hamper the swift movement of troops. Presumably the rest of the population had to fend for themselves.

All those arrangements related to Molland and to Devon, but should Napoleon's invasion have taken place in the South West, where successful invaders had landed before, then the people of Molland and the rest of Devon knew exactly their line of march. From Molland Town they were to proceed to Molland Common and thence to Dulverton. From there they were to 'cross the roads' to Wiveliscombe, on to the Gore Inn at Bishop's Lydeard (now the Lethbridge Arms, Gore Square), thence to Langport and the moors north of Somerton, where the government presumably considered they might be safe while the army stood and fought.

―――

In May 1803 Napoleon, aware or not of the measures taken by the British, vowed he would sacrifice 100,000 men in the invasion of England, and assembled a vast army in Boulogne, Dunkirk, Calais and Le Havre. Opposed to him by the beginning of August were nearly 10,500 hastily-recruited militiamen. By the end of the year there may have been as many as 400,000.

Among the first to come to the defence of their country, thanks to the enthusiasm of Henry Bull Strangways of Shapwick, was the Polden Hill Regiment of Volunteer Infantry consisting of eight companies of 60 privates each and a total of 29 officers, 24 sergeants, 24 corporals and 16 drummers: 573 men in all. Strangways himself was at the time a lieutenant in Lord Paget's regiment on leave of absence from his base in Plymouth and on half pay.

The first division of the new regiment assembled for the first time on 18 September 1803 in a field called Clover Close in Cossington. There Strangways, still a regular lieutenant but addressed by his men as Colonel, met what was probably a rather motley group of men coming from Shapwick and the rest of the Polden villages but also from as far afield at Stretcholt.

Equipment was, of course, both badly needed and in short supply. An order for weapons was sent to the Board of Ordnance and by late October delivery was promised from Plymouth. The sergeants were furnished with coloured pikes instead of the expected spears but there was, so it was claimed, only one drum maker in the kingdom and the Polden Hill drummers probably had to wait.

At the end of October the division was under orders to assemble at Crandon Bridge, ready in case the enemy should appear in the Bristol Channel. A month later the whole regiment, still without proper equipment, met for inspection at Shapwick by Lieutenant Colonel Kirkham, appearing on behalf of the Government Inspector of the Western Division. He must have been satisfied with their turnout and the rear ranks were duly presented with pikes.

And that, so far as one man's record is concerned, was the end of the excitement, although the regiment with others offered to find escorts for French prisoners between Plymouth and Bristol after Napoleon's threats had come to nothing and rather worse than nothing.

By 1808 invasion threats had long ago receded as Nelson had finally given the British command of the seas. Enthusiasm for volunteer soldiering had also waned, but still the government was wary and decided to offer volunteers a transfer to the status of militiamen. The Polden Hill Volunteers were rare among the Somerset fighting units in accepting the offer and each man received two guineas (£2.10p). Henry Bull Strangways was appointed Lieutenant Colonel Commandant of what was now called the Polden Hill Regiment of Local Militia.

Their name thus lived on when most of the county's Volunteer Force had been disbanded. Under the command of Captain King, perhaps the John King who had been an ensign when the regiment was first formed, 71 privates, 2 drummers, 4 corporals and 4 sergeants assembled at Taunton on 4 September 1813. They were, of course, still part-time soldiers yet no longer exclusively from the Poldens but from a wide area in the east of the county.

Sergeant Richard Banwell was a carpenter from Wedmore, Sergeants Thomas Jossey and George Twogood farmers from the same parish. Sergeant James Lovell was a hairdresser from Glastonbury. Most other ranks were labourers but among them were coal miners from Timsbury, Farmborough, High Littleton and Paulton, a paper maker from Stoke Lane, a basket maker and a fellmonger from Glastonbury, a silk dresser from Shepton Mallet and George Wall from Wedmore who described himself as a single-stick player. In fact Polden men were in a minority: three from Catcott, two from Burtle, only one from Ashcott.

113

Their trip to Taunton was on foot; most men were paid for six marching days to cover up to 44 miles there and back, the rest for four days. Sergeants, corporals and drummers were paid a little more and all received beer money and what were called 'sweets and sours'. Taunton's plentiful inns, to which every man was duly assigned, afforded beds and ample opportunities to spend the cash.

But why Taunton, and why just then? The columns of the *Taunton Courier* included reports, many days old and of doubtful veracity, that Austria had suddenly broken its cease-fire with the French and had joined the allies against Napoleon. There were despatches from Sir Arthur Wellesley that he was making progress against the French in Spain, and letters speaking of Russian victories and Russian defeats almost in the same sentence. There were also letters from French sources suggesting that Austrian resistance was no more. But there was no immediate invasion threat; it was simply that September was the time when Volunteers all over the country had their annual fourteen days of training and exercises, and Taunton was the base for the regular county regiment with associated high professional standards and fearsome bellows of command.

So the *Courier* published summonses to members of two Devon regiments, the Highridge Devon Local Militia to Tiverton, the East Devon or 7th Local Militia to Honiton, and the Polden Hill Regiment and the Somerton and Langport Militia (Colonel Pinney) to Taunton. Pinney and his men arrived in Taunton two days after the Polden and Mendip men had left. For a few days each was a more efficient fighting force since last they had been marched around a parade ground with the yell of a sergeant-major ringing in their ears.

11
ALL ABOUT MONEY

Ownership of a manor may have given a man considerable legal and political status, but with status came responsibility and that often cost money. Rare was the family in the Middle Ages where there was never a financial crisis: kings borrowed cash to go to war, noblemen hoped to take a rich prisoner and secure ransom money, knights hoped to find good lordship and thus ensure their exploits cost them as little as possible. A generous lord was valued above rubies. And there were debts and debts: honourable ones incurred in fighting for a noble cause or fulfilling family obligations, less honourable ones resulting from living above means. Yet all, somehow and at some time, had to be paid, and the manor was the best security.

"Each year he had to pay the king at Rouen a lance with the tail of a fox hanging from it"

Walter Hungerford, Baron Hungerford, was a great man. His father was Sir Thomas Hungerford of Farleigh Hungerford and Wellow, and Walter, then only twenty-one and a loyal supporter of Henry Bolingbroke, was made a Knight of the Bath at the coronation in 1399 when Bolingbroke became Henry IV. In 1400 he was elected MP for the first time and in 1414, when MP for Wiltshire, he was chosen to be Speaker of the House of Commons. In that same year he was also sheriff of Somerset and Dorset and ambassador to negotiate with the Emperor Sigismund. From the emperor's court he travelled on to attend the Council of Constance and returned with the emperor to England.

115

Yet he was, first and foremost, a military man. He fought at Agincourt, leading his own troop of twenty men-at-arms and sixty mounted archers, no doubt men from his estates in Somerset and Wiltshire; and very likely he uttered the words Shakespeare put in the mouth of the earl of Westmorland:
Oh that we now had here
But one ten thousand of those men in England
That do no work today!

Westmorland certainly did not say them because he was not at Agincourt. Hungerford was obviously close to Henry V, was executor of his will, and was a senior member of the government ruling in the name of the boy king Henry VI. His last important post was Lord High Treasurer of England, and his reward was a summons to be a member of the House of Lords.

Hungerford, it perhaps goes without saying, was a rich man. His Somerset estates included South Cadbury, Maperton, Holbrook, Wootton Courtenay (acquired through his wife), Backwell, Hallatrow, Wellow, Twerton and, of course, Farleigh; and there were more lands in Wiltshire, Berkshire, Dorset, Oxfordshire, Hampshire, London and even a castle in Normandy named Hommet. This last was given to him in 1418 with a rather peculiar obligation attached: each year he had to pay to the king at Rouen, the capital of the English lands in France, a lance with the tail of a fox hanging from it.

A man with such an income could afford luxuries like the silverwork undertaken by Thomas Goldsmyth of Shaftesbury which cost £10 in 1429–30 and more than twice that sum paid to John Ewley of Bristol, a smith, for ironwork for his private chapel in Salisbury cathedral. And such a man had a body of servants to do his bidding: for the estate a receiver-general (in 1429–30 John Carter who was also rector of Camerton) an auditor, a clerk of account, stewards in Somerset, Dorset, Devon and Wiltshire, and legal advisors wherever they were needed.

At home three men were paid special rewards in 1429–30: William Wardropere, John Janyn, the bakery boy, and John the chaplain at Farleigh. No doubt there were many more mentioned and paid in other years. Those were domestic servants. In the same account were men attached to various churches: £10 went to John Masson for building the church at 'Heightre' and another £8 and more to John Hogges, the carpenter working there. The rector of Farleigh had a smaller sum for new building. In the same year a friar called Curteys received a generous present and John the clerk of Keynsham a smaller one that Whitsun week.

What makes Hungerford a little unusual are payments in every year for which his estate records survive to the poor at the rate of 4d (1p) a week. So John Carter the receiver-general recorded in 1429–30 that he had paid 17s 4d (86p) to the poor of Farleigh, Saltford, Backwell, Maperton, South Cadbury and Wootton Courtenay. But in the account for the year 1455–6, some years after Walter's son Robert had succeeded to the estates, there is only a gift to two poor men at Hungerford and to 'the hermit' at South Cadbury.

It is, of course, no more than a wild guess, but travellers going between North and South Cadbury before the A303 was modernised, would have to halt at what was called Chapel Cross. There, on the South Cadbury side of the main road, was a cottage which, it was discovered in the early 1970s, was evidently medieval. What, it was asked at the time, was a chapel doing there? Could it have been a shrine for travellers to offer prayers for a safe journey and a swift return? Maybe a better answer can now be suggested, namely that it was the home of the hermit who lived there with the support of the rather pious and generous Robert, Baron Hungerford, Lord of Hungerford, Heytesbury and Hommet.

The Stawells were a Somerset family through and through; whether they or the Polden village came first no one could tell, but they can be traced there back in the mid thirteenth century and to Cothelstone in the twelfth. So they were a persistent family, and when it mattered they were loyal. It mattered most in the 1600s when the most loyal of all was Sir John Stawell, Knight of the Bath, who would undoubtedly have enjoyed his magnificent funeral at Cothelstone in February 1662. He deserved such a reward for he had been the most conspicuous opponent of Parliament in Somerset during the Civil War, lost his estates as a result, and was imprisoned in the Tower until 1653. He was then held in London under house arrest on £6 a week.

He had been MP twice for the county before the war and was for a short time again from 1661 until his death. He was remembered as a 'lofty, proud man' and was the father of nine sons and two daughters. He outlived all but three of his sons, and the oldest of those was *non compos mentis*. His second son Edward was also a cavalier and died in exile in 1653 and another son, Thomas, probably also died abroad.

George, the third son, managed to keep his head down and on. He succeeded to the family estates, was sheriff in 1667–8 and, perhaps in celebration, built the exquisite chapel in the field now beside a farm in Low Ham. It was consecrated in 1669 and the velvet altar frontal made in the following year is now preserved in the museum in Taunton Castle. George's initials and his coat of arms are carved on the north door of the chapel, and the text on the chancel screen, from Proverbs 24.21, gives more than a clue to the Stawell family attitude to politics and the world in general: My sonne, feare God and the Kinge and meddle not with them that are given to change.

George died in the year the chapel was consecrated and was followed by his rather more flamboyant brother Ralph. He, too, was loyal, serving as Deputy Lieutenant of both Somerset and Wiltshire (he had a house at Avebury) and Colonel of a militia regiment recruited in and around Bridgwater. In 1683, as a kind of posthumous reward for his father, he was created Baron Stawell of Somerton.

It was a reward, too, for Stawell's own activities in Bridgwater against Whigs and nonconformists (fanatics he called them) who were not too keen to see a Roman Catholic on the throne, but he must have felt a fool when most of his regiment melted away to join Monmouth. He himself thought it wiser to leave his home at Low Ham on 4 July 1685 when Monmouth was in Bridgwater and the royal army just up the road in Somerton. He came back four days later when the battle between them was over, and two days after that rewarded the watchmen handsomely for looking after his property. Stawell may have had some satisfaction when his father's old opponent Colonel Richard Bovett, now a Monmouth supporter, was hanged in front of his house at Cothelstone.

But loyalty could only be stretched so far. James II made him Lord Lieutenant in succession to the Catholic Lord Waldegrave to acquire some credibility when all around him was falling apart, but Lord Stawell changed sides when William of Orange landed on 5 November 1688. He was only forty-eight when he died nine months later.

Lord Stawell's son John was about twenty when his father died and did not reach his twenty-fourth birthday. He left a daughter and debts so enormous that sales were inevitable. Some said the disaster was his fault, some his father's. The father is usually blamed because he began to build an enormous mansion at Low Ham, planned to be 400 feet long and 100 feet deep that ran away with over £100,000 and was never finished.

Very fortunately an account book of Ralph and John Stawell survives covering the years 1682 to 1691. It makes fascinating reading and shows that Ralph had been borrowing money heavily from the beginning, and at least part of the debt was a matter of family honour, namely trying to find the enormous sum of £30,000 owed as the dowry of George Stawell's daughter Ursula when she married the earl of Coventry in 1681. The earl came down to stay with his wife's uncle in 1686, perhaps to remind him that it was still not paid in full, and broke some of the windows in Low Ham church. The cost of repairs was mentioned several times in the accounts.

And although those accounts manage to hide some of the details, it seems clear enough that if Ralph planned to build the mansion, John actually spent the money. The wages bill each month almost as soon as his father was dead rose enormously. No wonder the debt in 1694 amounted to £72,000 against income assessed at £4,300.

Part of the mansion was actually finished and lasted perhaps until the end of the nineteenth century. Visitors described painted and plastered ceilings and a large, square, detached kitchen furnished with a huge elm table. All that now survives of the building is a sort of triumphal arch, squeezed incongruously between two roads outside Sparkford, moved there by one of the Mildmay family to adorn his estate at Hazlegrove.

And there also survives George Stawell's chapel with the family monuments which give some idea of the important opinion the Stawell's had of themselves. The rather curious terracing stretching up the valley south of the chapel, surrounded still by a stone wall, marks a garden planned by John, Lord Stawell, with the help of Jacob Bobart of Oxford, one of the leading experts of his time. A survey by the Royal Commission on Historical Monuments has compared what remains on the surface with Bobart's own description of his plans: they match exactly.

In fact Ralph and John were both interested in gardens, the former spending money on African and French marigolds, larkspur and hotspur peas, the latter on orange trees. Those family accounts also have other touches: Ralph bought battledores for the young ladies, a beard comb and case for a friend, and an almanac and the latest part of Dryden's *Absalom and Achitophel* for his wife; John paid £20 to 'Mr Griffier, painter', presumably for one of those curious bird's-eye views of his house and garden from one of the famous family of landscape painters. If only it had survived!

It must be very unusual, if not unique, that two leading politicians should have come to live so near each other. In a sense it was not exactly by choice. William Pitt only came to Somerset because a rather eccentric retired politician, Sir William Pynsent, left him an estate. Lord North only came to live at Dillington because it had been inherited by his wife.

Neither man left much of a permanent mark on their erstwhile homes, although both are known to have created landscaped grounds that have largely disappeared. The most obvious survivor is the column at Burton Pynsent commemorating Pitt's benefactor which stands proudly on Troy Hill overlooking West Sedgemoor.

Pitt and North were, of course, of different generations and in that age of political intrigue their common political label, Whig, was no guarantee that they agreed about anything. In fact Pitt offered North a job in 1758 (which he declined because it would have meant going abroad) and again in 1766. On the second occasion he was not too happy (the job was joint Paymaster-General) 'but that his office had been offered him in such a manner that he could have no reason to refuse it'.

Those two job offers were made when Pitt was in power, the first time as Secretary of State under the nominal leadership of the duke of Devonshire when he, almost single-handedly, conducted a war against France. On the second occasion Pitt was earl of Chatham and ran the government from the House of Lords with the title of Lord Privy Seal: 'and a sad mess he made of it', the historian John Brooke declared.

In between Pitt did what he did best: opposed and criticised the king and his ministers, on one occasion in March 1763 speaking against the government's policy to levy a cider tax. One who heard Lord North said he replied to Pitt 'and (as usual) perfectly well'. Yet it was Pitt's stand on the cider tax that, it was said, inspired Sir William Pynsent to leave him the Burton estate. By the time of his death in 1765 Pynsent was eighty-five and lonely. His daughter Leonora (with whom it was said, he had lived 'in pretty notorious incest') had died in 1763. His wife and other children had gone long before. He had a nephew, a niece and three great-nephews, to whom he left 1000 guineas (£1,050) each; and he left annuities to his servants including his two gardeners.

But Pitt was the favoured heir, and he came to live at Burton with some despatch. It was, after all, much nearer Bath than his home at Hayes in Kent; and Bath, which he represented in parliament, held out prospects for some alleviation of his chronic gout. Yet the favoured heir was also the sole executor and it was thus his responsibility to find the cash for the discarded relatives and the faithful servants. The former Pynsent estates at Urchfont in Wiltshire and the manors of Burton, Moreton (Moortown) and Drayton may well have been stretched to produce fluid assets, although they were said to have been worth £3000 a year. More likely, mortgages were raised.

There were, inevitably, other calls on Pitt's purse. The mansion house at Burton obviously called for an extension and the column had to be paid for. After his brief return to political power was over Pitt came back to Burton to begin to transform the grounds, planting cedars, limes and elms to create his own version of his brother-in-law's park at Stowe on the ridge overlooking West Sedgemoor. Among his practical helpers was Captain Samuel Hood, later Admiral Viscount Hood, who when in command of the American station sent seeds and plants of birch, black spruce, ash, maple and buckthorn from Nova Scotia to be planted on Burton slopes. Hood himself was a Somerset man, the younger son of a vicar at Butleigh.

It was not long before more cash was required and in May 1771 Pitt arranged to borrow £4000 on the security of his three Somerset manors. The money came from Samuel Hood's elder brother Alexander, then a mere Post Captain but, more important for the occasion, Treasurer of Greenwich Hospital. Like his younger brother he was later to become an admiral and a viscount, Viscount Bridport of Cricket St Thomas. Like his brother he was also to become a Tory Member of Parliament.

Pitt's financial needs were evidently very pressing. By the time of his death in 1778 he had borrowed £13,000 from Hood, who must have been relieved when parliament voted £20,000 to discharge his debts. There were other creditors too, including Francis West who had lent a mere £3000.

But why Hood and West? It is a complicated tale, but Pitt's wife Hester and Hood's wife Mary were first cousins. Hester was daughter of Richard Grenville of Wootton, Buckinghamshire, by his wife Hester, Viscountess Cobham, sister of Richard Temple of Stowe, Viscount Cobham. Mary was daughter of the Viscountess's sister Mary by her husband Richard West, a clergyman and prebendary of Winchester. Mary brought Hood a large fortune, and large fortunes had to be invested.

Perhaps it was not just business and profitable risk. Pitt married Hester Grenville when he was forty-six and she about thirty-four. Their marriage was 'one of unalloyed happiness and mutual affection', which was remarkable given that Pitt was thought to be a loner who had no friends and could not bear his children living in the same house. However, Hester was not his first choice. Presumably in his youth and certainly before he had made any reasonable profit from the office of Paymaster-General, Pitt had fallen in love with a girl who then had but little but herself to offer. She was none other than Mary West. Was it her money rather than Hood's which helped to keep the Pitt fortunes afloat?

—*m*—

The little hamlet of Sutton Mallet is hardly on the tourist trail. Its church was declared redundant fifteen years ago, which means a key has to be found in order to gain entrance; its lanes are narrow, its houses unpretentious. A road sign warning of kangaroos is probably a joke, but as its name declares, the village once belonged to the ubiquitous family of Malet – in fact by 1166 until the end of the seventeenth century. It was also, for a time, known as Veny or Venus Sutton, a reference to the fenny character of much of its land on the edge of Sedgemoor.

The last male Malet owner, John Malet, died in 1656 and was succeeded by his daughter Elizabeth, wife of John Wilmot, earl of Rochester. Elizabeth, determined to keep the family name alive, had her youngest daughter christened Malet and it was she who in 1682 succeeded her mother in possession of Sutton. Malet Wilmot became Malet Vaughan when she married John Vaughan, Viscount Lisburne. Malet died in 1709 and in 1720 John broke the family chain of possession by selling to Robert Knight.

Probably very little changed for the people of Sutton. Malets had never lived there, neither did Wilmots or Vaughans or Knights: there was, after all, no suitable house. Robert Knight was forced to sell because of his grave financial embarrassment, but his son bought the estate back, presumably to save the family's honour. The ownership after that cannot be traced for some years, but the Bridgwater businessman Benjamin Allen was owner in 1785 when he sold to Richard Reynolds.

Reynolds died in 1816 leaving Sutton jointly to his daughter Hannah Mary, wife of William Rathbone, and to his son Joseph. Hannah later became sole owner and her sons Richard, Theodore and Benson followed her, bringing the descent of the manor of Sutton Mallet to the later nineteenth century. All rather boring, merely a collection of names. But those names are important far beyond Sutton Mallet.

John Wilmot, earl of Rochester, for instance, was a libertine: gentleman of the bedchamber to Charles II but frequently in disgrace, composer of amorous lyrics, obscene rhymes and mordant satires. Robert Knight the elder was cashier of the South Sea Company and thus in more than a little trouble when the Bubble burst. He fled to France in 1721, losing over £200,000 of assets but became a successful banker in Paris. His son, who sat as MP for Milborne Port 1770–2, received two Irish peerages through the influence of his mistress and was known from 1763 as the earl of Catherlough. Benjamin Allen was a little more respectable, serving as Bridgwater's MP between 1768 and 1781, working closely with Charles James Fox, but finally losing his seat for corruption at his final election. Someone described him as 'a fair, well-meaning man'.

Richard Reynolds was respectability personified, a Quaker iron-master from Ketley in Staffordshire who retired to Bristol where he became widely known as a philanthropist. His first wife was Mary Darby, a member of that family that was at the heart of the Industrial Revolution, and in his will he mentioned furnaces and forges in Coalbrookdale. Hannah Mary continued her father's tradition, marrying William Rathbone, a prominent merchant and philanthropist of Greenbank, Liverpool. Her eldest son, also William, was an eminent educationalist in the city and served as mayor in 1837. Two other sons, Theodore and Benson, shared Sutton, Gappers, and Godfreys farms although Theodore lived at Allerton Priory near Liverpool and Benson at Geldeston in Norfolk. Benson seems to have acquired at least some of the manorial papers, namely two leases granted in the 1720s by Robert Knight which are now in the Norfolk Record Office.

Visitors to Sutton Mallet will see no evidence of those remarkable owners: no grinding mills and throbbing furnaces (there was a windmill on the edge of the moor in 1685 but only a smith in 1851), no rich educational establishments (a day school closed in the 1870s), no formal philanthropy (no trace of a charity for the poor). William Malet was reported in debt in 1557 but hardly on the Knight scale, and as for profligacy, the best to be uncovered were that Thomas Haberfield in 1568 did not cohabit with his wife, that in 1600 divine service was not read 'orderly', the minister did not always wear a surplice, never prayed for the Queen, and did not keep a bull or a boar, the parson's customary responsibility on behalf of his farming community, and in 1666 that Charles Bryan, the curate of Sutton Mallet and Stawell, conducted private and clandestine weddings.

The church in which those ceremonies took place has disappeared like much of Sutton's history. A visitor in the 1780s described the building as 'very mean

... a dark and dismal looking place ... very dirty and much fitter for a stable than a place of worship'. The pulpit was 'wretchedly mean' although the visitor noted green cushions on the pulpit and a green fringed cloth on the good oak communion table. The communion rails were painted blue.

That church, desperately in need of Liverpool philanthropy, was almost entirely pulled down in 1827 and the County Surveyor, Richard Carver, produced a designed that retained only the tower, the east window and the communion rails. William Stagg, a carpenter, carried out most of the work and a Mr Chapple set up the font. The high box pews, each traditionally occupied by a family from each local farm, and the benches under the west gallery are a graphic reminder of the two classes in village society, and the three-decker pulpit a demonstration of the parson's omnipotence. The appearance of any one of the lords of the manor would have seriously upset that comfortable balance.

12
LEISURE PURSUITS

Of course they played, but they have left us few records to prove it. Children must have done, but was it children who made those marks on the stone benches in Blackford church porch and the cloisters at Wells which served as boards for a game with counters? Or at Wells was it idle clergymen with nothing to do between services? There may not have been all that much leisure time for adults, except on high feast days and especially at Christmas; and netting wild birds in the sixteenth century and killing vermin in the eighteenth and early nineteenth were less recreation and more a community necessity. But physical challenge and competition were always there, demonstrated in games of fives and cricket. Significant leisure time, at least for some, came from the 1880s onwards, and with the help first of the bicycle and later of the motor car and the charabanc quite ordinary people began to explore the county and to appreciate its beauty. And the cinema was a place to appreciate another kind of beauty

"Our ancestors four centuries ago seemed bent on destroying animals and birds"

O ur ancestors four centuries ago seemed bent on destroying animals and birds. In fact, public funds in the form of bounties were paid out to local hunters and snarers and were meticulously recorded in parish records in accordance with the requirements of Acts of Parliament. By one such Act of 1532–3 each parish was to have a net to catch rooks, crows and choughs (jackdaws) which presumably threatened crops, and 2d (1p) was to be paid for every twelve old crows, rooks or choughs caught by landlords or their tenants. Rather more expensive, though perhaps more effective, than the Tudor scarecrow.

The Act, perhaps not entirely successful, was extended in 1566 to threaten all 'noyfull fowles and vermyn' which damaged farmers' livelihoods. A penny was now offered for every three crow, chough, magpie or rook heads, the same for every three young owls and every six unbroken eggs. Kingsdon parish spent 5s 3d (26p) on a rook net in 1612 and 15s (75p) on another in 1676.

During the seventeenth century the same parish offered 2d (1p) a dozen for sparrows, 4d (2p) for a fitchet (polecat) or a hedgehog, a shilling (5p) for a fox. The sums varied from parish to parish and from time to time; Somerton, like Kingsdon, offered 4d (2p) for a hedgehog, but Haselbury Plucknett only 2d (1p). Winsford later paid 5s (25p) for a fox, considering the damage they could do to valuable lambs well worth the expense.

At Somerton and Long Sutton marten ('martin cats') were occasionally taken – like foxes worth 1s (5p) for the obvious skill and effort involved in catching them; at Queen Camel otters were sometimes taken. Doubtless a systematic search through the county's parish records would reveal either other victims or different names for the same creatures in different parts of the county. And also, of course, rather odd spellings, such as 'rouckhids', 'sparas', 'sparrers', 'higgogs', 'higghorkes' and the less obvious 'wood fulkes'.

Variety, of course, could be determined as much by parish policy as by the natural surroundings of each area. In 1765 Somerton parish authorities decided, for reasons not given, that they would make no further payments for vermin. Seven years later they resumed their campaign against sparrows, bullfinches, tom tits, foxes, hedgehogs and stoats. Presumably the farming lobby had become too vociferous and the apple crop had been poor. But in 1788 they decided not to pay for bullfinches and in 1806 agreed to give 2d (1p) a dozen for sparrows, chaffinches and yellow hammers. The paid slaughter went on in Somerton until the early 1840s, and it was lawful; and for many families it may have been a lifeline. To catch a fox or a marten could keep a hungry family for days. Many parishes actually employed a full-time mole-catcher, at East Lydford at a salary of 2 guineas (£2.10p).

In Queen Camel a separate account was kept of vermin payments and in just one year four families, the Willcoxes, the Willises, the Martins and the Brooks, between them accounted for 49 of the 58 stoats caught, 7 of the 9 marten, and 6 of the 7 polecats. Richard Willcox was clearly the expert – 7 stoats, 6 marten and 2 polecats – giving him a total of 7s 6d (37p). 'Different boys' of Long Sutton spent their days in the 1830s earning 3d a dozen for sparrows (708 caught in 1835, 1,170 in 1837) while in Muchelney at the same time Mr Walrond combined the duties of parish clerk and vermin controller. In 1848–9 he sent in as usual his bill for 'sparrows, parchment for baptisms and letters: one pound, ten shillings and seven and a half pence' (£1.53p). But Mr Walrond had an advantage over village boys because he had a gun and won prizes for shooting birds.

It is difficult to know quite why three hundred years of tradition should suddenly have been swept away in the 1840s when bounties ceased to be paid. Were there then, perhaps, enough small boys to be sent rook scaring, and hounds enough to deal with the fox and the otter? Certainly, parish paupers, formerly the expert hunters, found themselves breaking stones for parish roads. Uncontrolled vermin and 'noyfull fowles' remained a nuisance to small farmers and cottagers, although better crop yields meant that the damage done was of less significance. Rooks and crows still devasted newly-sown corn, magpies and jays were enemies in the poultry yard, foxes in the sheep-fold, sparrows in thatch. Worst of all, many thought, was the hedgehog whose sucking of cows at night was clearly responsible for the drop in milk yield. But what justified the death of kingfishers and yellow hammers?

We regret the absence of marten and polecat, now confined to remote parts of Wales or Scotland, but their disappearance is as much to do with change in natural habitat as the depredations of the bounty hunter. The kite and the otter fell to more sinister forces, but have marvellously returned. What will become of the fox and the stag now that hunting with hounds is so restricted?

—*wm*—

On 14 November 1623 a court held in St Mary's church, Taunton, by Dr Francis Gough in the name of Dr Samuel Ward, Archdeacon of Taunton, heard that several people from Durleigh and Fiddington had been playing fives against the walls or towers of their parish churches on various Sundays and holy days. The problem seems not to have been the game nor the venue, but the days which caused the trouble. Even more trouble came when Thomas Clement of Durleigh and three men from Fiddington defied the court by either refusing to appear or failing to do the penance required for the offence.

But the game evidently because more unpopular with the authorities. In 1629 men of Shepton Beauchamp were accused in a church court of using their church tower for play; and in 1633 the county magistrates at Quarter Sessions weighed in against players at Williton, though it emerged that the game was not under attack, only the players whose inaccurate play had resulted in damage to the church windows, leaving those with seats under those windows exposed to wind and rain during service time. A fives court was actually dug up in Bridgwater in 1678 and similar action was taken at Wrington.

The diarist John Cannon was certainly not against the game and recorded a 3-a-side game at West Pennard Revel in 1736 when the winners won a shilling each for a score of 21 up. He also noted the death of the landlord of the *George* at Glastonbury in 1735 'by his own carelessness and immoderate heats and colds at the game'. There was another fatality at Martock in 1758 when someone suffered a fractured skull from falling masonry dislodged by a player climbing to retrieve an errant ball. The Vestry, the combined church and parish council, which had earlier moved play from the south to the north side of the church, felt it then had to put a stop to the game. There were similar actions at Corston and Castle Cary. Minds were evidently broader at Babcary, where Parson Woodforde lost a wager on a game; and the sons of a vicar of Montacute are believed to have persuaded their indulgent father to allow them to cut away some of the decoration on the church tower there to improve the playing surface.

By the mid eighteenth century village innkeepers began to see the possibilities of encouraging the game on their premises. The *George* at Nether Stowey had a fives wall, called alternatively a tower, and there is another of similar date at the Blue Anchor at Combwich. A contemporary tower in brick survives at the Lethbridge Arms in Bishops Lydeard. The fine Ham stone towers at Hinton St George, Shepton Beauchamp, South Petherton and Stoke sub Hamdon are all obviously associated with village inns and there were fives courts at, for instance, the *Valiant Soldier* in Bridgwater and the *Swan* at North Petherton.

In the mid nineteenth century the game seems to have 'moved' yet again, this time to the more select surroundings of public schools (there were courts at Crewkerne, Bruton and Ilminster), but Milborne Port acquired one with a double wall as late as 1847, as if to prove that the game was still popular.

In the 1840s, in fact, south Somerset was quite a centre for the game, the players of Curry Rivel and Stoke leading the field. In July 1846 the *County Herald* reported a victory for Curry against Bridport and announced matches for purses of £30 against Bridport and £10 against Stoke. In the next year the

Curry court, belonging to the *Bull* inn and still to be seen, was 'well attended by lovers of that noble game, all of whom seemed highly gratified with the excellence of the play'. The village was en fête for the fatstock fair and the proceedings were enlivened by speeches from the two parliamentary election candidates who addressed the crowds from the inn window.

On the second day of the fair there were fewer dealers (and probably less money wagered) but 'some very good play and the prizes were well contested for. The company admired the good condition of the court and skittle ground'.

A year later and Stoke players challenged all-comers, but the visitors expected from Curry, Dorchester and Bridport did not arrive. The Stoke players, John Palmer and Frederick Fane, claimed to be the champions of England after beating Bath about 1855 and Palmer is credited with a record hit of 38 yards to the tower and back to the roof of the Fleur de Lys. No fractured skull resulted.

—*mm*—

Someone ought to study the prehistory of Somerset cricket. It will not be easy, for cricket clubs have not kept records well and reports in newspapers are patchy; but browse through the files of the *Western Flying Post*, the *Wells Journal* or the *Somerset County Herald* for the summer months in the 1840s and there will be found reports of Somerton's gentlemen pitting their skills against their rivals of South Petherton, Taunton playing Clifton, Banwell challenging Wraxall and Nailsea, Yeovil tackling their more senior cricketing neighbours at Sherborne, Bridgwater finding two teams to play each other.

Sometimes the reports were very short, confined simply to the score, which at least had the advantage of keeping individual failure from the public gaze: 31 August 1844, Somerton 97 and 87, Martock 96 and 73. When Banwell visited Wraxall a few years later there was no such reticence but rather fewer runs. The visitors made 57 in their first innings and 90 in their second, thanks to a good opening stand by R.B. Mills and T. Hancock, who made 32 and 23. Nailsea's first innings score of 77 in 41 overs including 23 byes, 3 leg byes and 3 wide balls. In their second innings extras again made the best score.

R.B. Mills was commended by the reporter for his twelve wickets in the match and T. Miles, with seven wickets 'bowled very well indeed, but not so swift as usual in the early part of the day; which was doubtless attributable to his having a strong breeze against him'.

The breeze was to be expected for the ground was on the top of Wraxall Hill, where the views were remarkable, though it was some way from the railway station, where the visitors had arrived. That was not made an excuse, for cricketers were 'not generally troubled with weak lungs' and such 'puffing' work was not the problem. But was the pitch satisfactory? 'The ground is a very good one for the purpose, if properly prepared and levelled behind as well as between the wickets'. Therein may lie the clue both to the low scores and the many byes.

One clear advantage of Wraxall Hill was the short distance from the local inn. When Taunton entertained the Clifton club at the North Town ground in August 1847 the landlord of the Railway Hotel provided a cold lunch for 100 players and spectators. That very same landlord in the next year produced 'selected viands' which took so long to consume ('the masticating function of the players' had to be 'fairly "played out"', so it was reported) that the match had to be abandoned when the 'shades of evening' overtook them. Mr Tapscott of the Bell, South Petherton, produced melon, ripe strawberries and cherries for the match luncheon in June 1844.

And there were the ladies. The Taunton v Yeovil match in August 1847 was graced by the ladies of Yeovil and the neighbourhood. They took (but of course did not provide) tea; and rejoiced, no doubt, at Yeovil's victory by eight wickets. And when play was over the Yeovil Band led the company in quadrilles and polkas.

A 'brilliant' array of ladies at South Petherton in June 1844 was part of the 'large number of visitors' attracted to the 'animated scene' when the home side made 79 and 55 and the visitors 37 and 68. The Revd W.R. Newbolt, vicar of Somerton, had a bad day: 0 and 0; Mr Custard of South Petherton and Mr Otway of Somerton distinguished themselves more positively. The Somerton Brass Band attended the dinner at the *Red Lion* after the return match which Somerton won by three runs. Mr Newbolt chaired the dinner with his 'usual good humour and ability'.

But just occasionally excitement had somehow to be engineered. In 1844 the Bridgwater club, established nearly ten years earlier, organised a match between twenty-two of their own members. Ladies and gentlemen assembled on the hill behind the Dock to see Mr Salmon's side dismissed for 57. Before Mr Manchip's side replied wagers were offered at 2-1 against. There were few takers because Dr Sewell and Mr Talbott were known to be 'cracksmen', but in the event their wickets were 'speedily lowered', as the reporter's phrase went.

Play continued until 7 o'clock and resumed the following afternoon when Mr Salmon's side won handsomely.

There is no mention of rain interrupting play in any of these games, although when Somerton played South Petherton on that June day in 1844 the weather was reported as 'most suspicious'.

—*mm*—

It is a tiny book, measuring about two inches by three inches, bound in soft, dark green leather, with marbled end papers and gilt-edged pages. The words 'Don't Forget' are inscribed in gold in a modern hand on the front cover. It was purchased (such an item was not bought) from J.J. Banks and Son of the Imperial Library in Cheltenham; the company's tiny dark red label with gold print says as much, and the owner wrote her name, Roberta Vine, her address and the date – April 1921 – on the fly leaf in her best handwriting. Probably it was a 25th birthday gift.

She was, to be precise, my first cousin once removed. As a small boy I called her, very respectfully, Auntie Ruby; as I grew older I thought of her simply as Ruby, the excitable, nervous, emotional, dotty-about-dogs half of what my own branch of the family usually referred to as the Weston girls. Hilda, the older, practical, down-to-earth one made a perfect foil.

They had come to Weston super Mare just after the First World War when their managing mother, my grandfather's eldest sister, had realised that her useless husband would never make a success of farming and she had better take over responsibility for making a decent living. What she did best was keep house, so why not buy a house in Weston large enough to accommodate the growing number of people with modest leisure. A double-fronted one in respectable Moorland Road suited admirably and there the family lived, Father coming and going as he pleased and the girls doing most of the work.

The establishment was clearly a success and Ruby, at any rate, was frequently invited to stay with people who had been so happy on their seaside holiday; and if she could not spare more than a day, then she and her sister would cycle into the country or meet up with cousins and friends. They were still going on jaunts when I remember them, not then by bicycle but in their Baby Austin, just the thing for a small boy much given to travel sickness. The short trip from Weston to Highbridge was more than I could endure.

The little 'Don't Forget' book was Ruby's record of such trips in the 1920s and 1930s, a record of how a girl of a certain age with very modest means and limited time for recreation could, nevertheless, find genuine enjoyment in the countryside.

But, to begin at the beginning, on the afternoon of 21 April 1921 there was a 'Spinster's Birthday Party' at which she, her sister, and some other unnamed 'single ladies' raised the sum of £27 0s 9½d (£27.4p). What for she did not record.

Six days later Ruby was rejoicing that her friend Ruth had entered the married state and that she spent her honeymoon in the house in Moorland Road. Ruby declared she herself had a 'lovely time with them' and after three days the happy couple left for their new home in Wincanton.

On a Monday afternoon in May that same year the two sisters cycled to Burnham on Sea, one and a half hours each way and 'rather blowy but not too hot'. They thoroughly enjoyed themselves. In July there was an evening steamer trip 'cruising round', a 'very good' performance of the *Quaker Girl* at the Knightstone Pavilion in mid August and a walk in Kewstoke woods in early September, the walk almost certainly in company with 'J.M.' A day or two after 'J.M.' had left there was a sea trip from Clevedon.

'Don't Forget' is not a diary, only the highlights of a rather ordinary life; but it was a life of commitment to causes. In March 1922 Ruby was in a party which went by charabanc to Bath for a Christian Science lecture. Another lecture was attended at Bristol in March 1927, and she recorded listening to a debate on the subject on the BBC in March 1933. She attended the three-day meeting of the Liberal Federation at Weston in June 1926 and her sister won first prize at the whist drive held during the conference.

On 9 June 1925 Ruby went to Bristol when the King and Queen opened the new university buildings, saw their Majesties pass by twice, had 'a good view of everything passing' and had a 'lovely day'. The Duke and Duchess of York visited Weston in July 1928 and were also seen twice. It was a great day for Weston, Ruby thought, and the weather was 'lovely'.

The sisters went to the Wembley Exhibition in June 1924 with every other self-respecting citizen. Mr Ladd took Ruby to the opera on Weston pier in 1924 ('had a good time') and she enjoyed listening to the voice of Miss Clara Serena and the playing of Mr Albert Sammons, the world-famous violinist, at the Knightstone in 1927. Twice she went to the Bath and West Show, in 1924 at Taunton, in 1932 at Yeovil. She and Hilda went over HMS *Malaya* in 1931 ('terrible crush'), Ruby alone joined a party to visit Fry's Chocolate Works at Somerdale in 1932.

In spite of her nervous disposition, my cousin once removed was determined to take risks. On 19 May 1933 she took her first air flight. 'Thrilling', she noted, 'but thoroughly enjoyed it'. Three years earlier as one of a party of six she spent a week in Belgium including a day in Holland. She kept her tickets, a map of the London Underground and her bill from Thomas Cook and Son for the rest of her life.

Not all was so exciting but it was generally 'lovely'. Usually little holidays to South Wales or Devon, attendances at cousins' weddings, weeks with relatives in Sussex or Dorset. Always welcomed, always the centre of laughter and quite often the object of much teasing. There is just the suspicion that Ruby was away from home rather more often than her practical sister. The boarding house, after all, was a business which had to be attended to.

～mm～

The local history of the cinema ought to be undertaken soon, before the memories of loyal patrons fade completely. The films themselves are well recorded, but what of those buildings, one or more in every self-respecting town in the land, where escapism and entertainment were available and where the interpersonal skills of several generations were tested and refined in some sort of privacy and relative comfort?

Memories will still be green for the Gaumont and the Odeon, the Central or the Regal where in the 1940s the sweet ration could be consumed at a sitting, local adverts raised hoots of derision and newsreels lent some sort of respectability to what was otherwise pure pleasure. But who now recalls the Electric Picture Palace and Variety Hall in Wells, the Picturedrome owned by the Bath Electric Theatre Company Limited, or Sydney Mille's Empire in the High Street, Midsomer Norton? Who remembers Saturday morning cinema clubs? Who enjoyed the war films projected out of the back of a grey van parked outside the school gates on a summer evening?

Someone with time for research will have discovered Somerset's oldest cinema, opened somewhere soon after 1906. Was it, perhaps, the Vaudeville in Bath or the Regent Street Picture House in Weston? The Corn Exchange in Taunton must have been one of the earliest; it was converted into a 'picturedrome' called the Exchange Theatre in 1910 and the Assembly Rooms at the London Hotel became the Empire Electric Theatre in the same year. In 1913 the Lyceum was built as both theatre and cinema. Curiously, *Kelly's Directory* for 1914 mentions only the Empire as a cinematograph hall and thus makes Taunton look rather less progressive than most other towns such as Bridgwater, where the Bijou was opened in 1912.

That 1914 edition of *Kelly's Directory* for the county lists thirteen 'cinematograph halls'; by 1919 there were nineteen, still not naming Taunton's Lyceum; by 1923 the total rose to twenty-six, by 1931 thirty-two, by 1939 forty-three. There were a few flamboyant names in the early days like the 'People's Perfect Picture Palace' in the Victoria Buildings, Crewkerne, but Empire and Electric and Palace were common themes. By the later 1930s, when many of the independent cinema companies had been swallowed up by the giants, there were five Odeons and two Gaumonts in the county and the Cosy (Minehead) and the prosaically-named Watchet, Portishead or Central had almost been revolutionised into Plazas, Regals, Regents, Rexes. A couple of Palaces still survived and so, praise be, did the Magnet Theatrical Talkie Company operating from the Town Hall, Castle Cary.

Names, mostly; and distant memories. But the proprietor or perhaps the accountant or lawyer of Highbridge Cinema Limited of Church Street, Highbridge, has left a glimpse of something more, for receipted bills have not been thrown away. And there revealed is the cinema in all its glory – two main films each week and more on Saturdays, but not just films. Who could resist the glamour of the posters full of promise for forthcoming attractions and who could possibly pass the confectionery counter where boxes of 'half-pound Popular' or 'half-pound Art' chocolate by Kunzle of Birmingham were so temptingly displayed?

It never occurred to customers unless the projector broke down or the place wasn't warm enough or the lights failed that behind the magic of the cinema were practical considerations. The coloured tickets which appeared at the touch of a button from the shining silver dispensing machine were, if one ever inspected them closely, coarse and shoddy productions, costing in the 1920s 10s 1d (50p) for 10,000 from Willsons of Leicester. One regular attender still remembers the manager's regular fight against invading flies as he sprayed the audience and the air above them with noxious 'Flit' during performances.

Posters, only slightly less ephemeral than most of the films themselves, were a vital part of the business, though whether they ever converted a reluctant cinema-goer must be open to question. They were, and still are, an art form in their own right and Mr Wheeler of the Highbridge Cinema dealt with Clages of Walthamstow and the Producers' Distribution Company. Burnham's United Bill Posting Company charged 18s (90p) for three weeks' work in November 1926.

In those far-off days the film distributors themselves had names almost as romantic and exciting as their products: the Famous Lasky Film Service of Cardiff, the Fox Film Company, also with an office in Cardiff; Allied Artists Corporation of London, Stoll Picture Productions of Oxford Street; the European Motion Picture Company Limited of Wardour Street, distributors of Universal Pictures; Jury-Metro-Goldwyn Limited; and Ideal Films.

And all those companies sent films to Highbridge Cinema, each accompanied by their account for hire for three days; and more than once sent a second account when the film was returned without payment. For times were evidently hard: new arc lamps from the Gaumont Company Limited of London were expensive items; J. S. Fry's account for Cokerbars, Milk Bars, Milk Croq, Milk Walnuts and Milk Naps was also pressing; and the novelty hats bought for Christmas 1926 might not bring extra business.

But surely the seasonal films would do the trick? Who could possibly have resisted *Troubled Wives*, showing from Monday 23 December 1926, *Coast of Folly* from the 27th and *Golden Princess* from the 30th, each costing the proprietor £2 plus carriage? Cheap at the price. *California Straight Ahead* from 16 December had cost £3 6s 8d (£3.33p) and perhaps sounded a little more interesting; and the January 1927 programme had to be better with *Pickle, Tin Ghost, Bear Cats, Cross Cruise* and *Soap Suds Lady*, surely for the Saturday Club, *Lord Jim* and *Wild Horse Mesa* for the grown ups, and *What Happened to Jones* for those who just wanted an hour or two with a nervous young lady in the dark.

13
CROSSING THE ATLANTIC

MAIDENS 1/6d each
4 for 4/0d

"John Watts of Westonzoyland received from Evans 4s (20p) for four maids"

The role of Bristol in the discovery of America brings the history of the New World very close to Somerset, and since then the connections have been many and various. Investors were necessarily fewer than labourers in the islands of the Caribbean and the plantations in the colonies on the American mainland, and many of the labourers were there under duress, transported for their part in the Monmouth Rebellion. Some of them eventually found their way as free men to the newly emerging settlements on the south-eastern American seaboard. Links with the mother country, more comfortably thought of by republicans as The Old Country, happily persist, to the very great benefit of the tourist industry, and descendants of Monmouth rebels should be proud of their transported ancestor.

136

B ermuda, or to be more accurate the Bermudas or Summer Islands, were once very unattractive. The Spanish left in 1612 because of the hurricanes that frequently devastated them. As soon as they left, the English, of course, moved in for the English have always ignored the weather, and naturally the Spanish then changed their minds and wanted to go back. But the government of James I would have none of that, especially when someone claimed that a piece of amber the size of a giant had been found there. Clearly, there was money to be made, so a group of City financiers calling themselves the Society of London persuaded the Crown to give them a charter of incorporation allowing them to establish a colony – they called it a plantation – in the Summer Islands. That meant that they acquired 'divers liberties', that is to make necessary laws to govern the new colony and to regulate trade. But there were problems. The same City businessmen were also involved in the Virginia colony and things were not going well there. In fact, so the government was told, the whole plantation idea 'sleeps'.

In 1617 the news from the Bermudas was worse. Rats destroyed everything that was planted and five men were so fed up they left in a small boat 'little bigger than a double wherry' but somehow reached England safely. Without them the new colony was thought likely to fail, and without new blood the whole enterprise looked very unattractive. Settlers were desperately needed, people who might be persuaded with the seventeenth century equivalent of a free cruise. That was why Owen Evans, evidently a smooth-tongued Welshman, turned up at Othery in 1618. He was entirely plausible. He showed people his badge of office as messenger of the king's chamber or royal pursuivant, an official whom anyone might be happy to invite into their home.

He declared that he had a royal commission not to invite but to impress, a word which did not mean to make an impression but instead to impress just as press gangs were later to impress, in other words to recruit by force. But Owen Evans was not looking for likely lads to be turned into drunken mariners; he was looking for maidens for both the Bermudas and Virginia colonies. He went about his business in the proper manner by approaching an influential local government officer, none other than Francis Prewe of Othery, constable of the hundred of Whitley, whose jurisdiction covered most of the Polden villages and stretched across the moors to High Ham and Compton Dundon. His duty, he was told by Evans, was to find maidens. Suspicious, he demanded to see some evidence of Evans's authority and was shown the badge and threatened for non-compliance. That was in the middle of October 1618.

Leaving Prewe to do his dirty work, Evans went across the moors to Beer and threatened to hang Thomas Crocker unless he found some maidens there. Amazingly there were some other men who went along with the scheme. John Watts of Westonzoyland received from Evans 4s (20p) for four maidens and Jacob Cryse was prepared to offer his own daughter at the same rate. William Michael of Othery decided a bribe was the answer and offered Evans 10s (50p) to go away. It seemed the obvious solution since the village's likely maidens had all fled.

The story soon spread. Only three days after Evans had first appeared in Othery the news reached Sir Edward Hext at Low Ham and he wrote to the Privy Council. Was this man on official government business or was he not? Sir Edward rather thought not, particularly because Evans was quite happy to take money instead of maidens, but you never knew with governments. Official business or not, the effect of his presence was most disturbing. As many as forty maidens had fled from one parish 'to such obscure places their parents cannot find them', he wrote. Whether he received a reply is not known but he soon took the matter into his own hands by arresting Evans. He was careful, as he wrote to the Privy Council again in November, 'to treat him with all the consideration due to a servant of the king', but arrest him he did and then sent him under escort to London, accompanied by detailed information on the whole affair.

What happened then is not known, but surely the Privy Council took action against such a blatant piece of trickery. The records of Othery parish are silent about the affair, but those who paid the cash bribe probably never saw their money again. Hopefully the maidens returned home safely, thankful they had escaped an unpleasant fate.

The Bermudas were certainly not all bad. The poet Andrew Marvell was glowing about them some years later – an 'island far kinder than our own ... safe from the storms ... eternal Spring'. He even mentioned 'the Ambergris on shoar', so he had heard the story, too.

———

For three hundred years or so south-east Somerset was distinctly industrial. The textile business involving weavers, worsted combers, dyers, button makers, linen and woollen drapers was everywhere. But not always prosperous. There were years in the early seventeenth century, in particular, when inflation and bad harvests threatened disaster and the government, concerned less for the workers than for loss of tax revenue, had to take a hand.

Government at the time meant the Privy Council, and every so often in times of particular crisis the council sent off orders to their stooges, the local Justices of the Peace, to make enquiries and to send back answers. Early in 1623 the council issued a Book of Orders in an attempt to keep down the price of those essential commodities, bread and ale. Farmers had been told that they could keep a 'competent' amount of 'bread corn' and malt for their own use but were to release the rest onto the market and not to keep it in store to force the price to rise. The justices were also to keep an eye on bakers and alehouse keepers to ensure that they did not produce inferior products – not too much rye or bean and pea flour in the bread, not too much water in the ale. That was in February 1623. Three months later Henry Berkeley, Matthew Ewens and James Farewell, Justices of the Peace in the hundreds of Catsash, Norton Ferris, Horethorne and Bruton, were asked to certify how much 'corn' was in store, how many maltsters were in business, how many decent alehouses were open.

Those were the days when south-east Somerset grew more grain than grass, and in store were 4472 bushels of wheat, 2500 of maslin (mixed grain, probably rye and wheat), 1496 of barley, 976 of beans, 914 of oats, 468 of peas and 308 of rye. Where it was and who had grown it we do not know. The justices also reported that there were thirty-nine maltsters in business, no bakers 'of note' and no brewers at all. As for alehouses, they rather smugly recorded that they had reduced them to as small a number as they thought 'convenient' (for whom they did not say) and had 'straightly charged' the owners to keep within the law.

Ten years later and there was a new crisis: simply too many unemployed, too many poor, too many people wandering about not seriously looking for work, and too many people 'idly tippling'. So again the justices went to work. Henry Berkeley and James Farewell met together at Castle Cary in July 1632 and produced some more statistics for the Privy Council. In total they reported that forty-two poor children had been bound apprentice by parish officers to some useful trade or occupation – Robert Love to Nicholas Watts in Cucklington, Robert Popley to James Kinge in Milborne Port, Christopher Marten to Thomas Gawyne in Horsington. As many as thirty-seven 'rogues and vagabonds' (unemployed strangers) had been arrested, whipped, and sent back to the places of birth or settlement, and five alehouse keepers had been convicted of tippling without licence.

Some parishes were obviously more prosperous and law-abiding than others. Bruton had bound out eleven apprentices but James Weekes and John Corpe had been found selling ale without licence. Yarlington, on the other hand, had no poor children, but eight rogues and vagabonds had been found elsewhere in Bruton hundred and had been duly removed. There were no poor children it was claimed, in Wincanton, Penselwood, Charlton Musgrove and Bratton. Perhaps the fears of the Privy Council had been exaggerated.

But there was evident distress; too many people were chasing too few jobs even if the clothmaking business was doing well, and Richard Eburne, vicar of Henstridge, had an answer: emigration. In a pamphlet entitled *A Plain Pathway to Plantations* published in 1624 he suggested that a colony in Newfoundland would be both a moral virtue and the only cure for the economic and social ills of England. There was, however, a difficulty. The Newfoundland colony would not welcome poor apprentice children, let alone tipplers, rogues and vagabonds. Gentlemen were required, or failing them yeomen, men of substance and courage.

Courage was certainly needed to face the uncertainties and privations of the New World, and there was courage enough in south-east Somerset. Masckiell Bernard and William Read from Batcombe, John and William Ames from Bruton, Hugh Mosier from Cucklington, and Mark, Roger and William Haskell from Charlton Musgrove are recorded among the early immigrants to New England, part of a sturdy band whose descendants regularly return to their mother county, hoping not to discover that their ancestors had been tipplers, rogues and vagabonds.

─────

Somerset for many reasons, mostly religious or economic, occasionally political, is the ancestral home of thousands, perhaps millions, of Americans, and among them at least five Presidents. When asked to suggest which, American audiences are not at all certain and begin by not being very impressed, for there have been presidents and presidents.

So beginning with the most modern there is Calvin Coolidge (president 1923–9), a Republican of great integrity who had to rescue his party from the scandals of his predecessor Warren Harding. Coolidge presided over a country bent on prohibition and the mob rule to which it gave rise; but it was still a prosperous country, and his rule kept it that way. Yet he is not remembered today with great respect or affection, partly because he said so little.

Indeed, he was known as 'Silent Cal': a lady sitting next to him at dinner confessed she had a wager that she could get him to say more than three words. 'You lose', was his reply.

The next 'Somerset' president before Coolidge was William Howard Taft (president 1909–13), another Republican and very fat, the only ex-president to become chief justice of the United States. Taft's great mistake was to fall out with the man who gave him power, Theodore Roosevelt, and between them they lost the 1913 election to the Democrats. Taft in old age became more and more reactionary.

And next before Taft was Millard Fillmore (president 1850–53), about whom most Americans known nothing. One of many vice-presidents to succeed, Fillmore was in office when Mrs Harriet Beecher Stowe wrote *Uncle Tom's Cabin*, a book that contributed to the break-up of his Whig party.

American audiences by this stage are still not very impressed with Somerset's contribution to their history, but when John Quincy Adams and his father John Adams are added to the list, then interest heightens. Here are the sixth and second presidents of the United States, both ministers for their country in England, both able lawyers from Massachusetts.

Whether any of these five knew much about their Somerset ancestry is not known, but the fact is they all spring from the same source, all descend from Henry Squire of Charlton Mackrell, whose daughter Edith married Henry Adams of Barton St David in 1609. Henry Adams was the fourth son of John Adams of Barton and could trace his ancestry at least back to John Adams who served as a billman for his village in the muster of 1539 and who had a brother Robert who farmed at Butleigh. Edith was the granddaughter of William Squire, rector of Charlton 1545–67 and had a sister Margaret. Margaret married John Shepard and was the ancestress of President Taft.

Henry Adams emigrated with at least some of his family in 1638 and settled in Braintree (later Quincy), Massachusetts. He was then well over fifty years of age; perhaps it was for his seventh son Joseph, born in Kingweston in 1626, that he went. Joseph was to be the great-grandfather of John, the great wheeler-dealer of the first Continental Congress, the 'colossus of the debate' on the Declaration of Independence. It is right and proper that the Stars and Stripes are displayed in Barton St David church beside a bronze plaque commemorating his family.

Five presidents put Somerset, surely, into some sort of hall of fame; and they might not be all, for recent research suggests a connection of President Rutherford Hayes (1877–81) with Crewkerne. Perhaps there will be more.

―✐―

When on Sunday 7 October 1787 James Hinton and Edith Page presented themselves at Long Ashton church after Morning Prayer to be married, there stood before them an elderly clergyman whose accent was quite unlike the cultured tone of the late vicar. They may have known that he was an American, but what was he doing so far from home?

It was a sad business. Henry Caner, clerk in Holy Orders, Master of Arts and Doctor of Divinity, was a political exile. The country which had replaced George III and a Crown with George Washington and a Presidency was not a comfortable home for such a loyal Anglican. He had thus resigned his living and had left his native land.

He had been born about 1699, for at his death in November 1792 he was said to have been ninety-three years old. He graduated from Yale in 1724 and in the following year he began to read prayers at the Anglican church at Fairfield on the Connecticut coast. He remained there for three years as a schoolmaster employed by the Society for the Propagation of the Gospel in Foreign Parts, but the writer of a letter of September 1727 said that by that time he had gone to England to seek Orders and hoped he could return to Fairfield.

He naturally went to London, for the bishop of London was then in charge of the Anglican church in the American colonies, but he went armed with a paper dated at Newport, Rhode Island, in May 1727 and signed by James Honyman, James McSparran and six others. In it they declared that they had known him for three years and stated, in Latin as befitted such a serious communication, that he was entirely respectable, pious, learned, a loyal Anglican and a devoted subject of King George. He was thus a proper person to receive Holy Orders. Henry was duly ordained at Fulham Palace on 24 August 1727 by Bishop Edmund Gibson.

On his return he was appointed to serve at Fairfield as an S.P.G missionary. The few official letters to survive from that time record that he was badly paid; that in 1736 he returned from another visit to England (this time to receive the degree of Master of Arts from Oxford by diploma); that by 1738 he had successfully preached at Norwalk, some mile down the Long Island Sound towards New York, but that the forty church families there needed support and could his brother be paid as his catechist and schoolmaster? The idea was accepted and in 1741 Richard Caner was appointed to assist in Norwalk, at Stamford, still nearer New York, and at Ridgefield, several miles up in the wooded interior. He was to receive £20 and was recommended in his turn for Holy Orders.

Then in April 1747 Henry received the due reward for his labours, appointment as rector of King's Chapel, Boston. The members of its ruling Vestry knew him as a preacher and wanted to make sure that he was present at the popular afternoon service on a Sunday rather than at the more formal morning service; the long-serving Lecturer who had run the afternoon service had to step aside.

Henry remained at his post in Boston for the next twenty-eight years, with the exception of a short exchange with the Revd Mr Gilchrist of Salem in 1752 because of an outbreak of smallpox at Boston, for Gilchrist had been inoculated and he had not. He continued to preach and occasionally his funeral sermons were printed: one on the death of Frederick, Prince of Wales, in 1751, another on the death of George II in 1760, and others commemorating prominent Bostonians. In 1763 he preached a thanksgiving sermon on the outbreak of peace. In 1766 the University of Oxford awarded him the degree of Doctor of Divinity.

There were, naturally, some problems in such a long ministry. A storm in his first year at Boston involved the rebuilding of his chapel. It was rebuilt again in 1753, the year when he had a bout of sickness. But the greatest problem was personal. Henry Caner was clearly a loyalist (they called them Tories then), in favour of King George and by implication in favour of taxation with no representation. Gradually, as republican fervour mounted, Caner and those who thought like him were isolated.

So in March 1775 he resigned his post and his pulpit. Boston and Massachusetts had recently supported a Declaration of Rights, an inevitable step towards independence. Only a month after his resignation the new governor of Massachusetts, General Gage, sent a party of men from Boston to seize arms at Concord that found its way barred at Lexington. Soon armed colonists surrounded Boston itself. That was no place for a Loyalist.

Exactly where Caner was in the next few years has yet to be found. He was evidently still in America when in 1783 he was among forty-six Anglican ministers from Massachusetts who petitioned for British help. At least the country he had so long supported with words eventually gave him a home. And why Long Ashton? Probably because his daughter by his wife Anne McKensey of Fairfield had married a Mr Gore of Boston, and Mr Gore had distant cousins at Barrow Gurney.

14
TRAVELLING IN SOMERSET

"... almost ended in tragedy when the car skidded more violently than expected, turned over, and threw the rugby types in all directions."

It was understood that when the weather was fine Somerset's roads were generally passable with care, but that come winter there were some routes which had to be abandoned. Improvement in the eighteenth century was the beginning of a transport revolution; canals came next, followed closely by the railways. Over the years the railways made a huge difference to life all across the county, and although those wonderful branch lines often lasted little more than a century and have now been gone for almost half that time, there are those (though perhaps only in Devon) who still look both ways at former crossings and fancy they hear the familiar whistle. What a revolution, which allowed farmers to send milk and cheese and strawberries and livestock (and rabbits) with speed and safety, to arrive fresh for sale in London! And in return came London newspapers and London time from the very beginning, and later on holidaymakers for coast or country; and later still thousands of scared children and not a few scared mothers, evacuated from vulnerable towns at the beginning of the Second World War.

But railways were for every day, for getting to school and to town or market, for visiting friends; trains were for watching in an idle moment as they made their way across the landscape; trains were part of a schoolboy's dream who had a clockwork model at home and craved to drive the real thing when he grew up; and locomotives, when they were driven by steam and had proper names and fascinating wheels and pistons and delicate liveries, were for respectable adults.

—*mm*—

A Dutch artist and his young companion visited Somerset in the year after Charles II was restored to his throne. The artist was William Schellinks, known now only to a few not because his work was second-rate but simply because he lived and worked in Amsterdam and had to compete with Rembrandt, Frans Hals and Vermeer. His companion was a thirteen-year-old Huguenot, also from Amsterdam, named Jacobi Thierry. The purpose of the journey, which continued through France, Italy, Sicily, Malta, Germany, and Switzerland, was educational and was probably financed by Thierry's father, a prosperous merchant.

At the time and since there were those who thought that the pair were spies, for Holland had recently been at war with England and would be again before too long, and certainly their journal, a copy of which is in the Bodleian Library at Oxford, revealed a sharp-eyed writer who never missed details of shipping and tides and of the damage caused by the recent Civil War.

The journey began in London with forays into Kent, Hampton Court, Windsor and the country houses on the London fringe. In the city there were plays, the Lord Mayor's Show, and the execution of three men who had sent Charles I to the scaffold. There was even the excitement of a tennis match. Then off to Oxford, Gloucester, Bristol and eventually to Bath through Keynsham and Weston, 'a pleasant good road in summer'.

In Bath they put up at the *Bear* and on their first day saw the baths, the Abbey and a bowling green. They were obviously fascinated by the baths and went again at 5 o'clock the next morning, presumably stripped to their underpants like the rest of the gentlemen, and sat in one of the recesses around the bath drinking mulled wine and watching some of the regulars having the water pumped over their limbs or heads. They had perch and artichokes for lunch, not cooked entirely to their satisfaction. Bath, they concluded, depended on visitors for its prosperity.

146

Before they left late in the afternoon Schellinks climbed Beechen Cliff and made a drawing of the city, having already sketched the King's Bath. Those two drawings, the only two he made in Somerset, are to be found in the famous Van der Hem Atlas, one of the most prized possessions of the National Library in Vienna.

From Bath they rode through Paulton and Chewton to Wells; or rather they rode to the top of the Mendip scarp and had to dismount and lead their horses because of the 'very dreadful, rocky, stony descent'. They stayed at the *George* in Wells. The cathedral, of course, caught Schellinks' eye, its west front then in bad condition because of its age and perhaps also the war, 'but all is being repaired'. A very large organ was 'in hand to be installed'. The bishop's palace, Schellinks thought, had been badly damaged but its hall was still 'very beautiful'. In the High Street was 'a very old, high and graceful stone building or Cross, and next to it a large market and assize or court house was being built. The principal trade of the city was stocking knitting.

Their guide at Wookey Hole showed them the so-called Brewery 'where the fermentation of fresh beer is very realistically depicted in stone' and other chambers called the Hall, the Dining Room, the Table, the Cellar, the Oven and so on, and they were told how the locals took bottles of wine to drink in the caves. They climbed both Glastonbury Tor and Wearyall Hill, saw the abbey ruins but moved on after refreshment to Street, Walton, Ashcott and Pedwell. The road over what Schellinks called the 'dry heath or pasture' was very good, and he noticed herds of cattle by the way.

Between Burrowbridge and Lyng Schellinks rode on the high footpath on the river bank beside the Tone and Thierry on the sunken road below. Here they were held up by an armed rider, taken to a nearby farmhouse and after a long wait escorted at sword point to Taunton castle. Explaining they were Dutch merchants on their lawful occasions they were soon set free and found a lodging at the *Three Cups*. Despite such treatment Schellinks liked Taunton: 'a nice and large market town and one of the most beautiful of this country'. Its long, wide streets 'full of shops and spacious market places' and its 'graceful high towers' evidently appealed to him, but there is no note in the journal that he was inspired to draw a picture.

Next morning the commander of the garrison apologised for their treatment, explaining that fear of a conspiracy had resulted in the arrival of 2000 soldiers and the arrest of a few people 'taken by the neck' and put in the castle. They were stopped again in Wellington, but were soon allowed to pass on their way to Exeter. They went so far west as Falmouth and then returned to London via Stonehenge. Their journey took them to Rye where they crossed to Dieppe in an open boat owned by Frenchmen, 'the worst rogues and swindlers in the world'.

—*mm*—

'Railways and Civilisation' and 'Where there's a Will there's a Way' declared two huge banners carried by some of the 800 working folk who, with about 500 gentlefolk, celebrated the opening of the railway across the moor from Highbridge to Glastonbury in August 1854. Each of the celebrating group enjoyed a cold meal in large tents and paraded around the Abbey grounds. A great day for the little town, though some feared that excursion trains might disturb its quiet character.

In its first year the Somerset Central railway planned six trains a day in each direction on weekdays, calling at Shapwick and Ashcott, and two on Sundays. Five years later a line reached Wells and another was well on its way to Cole near Bruton where by 1862 it joined the Dorset Central line. So travellers from Glastonbury could reach the English and the Bristol channels via what had become the Somerset and Dorset railway.

By 1863 there were five trains a day between Burnham and Templecombe, five between Wells and Highbridge, two passenger trains and a goods between Bristol and Wells via Highbridge, and four trains for passengers and two for goods direct leaving Burnham after the arrival of the Cardiff ferry and bound for Hamworthy beside Poole.

It all sounded almost too good to be true, and so it was. The last through train between Burnham and Poole ran in 1874. The Somerset and Dorset saw better prospects of business between Bath and Bournemouth once the notion of Burnham as an Atlantic port had disappeared, though there was still a through express between Bridgwater and Templecombe in 1890. Still, Glastonbury as a junction for Wells had its own, rather limited, importance – provided ... and that was part of the problem.

Provided ... there was cooperation. To operate successfully the Somerset and Dorset needed to work closely with the Great Western Railway at Highbridge and with what came to be the Southern at Templecombe. Dr Beeching devised its eventual closure by the same expedient of disjoined timetables in the 1960s. It was a device which rival companies were using in the 1890s and the people of Glastonbury were not alone in their indignation.

Much concern was expressed about the unpunctuality of services at a meeting of Glastonbury Town Council in 1897 and the Town Clerk was instructed to demand three new trains: one from Bristol via Highbridge in the late afternoon or early evening, one from Bath through Evercreech, another from Templecombe to connect with the 9.18am to Wells, since no-one travelling between Templecombe and Glastonbury could reach Wells before 11.18am.

The Town Clerk was also instructed to request that the 7.10pm Burnham train might run through to Glastonbury, leaving Highbridge at 7.35pm, thus providing a connection from Taunton. It would be, he declared, particularly convenient for many people, especially visitors to Burnham, County Councillors (who then often met at Highbridge), cricketers and others from Taunton.

Furthermore, the Town Clerk continued in his letter to the railway company, there was no train from the town for Burnham between 4.45pm and 9.20pm, and it was a fact that all the best tides were at or after 6 o'clock. In support of the suggested new services he pointed to the 'importance for fruit and perishable goods going northward' and the inconvenience of trains passing each other at West Pennard rather than at Glastonbury because of lateness. The railway company, of course, rejected the ideas.

Early in December 1899 the Town Clerk had a splendid excuse to resume the correspondence, and he addressed Mr R.A. Dyke, the Traffic Superintendent at Green Park station in Bath in high dudgeon. On Thursday 30 November, he wrote, a 'considerable number' of people had bought 'market tickets' for Bristol. They left on their return journey at 8.53pm but on arriving at Highbridge found that the last train for Glastonbury had already left.

It had 'always been understood', he declared, that the Glastonbury train would wait; it was only going to Wells, after all, and had no other connection to make. But in this particular night fourteen Glastonbury people were stranded at Highbridge and had to drive home at considerable expense. One lady was seriously ill as a result. The travellers felt they had been 'wantonly victimised' and Glastonbury people wished to be assured by the Traffic Superintendent that no such 'scandalous treatment' would occur again.

'I am favoured with your letter of 8 December' was the polite and empty phrase with which Mr Dyke began his reply; and he went on to declare the Great Western Railway entirely at fault. The Bristol train had been getting later and later; on the night in question it was 38 minutes behind schedule. It would not have been right to keep the Burnham passengers waiting at Highbridge for Glastonbury any longer. Mr Dyke went on to take exception to the Town Clerk's phrases and added one of his own about what suited one section of Glastonbury townspeople would not be satisfactory for another.

The Town Clerk, of course, had a ready reply: had they known that the Glastonbury train would not wait 'it is inconceivable to suppose that ladies would run the risk of being left behind on a cold winter's night at Highbridge'. Further, there were only four or five people in that train that did not wait; surely 'better a few incommoded' and the GWR blamed. The Town Clerk would not withdraw his accusations.

'We do the very best we can', came the rather softer reply from the Traffic Superintendent, who claimed that his company operated with a more liberal spirit than the GWR which refused to wait more than ten minutes for the Somerset and Dorset.

If getting two railway companies to work together was clearly difficult, the idea of adding others would surely have been disastrous. Yet two light railway schemes were drawn up in 1899. One was to link Glastonbury to Taunton via Street and North Curry, the other a single line between Bridgwater, Glastonbury and Langport. Glastonbury, so the Town Clerk wrote, would not support the second plan unless the line was doubled and continued to Taunton. Both plans were soon abandoned.

In 1900, however, came both a complaint and a proposal. The complaint was that the 10.52am from Glastonbury did not connect with the 11.45am at Templecombe for Waterloo and therefore passengers had to catch the 9.35am, making the whole journey far too long.

The second was a proposal from the people of Castle Cary for an early morning train from Templecombe to Bridgwater and Highbridge with a connection to Wells. There were quite urgent reasons: to enable boys and girls from Templecombe and Wincanton to attend Sexey's Trade school and Sunny Hill school at Bruton as day pupils; to convey magistrates, jurors, lawyers and suitors to the various courts at Wells; to convey clergy to diocesan meetings in the city; to serve the markets and fairs of the entire neighbourhood; and to improve services to the seaside (they called them watering places) at Weston and Burnham. They had in mind a rail network to serve the whole community. Whether the railway company complied is unknown, but for all its failings the Somerset and Dorset, known as the Slow and Dirty, won the hearts and minds of the people of Central Somerset and was deeply mourned when it closed in

1966. Someone said when it was first proposed that it was 'a track from nowhere to nowhere over a turf moor'; for more than a century people used it regularly to get somewhere.

—*****—

The young man appointed to manage the bookstall on Taunton station in 1868 was enormously proud of his post, and so he should have been for he had previously worked as a junior at Tiverton Junction and Didcot, and to be manager at Taunton was a considerable promotion. William Vincent was a man going places, a man of literary bent and ambition who moved on from Taunton to Swansea and ended his forty-seven-year career in charge of all railway bookstalls in Wales with his office, of course, in Shrewsbury.

The first railway bookstall is thought to have been opened at Fenchurch Street station in London in 1841. Taunton's must have come rather later and was not then much to be proud of: mostly shelves and cupboards without any shelter from the chill winds that swept up the new platform, opened after the Board of Trade had condemned Taunton's single platform. Its business, however, represented another of those inestimable benefits conferred when a permanent way snaked across the countryside.

Everywhere, Station Roads sprang up linking towns, and occasionally villages, to the new tracks. Station Hotels and Railway Inns took their proud though often rather brash places as near to prospective customers as possible, challenging the more ancient establishments to provide omnibuses to meet every arrival. Thanks to the railway London business was soon in touch with the provinces as never before and the commercial traveller began to cover long distances, seeking out hotels described as 'Commercial and Family'.

The railway company became almost overnight a considerable employer and the local station master a man of consequence. In Taunton in the early 1880s Mr Alexander Gibson lived in a villa, in Station Road, of course; the manager of the bookstall was only in lodgings, but his landlady had been seamstress to the Revd. Sydney Smith at Combe Florey, and her stories of his eccentricities delighted her would-be literary gentleman.

From 1842, when the first locomotive arrived in Taunton, the northern edge of the town began to change, and within two years a church, the forerunner of St Andrew's, had been built for the platelayers and porters, the clerks, inspectors and guards, the drivers and firemen who made their homes in and around the suburb of Rowbarton. The railway brought business to the town, quick access to the markets of Bristol and London. It brought employment, and, of course, it brought London time, that great universal by which the duties of the day could be regulated and every church clock be encouraged to tell the same story.

And the railway bookstall of the 1860s brought national news and the essential means of education. The *Somerset County Gazette*, the *Taunton Courier* and other local newspapers could offer national and international news, but often a week or two old. The railway bookstall could offer London newspapers by the 1 o'clock train on the day of publication, as well as the growing number of London-based magazines.

Among those magazines was the *Illustrated London News*, which until 1868 arrived at Taunton each week in unfolded sheets. William Vincent and his staff had to fold and collate them, getting their hands black in the process before they could be offered for sale at 5d. (2p) each. When the *Graphic* first appeared it was folded and stitched for 6d. (5p) The bookstall staff were much relieved when the *Illustrated* followed suit.

William Vincent, on behalf of his employers, W. H. Smith and Son, offered not just books and magazines but a lending library and most attentive service. Every weekday afternoon the bookstall lads delivered newspapers in the town, and at the time there were about seventy subscribers to the lending library for over two hundred volumes.

One subscriber expected his twelve volumes to arrive at his home by the weekly carrier, but on one rare occasion parcels from London were delayed. So Mr Vincent took the 7.40pm train from Taunton to Wellington and walked the remaining five miles to the subscriber's home. He missed the last train back so slept in a damp bed at the White Horse in Wellington in his overcoat and caught the first train back in the morning in order to open the bookstall on time.

Although he worked for W. H. Smith, Mr Vincent himself was considered a member of the railway staff. He was thus invited to the Christmas staff supper, and on one special occasion was asked to accompany an excursion train to Chard to help collect tickets at Ilminster at 8.30pm. He often found himself giving travel advice to his customers and they appreciated his attention, one invalid lady library subscriber presenting him with knitted mittens and a hot water bottle.

William Vincent left Taunton in 1871 to take over the stall and its satellites based at Swansea. From there the was promoted to Reading and Euston, and the last gave him much satisfaction, since he was able to speak to many of the leading figures of the day as they called at his stall or waited on platforms for trains that, of course, arrived on time.

—*mm*—

What could possibly have brought members of Bath Rugby Club to Camerton in 1931? The answer is that they were hired by the Gainsborough Film Company to act as a gang of policemen in a film which Herbert Wilcox was making of Arnold Ridley's famous play *The Ghost Train*.

Their role was to arrive suddenly on the scene in an old car down the steep approach to Camerton station where a hinged wooden platform had replaced the weighbridge. The idea was that when subjected to pressure the platform would tip up. The car was supposed to skid on a patch of grease and would conveniently move with the platform, thus disgorging the police on to the roadway. The scene was rehearsed and filmed several times but almost ended in tragedy when the car skidded more violently than expected, turned over, and threw the rugby types in all directions.

That scene was just part of the excitement which drew people from Bath and even Bristol as well as crowds of locals. Jack Hulbert and Cicely Courtneidge, the stars of the film, were famous then. Supporting them were Angela Baddeley, Carol Coombe, Ann Todd, Allan Jeans, Donald Calthorp and Cyril Raymond, all to be well known if not famous later.

Spectators watched as the picturesque Cam Valley in the heart of the Somerset coalfield was transformed into Cam Vale in Cornwall. The little branch line which had been built to take coal from Dunkerton and Camerton pits to Hallatrow on the Radstock-Bristol line now had the great honour of hosting the Cornish Riviera Express which, for the purposes of the film, thundered down under arc lights from Durcott through the little station at Camerton at night, enveloped in clouds of white smoke.

It was a balmy June, but the film required a rainy night. Radstock Fire Brigade obliged with their hand pumps and yards of hose snaking into the Cam brook. Each man stood on a small box at various points along the platform, unseen by the cameras, controlling the flow from each nozzle with his thumb. Angela Baddeley had to run along the platform to the station door in the drenching rain and was duly drenched. Many of the watching crowd were too when the hoses not infrequently burst.

Cicely Courtneidge was required to arrive by the train carrying a large green parrot in a cage and a heavy travelling rug which was supposed to become entangled with the carriage door. Watching her every move were lucky extras who had secured seats in the train as passengers. The less lucky watched from across the tracks, squatting on their haunches to avoid the cameras. So many came and became such a nuisance asking for autographs and getting in the way that the film company thought of removing themselves to another site.

The film was evidently good for the local economy. The disused station and coal pit at Dunkerton was the scene of a gun-running episode; a Bath antique shop provided several Victorian gilt-framed mirrors which allowed the cameramen, carefully protected, to film the oncoming train by reflection before each mirror was smashed. The nearby *Jolly Collier* did wonderful business.

The stars, of course, and the technicians stayed in Bath and came to Camerton each day by bus. The extras and onlookers entertained each other at impromptu concerts with violins, mouth organs and concertinas. The local policeman was once found drunk and incapable in a nearby field. Jack Hulbert when not filming collected fossils in local quarries.

The film was in black and white, of course, and only film buffs will know about it. Jerome Ltd., of Holloway Road, London, N 7 sold postcards of the action, and one young onlooker among many took snapshots and armed with his autograph album made himself enough of a nuisance to secure the coveted names. He also kept with the autographs a piece of exposed film and a Great Western Railway Passenger Rated Traffic label which came, perhaps with rolls of film, on the 10.35 on 17 June 1931, consigned to 'Ghost Train, Camerton'.

───

More than one writer has been inspired by a railway station. Edward Thomas's train stopped at Adlestrop on a late June day of heat and meadowsweet and blackbirds, and he recorded the hiss of the engine as it came to a standstill 'unwontedly'. 'Yes. I remember Adlestrop – The name ...'.

Adlestrop was on the line between Oxford and Worcester and the station opened with the track in 1853; and actually it stood not in Adlestrop at all but in the parish of Oddington. Such is often the way with country stations, decently, at a distance.

Keinton Mandeville was another of the kind. It opened with the track between Castle Cary and Langport on the new loop which allowed expresses to go from Westbury westwards without the detour to Yeovil. That was on 1 July 1905; and the station was actually in the parish of East Lydford.

It was not a particularly impressive station: two long platforms and a small siding for goods; a covered bridge and the usual small waiting rooms. Neither Keinton, Alford Halt nor Charlton Mackrell, according to Robin Madge, the historian of Somerset railways, 'ever really justified their existence, other than making some characteristic Somerset names vaguely familiar to a large number of holiday makers as they sped past'. If, that is, the train was not speeding too fast for the name-board to be read.

'Justify' is a word involving, for instance, the concept of value for money which Dr Beeching and his political masters understood, leading to the closure of Keinton Mandeville station and its neighbours on 10 September 1962.

But there are other kinds of justification. One autumn day in 1936 the Cornish Riviera Express stopped there unwontedly. At least two passengers went out into the corridor to discover why and where they were; one was a strikingly beautiful boy, the other a Welsh-born journalist returning from holiday. The boy's real name is not known but it became Absalom; he reminded the journalist of Rupert Brooke and he became an unlikely-looking murderer.

The journalist saw the station name-board and did not known then that Keinton Mandeville had been the birthplace of John Henry Brodribb, better known as the great actor Sir Henry Irving. Yet as he stood in that corridor he found himself looking at some rusting iron stock pens; rusting because farmers had already forsaken the railway for the greater convenience of motor lorries which could call at their farms and drive with comparative ease to the most appropriate market.

He saw, too, a zinc trough standing on posts, once ready to supply water to thirsty animals driven from the farms. Water from that trough would also have been used by the most junior porter to clean up after those same beasts had been jostled into cattle trucks and sent on their way.

Unlikely things to inspire a writer, but inspired he was. He had been reading a book for review and he had it in his hand as he stood in the corridor, looking out of the window. In it was the usual publisher's slip naming the publication date. He began covering the slip with notes in long- and shorthand, some of which he later could not read.

'At Keinton Mandeville there is a ...' – the word eluded him when he came to read it again. 'A lot of rusting iron beast-pens. A zinc water trough on posts over all. Here he hid in the water'. The there were notes about an emerging plot, soon forming the complete skeleton of a novel which had 'rushed into' the writer's mind 'from Heaven knows where'. The train had stood in Keinton Mandeville station for about five minutes.

On that publisher's slip, too, was the name the writer gave to the boy in the train, Absalom. And when the book came to be finished, fourteen months later – not bad for a writer working in spare evening hours – he inspired the title. It was O Absalom!

The book was a great success – three quarters of a million copies sold in about four years, and more since. But if the title O Absalom! is not exactly familiar, there is a good reason. When the book was about to be published in the United States it was discovered that William Faulkner had just published a novel with the title *Absalom, Absalom*. So instead, as usual ignoring the author's views, it was given the title *My Son, My Son*.

And so it has been known ever since, except by the Dutch, who kept the original title, the Germans who called it *Geliebte Sohne*, the Norwegians, who wanted the best of both worlds and called it *Absalom, My Son, My Son*, and the French, who did not care for either and were still undecided when the German army arrived for their second visit to Paris in the century. In several countries the book ran as a serial; films turned it, so the author thought, into a farce.

And the author, who told the whole story of its birth in Somerset in his auto biographical book *In The Meantime*, published at the height of the Second World War, was Howard Spring. Born in Cardiff in 1889, Spring rose from errand boy to newspaper reporter and literary critic. He was author of a string of novels after his Keinton Mandeville experience whose titles were once so very well known: *Fame is the Spur, These Lovers Fled Away*, and *Time and the Hour*.

At the beginning of the war in 1939 Spring went to live in Cornwall and probably rushed through Keinton Mandeville station more than once. If his train stopped unwontedly again he never recorded the fact. One novel from a station was more than could have been expected, but surely justification enough for its existence.

THREE MEN OF THE CLOTH

The choice of Church or Army often faced young men who had no prospect of succeeding to a landed estate; either one was a respectable profession for an educated man, and while gaming and other forms of high living might have to be shunned by a clergyman, dining, hunting, travelling or acting as a magistrate were permissible if not expected. Thomas Ken was modest, learned and pious, an outstanding and unusual ornament to his profession; Huntingford and Whalley, on the other hand, were much more typical of their time, conservative and more than a little eccentric, and well content to leave the care of a parish to others less well paid than themselves.

"And at the end of 1703 a great storm which swept the whole country caused the fall of a chimney at the Palace in Wells which crushed both Bishop Kidder and his wife."

Perhaps the best known occupant of the Bishop's Palace at Wells was the saintly Thomas Ken who, in 1691, found himself unable to continue as bishop of the diocese he had ruled with distinction for six years. His conscience would not permit him to swear allegiance to the new king, William III, since he had already, when he first became a bishop, sworn allegiance to Charles II and, after Charles's death, to his successor James II. For Ken James II, whatever his faults, was still the lawful king. William had taken the throne by force.

This brave action was not, of course, evidence of his sanctity. The one action more people remember, perhaps, is the one Charles II was later to recall. The king was planning to stay at the Deanery in Winchester on a visit to the city to oversee the progress of plans for a huge royal palace there. His Majesty was to be accompanied by the whole panoply of the Royal Household which meant, of course, Nell Gwyn. The royal billeting officer considered a house near the Deanery would be most convenient for her but its occupant, Prebendary Thomas Ken, had other ideas.

There was no confrontation, but Ken would not allow his position as a clergy-man to be compromised. The dean might have liberal views and a convenient conscience, and he later arranged for rooms to be added to his own house for Nell to occupy, but Ken would have none of it. No doubt he risked royal displeasure, which might have included his removal in disgrace from the College of Royal Chaplains. So be it; at least that would save him from preaching at Court every year.

The matter was obviously reported to the king and the king remembered. Two years or so later, two days after Peter Mews was promoted from Wells to the see of Winchester, Charles decided that his successor at Wells should be 'the little fellow who refused poor Nelly a lodging'. The little fellow, nearly always portrayed in a close-fitting black cap and simple clerical dress, was Thomas Ken.

Five years later, after the tragedy of the Monmouth Rebellion and Ken's own trial and imprisonment in the Tower with six other bishops, came the Revolution which put William III on the throne. Ken was only one of many who could not in conscience take another oath and became known as non-jurors. More extreme spirits toasted the 'King beyond the Water' and sympa-thised with the vain attempts to assassinate King William.

Early in September 1701, when Ken and James had both been exiles in their different ways for more than a decade, James Stuart died at St Germain, his home outside Paris. Ken's oath was cancelled by death, so could he not be bishop again? Well, he had only ever been bishop of Bath and Wells, but his successor, Richard Kidder, now held the post. Six months later and William III was dead, too; dead on 8 March 1702 from the effects of a fall from his horse after it stumbled over a mole-hill. The Jacobite toasts from then onwards were to the health of the new King James over the water and the health, too, of a little gentleman in black velvet who had compassed the death of their enemy. And at the end of 1703 a great storm which swept much of southern England caused the fall of a chimney in Ken's old home in Wells. Both Bishop Kidder and his wife were crushed to death. The throne of England was now filled (very amply) by James II's younger daughter Anne, and the throne of which Ken had been deprived was vacant, too.

The new queen, as Archbishop Runcie once reminded an audience at Wells, 'was as devout a High Church Anglican as any but the most grudging non-juror could wish', and she wanted Ken back at Wells where he belonged. But Ken's principles were rigid. The king over the water was still the legitimate king for he was James II's legitimate heir. According to the law that had governed the succession to the English throne for generations, he should be king. So Ken refused.

But there followed a kind of compromise. The vacant throne at Wells was filled by one of Ken's own close friends, George Hooper. In a letter to Hooper urging him to accept, Ken said how happy he had always been to surrender his claims to a worthy person (Kidder clearly was not) and he signed his letter 'T.K., late Bishop'. His real retirement had begun.

The storm that killed Bishop Kidder at Wells and destroyed the Eddystone lighthouse so shook the roof of the Vicarage at Poulshot that its principal beam was forced out of true, leaving it supported by only half an inch of masonry. Ken, who was asleep under it, was more fortunate than Kidder on that same night. Thereafter Ken's life was largely without incident although a group of Jacobites in Bristol caused him some trouble, accusing him of letting down the cause by accepting Hooper as his successor.

A chalice and paten claimed in the 1920s to be a relic of Ken when it was given to Wells Theological College was, its donor assured the college, given to Ken's chaplain, whose name is not known. That chaplain, himself a non-juror, went to the American colonies and was one of those still supporting the cause in the State of Connecticut in the 1720s. From him the chalice is said to have passed to John Boucher, an orthodox Anglican born in Blencogo, Bromfield, Virginia, in 1737 and ordained in 1761. He evidently left during the Revolution and brought the relics back to England where they can be traced to Hackney Rectory.

Chalice and paten are now in safe keeping in Wells Cathedral but were not included with Ken's silver chocolate or coffee pot in an exhibition in the cathedral library. There is a nagging doubt; they emerged at a time when Ken relics were becoming the rage, and better proof of their authenticity is needed. The non-juring chaplain must first be identified.

Commercialism has triumphed over antiquity in Hereford cathedral; well, almost triumphed. Only a small part of the evidently rather impressive monument to one of Hereford's less impressive bishops can be seen behind the shelves of the cathedral shop. Perhaps he deserves no better; he certainly would not have approved. The bishop was George Isaac Huntingford, bishop of Hereford 1815–32 and before that bishop of Gloucester from 1802. For the whole of the time he was bishop and for thirteen years before that he was also Warden of Winchester College, where for most of the time he lived.

And if that was not enough Huntingford was from 1789 until 1825 vicar of Milborne Port, to which he was appointed by the Warden and Fellows of Winchester College. In case it might be thought that there was something just a little improper in the appointment, it should be understood that he became vicar several months before he was appointed Warden, although he was already a Fellow and therefore had a voice in his own promotion.

In 1789 he was much in need of money and the income from Milborne Port, reduced to pay for a resident curate, was still important. His father had been a Winchester dancing master and there was no family fortune to fall back on. Huntingford's nickname 'Tiptoe' may have alluded either to his father's profession or to a word which appeared in one of the Greek school textbooks he wrote.

He became a pupil at Winchester College in 1762, went on to New College, Oxford, and returned to become a schoolmaster at college with the title of Commoner Tutor. He was not entirely happy or successful. In 1774 a particular clash with riotous boys who had been unduly blamed for imitating a hunch-backed housekeeper involved the removal of forty of them from school, though the boys had demanded that he should go.

Two years later there was another ugly incident and Huntingford begged the headmaster for the help of a colleague. It was probably not his fault again; the headmaster was no disciplinarian and the behaviour at Winchester, no worse than at any other school of the time, was dreadful. Yet he cared deeply for the school and for his Classical teaching. Indeed, he tried to supplement his income by producing books – rather unsuccessfully except for textbooks.

As a Fellow of Winchester he could afford to give up the challenge of facing recalcitrant boys, and for a time he went to live in Salisbury. The sudden death of his brother, however, left him with a sister-in-law and her six small children to support, and so he took on his late brother's school at Warminster, where he hoped to inculcate 'sound education and morals'. His boys had to understand every word of their lessons and on no account to cheat.

And so the idea of becoming vicar of Milborne Port was not all that ridiculous; many ministers lived much further away from their parishes than the distance between Warminster and Milborne Port. Why he did not give it up when at the end of the year he became Warden and moved back to Winchester is impossible to say, except that growing nephews and nieces grow ever more expensive. The difference between what he as vicar received in tithes and what he had to pay a curate was something over £100 a year.

His curate, William Owen, was probably happy enough with his lot, for he was at Milborne before Huntingford was appointed vicar and remained there until 1823, living in the house the vicar described as old and inconvenient, taking all the fees payable for his services, and leasing out the small glebe worth £20 a year. Probably most of the parishioners thought he was vicar.

The records of the parish mention Huntingford's name just once, in 1816, when Charles Earith's bill for some splendid embroidered and tasselled velvet cloths for the pulpit and reading desk totalled the outrageous sum of £36 12s (£36.60p). The bishop of Hereford topped the subscription list with five guineas (£5.25p). William Owen and Mrs Steele each gave two guineas (£2.10p), Lady Medlycott of Ven House, Miss Hutchings and Mrs Glasse each one guinea (£1.5p).

One other reference linking Huntingford with Milborne Port is a lease of his tithes to a local gentleman farmer, James Highmore, the tenant of the Winchester College farm called Canon Court. Cash down was obviously more convenient than the trouble of annual collection, and so in 1812 the bishop of Gloucester, as he then was, let the tithes for six years for the sum of £300. In 1818 the same man, then bishop of Hereford, renewed the lease for the same sum.

The letter to a solicitor accompanying the renewal of the lease was addressed from Winchester College, for that is where the bishop of Hereford continued to live. Candidates for ordination from the diocese had to go from Hereford to kneel before their bishop in the college chapel. He was, it must be said, a better bishop of Hereford than vicar of Milborne Port. He conducted diocesan business with care, concern and despatch until illness in 1827 severely curtailed his activities. By then he had at least resigned Milborne and was nearly eighty.

He is remembered at Winchester not as vicar or bishop but as Warden, and a very conservative one. Remembered, too, for an early and favourite pupil, Henry Addington, who as First Lord of the Treasury and Home Secretary was responsible for his appointment as bishop and his translation from Gloucester to Hereford. Huntingford would be less happy to be remembered for his reaction to a college rebellion in 1818 when almost all the pupils were in revolt and having been promised a fortnight's holiday in return for capitulation found themselves confronted by a party of soldiers with fixed bayonets. The list of the boys' grievances began with the accusation that the Warden was ugly.

Francis Squire, canon and chancellor of Wells cathedral from 1739 until his death in 1750, had a very remarkable grandson, by name Thomas Sedgwick Whalley. Thomas's father, Master of Peterhouse, Cambridge, and Regius Professor of Divinity at that university, died when he was only two years old and his mother brought him and his three brothers to Wells. John, the eldest, joined the Welch Fusiliers but died young on his way home from India; Francis, the second, was also a military man and lived at Winscombe Court. Richard, the youngest and rector of Horsington, was much admired by Hannah More, who thought he lived much of his time in heaven. So the Whalleys must count as a Somerset family.

Thomas, the third son, was educated at Charterhouse and at Cambridge, where he excelled in languages. He took Holy Orders and was presented to a living in Lincolnshire on condition that he did not live there since the air of the Fens was fatal to any but a native. He remained rector of the parish for more than fifty years.

Early in 1774, at the mature age of thirty-one, he married a lady with a considerable fortune, and for the rest of his long life he endeavoured to spend it. They set up home together not in some modest parsonage house in the country but at Langford Court, where for part of the year they were extremely hospitable. For the rest of the year they were equally hospitable in the centre house in the Royal Crescent in Bath.

There the Reverend Mr Whalley lived the life of an aesthete, writing dreadful poetry and either conversing or corresponding with a curious group of people including the actress Mrs Siddons, Dr Johnson's friend Mrs Thrale, and the novelist Fanny Burney. Fanny described him as 'immensely tall, thin and handsome but affected; delicate and sentimentally pathetic'. He was for ever speaking of his feelings and about amiable motives.

From 1783 the Whalleys travelled for four years through Europe, meeting as many titled people as possible. Marie Antoinette, Thomas was delighted to recall, called him *le Bel Anglais*. They returned in the summer of 1787 but Langford Court was let and nobody went to Bath at that time of year, so they began to build what was to become almost an obsession – a cottage on the top of the Mendips near Dolebury Warren. The aesthete did his best to become a country gentleman and made himself locally famous by hunting at Dolebury with spotted liver-and-white dogs from Denmark 'of great sagacity'.

The cottage grew and grew and became a Lodge – Mendip Lodge – and the original bare surroundings were covered with lawns and trees. In fact it became a villa, Italian, some thought, a *villa urbana* seen from the front; 'the loveliest architectural luxury I ever traversed' said his rather ignorant admirer Miss Seward. The service rooms were on the ground floor and the guests had sitting rooms leading to a verandah on the floor above. There, too, was a 'noble' dining room hung with fine pictures including a full-length portrait of Mrs Siddons. The kitchens were in a *villa rustica* at the rear.

Poetry continued to flow, still without much improvement. In 1799 Mrs Siddons and two other members of the Kemble family played at Drury Lane in a verse-tragedy he wrote, but it closed after nine nights. A greater tragedy was the death of his wife in 1801 from the effects of a carriage accident. A second wife died in 1805 and from then onwards Thomas seems to have indulged himself in buying paintings and jewellery. The University of Edinburgh awarded him the degree of Doctor of Divinity at the request of Sir Walter Scott.

A third marriage was a disaster and after a year he went off to France, in the circumstances not the safest country for an Englishman to visit. When Napoleon returned to power Thomas fled to Louvain and spent an exciting winter in Brussels. In 1818 he came home and bought the centre house in Bath's Portland Place; his wife set up home in Catherine Place. But he soon turned to travel again until setting up home for the last time in the West Country at Windsor Terrace in Clifton, the house where Hannah More was to spend her last years. In the summer of 1828 he went to France again, to stay with a niece, and it was there at La Fleche that he died soon after his arrival at the age of eighty-three.

William Wilberforce rather liked Dr Whalley, thinking him sensible, educated, well-informed and polished; a frequenter of noblemen's and gentlemen's houses, a 'literary and chess-playing divine of the best sort'. His memory was kept alive by a descendant who published his journals and correspondence.

Mendip Lodge, his fantastic house, lasted a little longer than its creator. It passed after some legal dispute to Benjamin Somers, who built stables and a coach house but left two grottoes formed by Dr Whalley – called the King of Mendip at the east end of the wood, and the Queen of Mendip' – in a state of collapse. The Somers family continued to occupy the remote house until about 1900 but thereafter it seems to have been forgotten. By the 1950s the twin lodges were in ruins, the drive overgrown. The house appeared at a distance to be intact but on close inspection the roof had gone, wallpaper hung in festoons, mirrors inside shutters had lost their silvering. What remained was demolished in the autumn of 1954; some of the stone was used to repair the floor of Banwell church.

16

DAY SCHOOL AND NIGHT SCHOOL

*"Young William Warren, a clergyman's son, was about twelve years old...
...would like 'to see him a little more manly in his behaviour.'"*

Somerset has a long and honourable history of education, from the time when boys likely to become clergy were taught in the cathedral and monastic schools. Bath had a group of scholars in the town as early as 1113, Taunton had a school in the town by 1286, Bridgwater in 1298, and others before the end of the Middle Ages at Dunster, Ilminster and Wellington. Rare surviving references to schools in smaller places such as Mells and Woolavington suggest the probability of many more. By the nineteenth century Ilminster grammar school was old and its reputation not high, in the 1830s waiting for the arrival of one of those reforming headmasters who in many places created the famous public schools which educated the governing classes of Victorian and Edwardian England. The education reforms of the nineteenth century that encouraged elementary schools in every town and village and demanded attendance at them opened the minds, revealed the talents and harnessed the energies of the whole population.

Young William Halliday of Chapel Cleeve, aged only ten, told his widowed mother in his first letter from school at Ilminster in 1830 that he didn't like it as much as home, that some of the boys were gluttons, and that he hadn't yet been 'folaged'; but, he added, 'Mr Allen has had many attentions to it'. His two elder brothers, John and George, were already at the same school, getting up at 6 o'clock, starting lessons at 6.30, stopping for breakfast at 8.30 and dining at 1.30.

George told his mother he liked Mr Allen 'pretty well' but Mr Bradley 'a little better'. John sounded quite enthusiastic about the gardens Mr Allen permitted them to make in the playground and reported in 1828 that he and George were 'attending a short course of lectures on optics and astronomy' given in the town.

In another letter George reported that Mr Allen had taken the whole school on two successive days to the fair where they saw two shows; and that their holiday tasks had been rewarded with an *optime* (John) and a *bene* (George).

Mr Allen had written to Mrs Halliday in 1829 – perhaps conscious that she was a good customer with two sons and possibly a third to come – apologising that dancing classes were impractical because only three boys attended and then openly to avoid Latin lessons. He confessed to no success, either, with Gymnastics, for a master was too expensive to employ. He had, he added, noticed the defects in George's reading ability but trusted that matters could be improved: 'his natural nervousness is, however, considerably increased by any observations from me, however mild'.

Can this be the same headmaster who was remembered from years later and then at a distance of almost a lifetime, as a veritable ogre? Perhaps another decade of teaching boys had soured Mr Allen; or perhaps William Halliday had been right about the imminent 'folaging'. Certainly young Charles Kegan Paul, son of the vicar of Writhlington, was sent to the same school in 1836 aged eight, and his memory remained all too vivid sixty years later.

School for Kegan Paul was 'a hell where life was one long misery' and Mr Allen 'the least fitted to train the young ... a little, wiry, energetic man, with a keen eye, sharp-cut features, and short hair like a blacking brush'. He certainly produced some good scholars and the nervous George Halliday became an army captain. Poor William, his wife and daughter perished in the Indian Mutiny in 1857. Allen excelled with the cane, a collection of which he kept in a cupboard slightly too short for its precious contents, whilst a spring catch on his desk controlled a lid which, when opened, allowed a cane to spring out to hand.

Kegan Paul recalled graphically how Allen, having found a victim – one almost every day – would fling his gown over his chair, touch the spring catch, seize both a cane and a boy and, having flogged until he was tired, would shut the wretch in a cupboard for an hour or two. The bruises could often last a month.

Readers of Dickens will recognise the type, and Ilminster Grammar School was one of many, though rarely, as in this case, do letters and memoirs survive to prove it. Censuses and Directories, however, contain the names of proprietors and pupils of boarding schools for young ladies and young gentlemen by means of which Victorian entrepreneurs managed to make at least a living if not a vast profit.

Joseph Stancomb of East Coker admitted to the census enumerator in 1861 that he lived partly on the fees paid to his wife by her boarding pupils, and Kegan Paul himself was later to take boys to eke out the poor income he received as rector of Sturminster Marshall in Dorset. Mrs Stancomb had thirteen paying pupils aged between six and sixteen as well as three of her own daughters, and her staff comprised two assistants and two 'assistants in tuition', her own two eldest daughters.

The Stancombs' school was still going strong in 1871 with thirteen pupils aged between thirteen and nineteen, with her husband and four daughters teaching as well as a 'foreign governess' from Germany. The household also included a cook and two housemaids.

Statistics like these cannot bring the school to life, though the Stancombs are known to have been members of the Christian Brethren movement and there can be no doubt about the moral standards taught there. Victorian governments had not considered the idea of league tables although Mr Allen's letter to Mrs Halliday suggests that parent power was not invented at the end of the twentieth century – it was simply a question of market forces. Certainly the Stancombs achieved the right balance and the two eldest daughters, having left Coker, continued in the education business in Hendford Hill, Yeovil, until the beginning of the First World War. Ilminster Grammar School, enjoying a small private endowment from the time of its foundation in the 1500s, continued rather longer in the same buildings and in a different guise as a school for girls within the State system until the second half of the twentieth century.

Burnham on Sea was a typical small seaside town of its time in the later nineteenth century: rather more apartment houses for the summer visitors and other signs of leisure activities like the two 'puzzle gardens' or mazes, but otherwise unremarkable.

Early in the 1870s there were five private schools there catering for those families who considered themselves a little above the National school on the Esplanade kept by Mr and Mrs Fisher which had been going for at least twenty years. First in alphabetical order in the *Directory* published by Morris & Co. was the preparatory school for young gentlemen kept by the Misses Frances, Jane and Ellen Bailey in College Street. The Misses Bailey had not been in the town more than about five years and within another three they had obviously decided that young gentlemen were too rough and instead for a few years kept a boarding school for young ladies.

Next in order came the well-established boarding and day school of Miss Anne Elizabeth Hobbs at Alfred House, also in College Street. It was simply described as a boarding school in 1861, as a ladies' boarding and day school in 1872, and still as a ladies' boarding school in 1889. Alfred House was also the home of Miss Hobbs' brother, a solicitor.

College Street was obviously something of the educational centre of the town, for at No. 8 lived Mrs Rosser, who also kept a school for ladies, some living in and some attending daily. And not far away in Oxford Street was a day school kept by Charles Way. The last two had closed by 1875, but Simon Harris in Victoria Street perhaps took some of their former pupils. In 1875 the educational scene was broadened by the appearance of Thomas Crabb of Sea View Villa on the Esplanade who described himself as a Professor of Music.

By 1883 only Professor Crabb and Miss Hobbs remained in business besides the National School, but three new schools had opened. Parents thus had a wide choice: Brean Down House for girls in Julia Terrace under Miss Fanny Dows; Ravensworth House School for boys under William Clarke; Burnham College, evidently superior if its name was any guide, under Ernest Albert Russell; and Steart House School for boys under Henry Edward Compson. Six years later all but one had gone, among them Steart House, but at least two valuable clues from it survive in the form of a pupil's report of academic achievement and that same pupil's account of costs for the summer term of 1886.

Young William Warren, a clergyman's son, was then about twelve years old and was soon to find himself a pupil at Malvern College. Mr Compson found the lad's conduct to be satisfactory, but would have liked 'to see him a little more manly in his behaviour'. His reading skills were 'fair', his writing 'fair when he takes pains'; History and Geography were also 'fair' but he was fifth in his class. Divinity was 'very fair', dictation 'still very poor' and bottom in his class of nine. Out of ten pupils taking Latin and Greek he was placed seventh: 'he wants intelligence in his work; he can work well enough in a groove, but fails when he has to think'.

All these were the opinions of Mr Compson. French and Mathematics were taught by a master only known to us as 'J.H.P' and for him Warren was much more satisfactory: third in his class for French and 'good', second in Arithmetic and 'very fair', top and 'good' in Algebra and fourth out of six in Geometry, then usually called 'Euclid'.

Private education cost money. Mr Compson sent the Revd Mr Warren a bill for £22 17s (£22.85p) for the summer term 1886, of which £20 covered the term's fees; £1 10s (£1.50p) was the fee for 'Drawing', extra lessons with a part-time, and probably ill-paid, teacher. Exercise for growing boys was important but also extra, which explains the 8s for a drill jacket, a useful grounding for most boys probably found their way to public school and then the army. Drill was no doubt the task of a retired military man in the town who might be willing to supplement his pension by putting young gentlemen through their paces. Perhaps Warren's lack of enthusiasm for that kind of exercise made him less manly than the headmaster desired. A further 2s 6d (12p) appears in the account as a subscription to 'school games', presumably the cost in the summer of cricket equipment. And 2s (10p) was spent on bathing machines; the sea was, after all, there or thereabouts.

And books had to be paid for: a Latin text, an English-Latin Dictionary and a French Reader, the first two so obviously favourites with young Warren, cost his father 14s 6d (72p). The expense was surely justified. After Malvern, Warren went to Oriel College, Oxford, and then to Wells Theological College, and was successively curate of Bridgwater, vicar of Meare, rector of Charlinch and vicar of Binegar.

—mm—

On Thursday evening, the 24 October 1895, thirteen lads went back to school. The master, whom they clearly respected, had persuaded them to spend at least one night a week improving themselves, and at the first session he 'explained as far as possible the usefulness in coming, and gave an outline of the work to be done'. And the work on that first evening was science and geography – matter and its properties first and then, to sugar the pill, an introduction to New Zealand with the help of lantern slides.

If the first evening was a modest success, the second was a disaster. Bridgwater Carnival, as the master ruefully wrote in his log book, proved 'a greater attraction than school'. And two or three lads 'dropped off coming', but two new ones arrived to hear more about matter, the means of production, fresh and foul air, and, having finished off New Zealand, were introduced to Australia. Then came another rival attraction on the first Thursday in December, an 'entertainment' at the Wesleyan chapel.

On the first week in February 1896 C. H. Bothamley, the county's Director of Technical Education, declared that the school had made a satisfactory beginning but suggested that a map of the country being studied might be useful, that illustrations of scientific points were not very good, and that the schoolroom was cold. It was also occupied for a concert a fortnight later and when the school inspector came on the following week numbers were down because a lecture elsewhere had seemed more interesting. At the end of March school closed; the attractions or demands of paid work during the spring and summer would clearly prove too great.

Yet the school continued with great regularity and success. In fact in January 1898 it was decided to hold it twice a week, and from October 1898 three times, on Mondays, Tuesdays and Thursdays. The topics appear to have become more advanced: elementary physiography and mensuration, volcanoes and earthquakes, subtraction of fractions, chlorine and oxygen, French standards of measure and weight, pulleys, isosceles triangles and commercial geography.

There continued, of course, to be occasional distractions. Behaviour was hardly ever mentioned by the master, though once two boys were sent out of the room. A concert took some away, the schoolroom was sometimes required for meetings of the parish council or for missionary or political gatherings. Yet in spite of interruptions the reports of inspectors were always good: 'very well attended ... instruction intelligent and effective'; 'results are most praiseworthy'; 'carefully taught'.

Almost a revolution took place in November 1900 when a girls' class was started, meeting on Tuesdays and Thursdays from 6.30 to 8.35 for needlework and cutting out, geography and domestic economy. The boys now met on Mondays, Wednesdays and Fridays between 7.00 and 8.35. Mr Bothamley was

170

very pleased and the Government Inspector said the school was well attended, the pupils well behaved.

Unfortunately the girls' class did not last for long because the teacher left, but it was revived in 1911 and attracted eleven attenders. At least one of the school managers did not approve, and the county authorities would not recognise the validity of the First Aid class because it was not conducted by a medical man.

And then came a greater conflict. On 28 September 1914 the master found that an English lesson 'resolved itself into a talk about the causes of the present war'. By November attendance was down because some of the lads had already enlisted although several managed to attend the Christmas social evening. Early in January two of the boys, then on active service in Bath, were presented with pocket Bibles and their fees were returned to them. All were, of course, invited to the end-of-term party at Easter 1915 but most of them had other, and more serious, duties.

At the beginning of the following term the master was worried about wartime security, and lighting restrictions required that he use maps for blinds in the schoolroom. The Authorities, looking ahead to the prospects for rural employment after the war, encouraged the visiting inspector to ask searching questions that foreshadowed compulsory day continuation classes.

By November 1916 compulsory military service or work on the land had deprived the night school of so many boys that the girls and boys were taught together in December and the school closed in January instead of Easter as usual. But there were 24 pupils in October 1917 and only one session had to be postponed because of a lecture elsewhere on the war at sea.

Classes were amalgamated again in January 1918 and the school could only manage a wartime 'break-up party' but when the next year's pupils met in the schoolroom on 11 November 1918 'the evening was devoted to patriotic songs, etc.' And two days later the master explained the terms of the Armistice.

After such difficulties it was good to know that the needlework, especially white embroidery, was of a 'really excellent' standard, though it was disappointing (but probably no great surprise) that elementary science had not 'much personal value for the students'. There was, of course, a counter-attraction, the world of work away from the countryside. The school struggled on until 1921, but the lads who had before been content to sit in the warm during winter evenings left villages for urban jobs and urban pay.

The evening school, held at the school shared between Chilton Polden and Edington but attracting pupils from Cossington as well, was not unique, though the embroidery skills learned there were clearly outstanding. It was but one attempt to improve educational standards beyond that which could be achieved during the basic school day. In its own time it was proof that the demands of a post war world involved better educational opportunities and that the challenge facing country villages was serious. The same thoughts and actions came after the Second World War; and educational improvement is still at the heart of measures for facing the future at the beginning of the twenty-first century.

17

MODERN WAR

Burrow Mump, standing proud over the Somerset Levels, was given to the National Trust in 1946 as a War Memorial recalling the lives sacrificed in the Second World War. It stands, with the Book of Remembrance in Wells Cathedral and memorials in towns and villages throughout the county recording the even greater losses in the First World War. For those who survived there were bitter and horrific memories, but experiences which humdrum jobs at home could never reproduce; and comradeship still recalled and never matched.

"... an illegal still in a wood behind the Cross Keys camp where booze was made from raisins stolen from the stores."

Siegfried Sassoon's bitter First World War poem 'They' recalls the Church Militant of the time, a bishop preaching war as a just cause and by implication encouraging his hearers to volunteer. The reward of the brave volunteers, he promises, having 'challenged death and dared him face to face', would be the knowledge that they had saved civilisation. Sassoon himself profoundly challenged by his experiences in the trenches, was not impressed; his returning boys were certainly changed: legless, blind and dying; and seeing them the bishop was not so sure he had been right.

The Reverend J.E. Loughnan, vicar of Walton since 1889 and an Irishman, was never in doubt. He was obviously one of those convinced that God was on England's side, and encouraging volunteers from among his flock was his clear duty. No matter how many lads fell, his views seem to have remained unchanged, and he not only recruited from the pulpit but also used scripture lessons in the village school to spread his anti-German attitudes.

His parish was not fruitful ground. There were too many socialists for his liking and too many Quakers. The former, he believed, did not care who ruled England (provided, he thought, they were well fed); the latter were pacifists who were, nevertheless, happy to practice trade warfare.

When the vicar visited the school before war actually broke out he discovered with horror that the youngsters could not believe the Germans were at all likely to fight; war was a thing of the past. But when war came young George Fisher from Walton, already a member of the yeomanry, was called up and John Norton and Harry Howe, older than George, were already members of the National Guard. Yet preach as he often did (the pacifists called his sermons recruiting harangues) he could not persuade others to follow. He evidently had his own list of potential recruits, 'possibles' he called them, but to his disgust few had 'any principle and courage', and failed to answer his call.

Mr Loughnan was not alone, for the clergy in general were used as recruiting officers in an amazing way, being asked to name those they thought fit to serve. Such pressure was perhaps more effective than the bands, usually of drums, outside public houses and processions of 'cheering Tommies' in army lorries and ambulances – who would have thought ambulances at all attractive?

Young farmers, especially, realised that prices would soon be rising; this was no time to leave home. A killing of a different kind was to be made and until controls were imposed, eggs went up in price to 5s (25p) a dozen and in town to as much as 8d (3p) each. Mr Loughnan's income from his tithe rose from over £75 in 1914 to over £109 in 1918 with the value of land and its produce.

Eventually compulsory military service was introduced. Some lads were now willing to 'go if they must' but waited, commented the vicar, as long as they could for the 'must'. Local Quakers, 'notably one Whitelaw and one Stephens of Ashcott', coached others how to secure exemption as conscientious objectors (a fee of 1s (5p) was asked for instruction) but only one Walton family, in the vicar's words, 'disgraced themselves'.

Exemption, for six months or permanent, was achieved by what the vicar called 'every foxy trick, so well known to Somerset folk' with the best liars coming off best. Sons of farmers became shepherds, ploughmen, horsetenders, cowmen and milkers on their fathers' farms, but the best excuse was to have a widowed mother. One family of three brothers escaped altogether; in another of two brothers and an uncle, the two brothers went and one did not return.

In church the vicar insisted on the singing of the National Anthem after Evensong every Sunday. Many of his flock objected, wanting the soldiers to be saved rather than the king. One choirboy was sacked for refusal. The lad's oldest brother was the first pressed man from the village to be killed. In total the village lost only five, among them William Summers, the only Walton man to win a medal. Eventually the vicar added the hymn for absent friends after the National Anthem, which he admitted proved a popular alternative.

Life in Walton during the war was anything but comfortable. Food became scarce, tradesmen no longer called, and the vicar like the rest of his flock had to walk into Street for supplies. Those were obtainable, if at all, only on Fridays and Saturdays in return for coupons. The farmers, of course, looked after themselves well enough – they would hardly offer Mr Loughnan anything after his tirades against them and must have begrudged paying him tithes. And 'idiotic government' made matters worse.

When the war eventually ended, what then? Mr Loughnan long before that happy event realised that a new era would soon dawn. Writing in his parish magazine about the proposal to make all seats in church free, he said that to claim privileges of any kind on what seemed a class basis was unthinkable after the sacrifices all families had made. Conversion is the word that springs to mind.

Mr Loughnan stayed in his post until 1931, doing his duty as he saw it in total for more than forty years, and at some stage during those post-war years summarised his views and his memories of the war that are preserved among the Walton parish papers.

~~~

Drilling in full kit under the June sun in 1917 at the camp for army conscripts at Sutton Veny in Wiltshire was not fun, but a cycling pass home to Somerset for the weekend was like gold and James Wedlake relished it, for it was a chance to see his wife and two young children again. It turned out to be embarkation leave, for a month later James and his comrades were parading on Salisbury Plain in their new Indian issue uniforms before two visiting generals.

His next letter home was from Cape Town where at the Visiting Troop Entertainment Establishment the young soldiers, James among them, were given tea and attended concerts. Then on to Durban where he and a few others contracted scabies and found themselves using the 'Rest, Refreshment and Writing Room' at Central West Street. Perhaps it was there James had time to study a useful booklet issued by the YMCA called The Brightest Jewel, a useful guide to India with some tips on elementary Hindustani and hints of how to keep healthy.

India was a great shock to lads from rural Somerset. When he first arrived in Bombay James sent his mother back in Houndsley near Winford the army issue post card with the printed message 'All's Well'. From Pashan Camp, Kirkee, two weeks or so later, he wrote of jackals roaming about, hundreds of different coloured birds, wild parrots and swarms of flying foxes. The nearest town he thought a 'horrible native place' full of bad smells and 'the lowest type of Indians ... called hindus ... very filthy and dirty and go about half dressed almost naked ... If ever missionaries were needed in this world it is here'. The army had the matter in hand. A collection was organised on the following Sunday 'towards helping to teach these unfortunates the Gospel and Christian Knowledge'. Missionary success would surely put an end to the need for a rifle on church parade.

The tented camp at Trimulgherry brought James in sight of temples, monkeys and snakes and also unbearable heat. Doses of quinine three days a week kept fever largely at bay, but men were falling at the rate of twenty a day. Mail from home was irregular but so very much looked forward to; one delivery brought local papers from Radstock and four copies of John Bull, but letters told of food shortages and of his sister working in a restaurant in Wales 'amongst nothing else but colliers'.

But now Indians became interesting, especially the Nizam of Hyderabad, in whose territory they were stationed. He, possessor of 200 wives, his own railway and currency, even offered every soldier a rupee a week if the British government would permit him to be saluted.

James Wedlake was lucky. Promotion to lance-corporal gave him enough money for a camera but many of his fellows were already quinine addicts. Then he became sergeant-instructor with an extra 20 rupees a month,

Thursday afternoons and Sundays off, and plenty of time in the sergeants' mess with billiard and reading rooms to relax in. Now he could afford to send his mother a little silk shawl and was proud to know it had been admired by his aunt at Felton – but Felton reminded him of orchards, and orchards that a drop of cider would not come amiss.

By 1 November 1918 Turkey had collapsed and the threat facing James and his comrades was not invasion over the Khyber Pass but influenza: thirty men in his own camp died in a month. But peace meant being a lance-corporal again. 'They are welcome to their stripes', he wrote rather bitterly, 'all I want is to get home as soon as possible'. Instead he went down with fever, which at least stopped him from serving in the army of occupation in Europe; instead he served in Ireland, from which no snapshots and no letters survive.

—*m*—

In 1993 an American tour operator had plans for a rather low-key trip that studiously avoided the overcrowding and overcharging to be anticipated in Normandy in 1994 for the fiftieth anniversary of Operation Overlord and instead proposed to take customers back to the places where they had served in England.

The *Old England Clarion* announced at the beginning of 1994 for the benefit of visiting veterans and their wives, some of them surely GI Brides, that there would be a host of natives whose memories stretched back fifty years and who would flock to rallies, air shows, tea dances, parades, exhibitions and films with a wartime theme. In the event the tour was cancelled, for potential partic-ipants felt too old to travel. Those veterans still alive in 2004 remembered with a poignant mixture of diffidence and sadness the sixtieth anniversary.

With much more enthusiasm men too young to have fought in 1944 have tramped the English countryside in search of pillboxes, gun emplacements, barrage balloon sites and, of course, airfields: the archaeology of war. Those sites, like those of an earlier age, have a habit of merging into the landscape. Visiting GIs have so often been frustrated and disappointed that their memo-ries of the 1940s have played them false. Gone is the concrete, the noise, the smell, the excitement; absent are those companions with whom those heady days were spent.

But there are some sites that even the most unobservant realise had something to do with war. One of them is General Dept G-50, otherwise Blinkhorn Siding, one of only eighteen depots in the UK which made the success of Operation Overlord possible. Anyone who worked there sixty years later would not be entirely disappointed on their return. The location of the PX, the Red Cross Club, the dispensary, the dental clinic, the fire department and the constabulary might cause problems; and the rail sidings have mostly disappeared. But anyone travelling west from Taunton on the Wiveliscombe road at Cross Keys will see the unmistakeable shapes of the Romney huts and the massive sheds, each about the size of three football fields. Nowadays it is the Norton Trading Estate.

From adding machines to zippers, goods came across the Atlantic to Swansea, Cardiff or Bristol and were transported to G-50 usually by rail. The Quartermaster Corps was responsible for something like seventy thousand different items, all of which were vital to the war effort. Class I items were things like rations, to be consumed roughly at a uniform rate; Class II items included military equipment, office supplies and other items issued on a more limited basis; Class III items included engine fuel, coal and wood; Class IV might be materials for construction and fortification.

Lt Roland Schoepf of Manchester, New Hampshire, an original member of Company C, forty-fifth Armored Medical Batallion, Third Armored Division, found himself one of several thousand military personnel at G-50 from February 1944. Nearly fifty years later Lt Schoepf published his wartime memoirs entitled *The Generally Unknown Soldier*.

Coming to Somerset was a culture shock for Lt Schoepf. First there was the problem of language, then of Double Summer Time, then the discovery of an illegal still in a wood behind the Cross Keys camp where booze was made from raisins stolen from the stores. Not all went smoothly, and the temptation to blame the British railway system was rather strong. At all times there should have been 500 tons of evaporated milk at G-50, and the variation need to be investigated; there was almost disaster when in the late spring the canned fruit stocks were completely exhausted, and the only solution was to substitute raisins to make the schedules balance. The result, of course, was that throughout the entire US army in Europe raisin cookies, raisin bread and raisin pie were on mess menus, and bowls of raisins could not be given away. At last they went, to be replaced by prunes that someone had over ordered.

Roland Schoepf all those years later remembered bicycle trips to the Quantocks, films at the Empire Hall in Taunton, a trip to Weston; the discovery that a sick Englishman would say he felt queer; that General Omar Bradley had driven through Taunton on his way to Plymouth and embarkation to Normandy. One man's memory of war.

—*mm*—

The fiftieth anniversary of the end of the Second World War in Europe has been much celebrated in 2005 and exhibitions in local museums have been moving reminders to those of a certain age and a great fascination to the young. Still around us in our countryside are those solid concrete pillboxes with which we somehow intended to hold up an invasion force, and every so often someone finds rusting ammunition or some carbon rods from a searchlight battery, evidence that we were under siege and desperately defending ourselves. Someone creating a garden around his home at High Ham found cutlery from a wartime mess at Westonzoyland, perhaps evidence of a picnic rudely interrupted by the sound of the claxon announcing yet another scramble. Pillboxes, ammunition, carbon rods and cutlery are part of the archaeology of the Second World War; and so too are the visible remains of wartime

Yeovilton has had a continuous military role since 1939 and has for many years welcomed visitors to share the stirring story of naval flying. Broadfield Down, later Lulsgate Bottom, is also still in the flying business, sending businessmen and holiday makers on peaceful missions all over the world from Bristol International Airport. Helicopter pilots still sharpen their skills over the concrete and grass of Merryfield, and many a would-be driver practised up and down the old runways at Westonzoyland without too much risk to the family car.

But who remembers HMS *Dipper* at Henstridge, who served at Churchstanton (Culmhead), whatever went on at Doniford, and who and what were stationed at Charmy Down? They and the fields at Charlton Horethorne, Weston super Mare, Yeovil and Whitchurch were Somerset's contribution to the airborne war effort more than half a century ago.

Over 350 acres of land at Henstridge were commandeered from farmers in 1941 to provide five runways over which young naval pilots could practice deck landing. Construction took eighteen months and, in April 1943, HMS *Dipper* was commissioned, but it was used for only about a year by the Fighter Wing. The station continued in use in so-called peacetime until 1957, still masquerading as the deck of a carrier. Until the same year, incidentally, helicopters received their annual overhaul there after service whale-spotting in the Antarctic.

Churchstanton (Culmhead) has different claims to fame. Poles and then Czechs were stationed there between 1941 and June 1943, and after that date Spitfires there were engaged on deck landing practice and Wellingtons on low-level bombing training. There were also some boffins from Farnborough testing balloon cable-cutters – or rather getting RAF pilots to fly into the cables suspended from barrage balloons. The CO himself had to bale out of his Wellington when the blades on his wings would not operate and he became entangled.

In June 1944 Culmhead boasted for a few weeks the first allied operational jet propelled unit when Meteors screamed across the Blackdowns, but they soon left for Kent, and by that time the airfield was becoming remote from the focus of war. For a time it was a glider training school and after the war a glorified parking lot for mobile dental surgeries.

Doniford had been militarised since the 1920s when the army established an anti-aircraft gunnery range there every summer, firing at targets towed by aircraft based at Westonzoyland. In the 1930s they used radio-controlled Tiger Moths called 'Queen Bees', launched from a catapult, to make the gunners' work harder. There was a small airstrip still used in the 1940s by Lysanders and Piper Cubs.

Charmy Down, just outside Bath, was home in 1940 to Hurricanes defending Bath and Bristol, for two years was used by Canadians on work-up periods, and was the base for bomber squadrons raiding Cherbourg and other Continental targets. The Americans took it over in November 1943 as a tactical air depot for a few months and then handed it over to Flying Training Command.

Bare facts about these and other Somerset airfields may well jog memories; they cannot hope to convey the tedium, the excitement, the occasional tragedy of life on a Somerset airfield more than sixty years ago. A stroll through Charlton Horethorne for someone stationed there at the Air Direction School may still bring recognition, even if the grass runways have long been obliterated. A drive from Westonzoyland to Othery may at first be a little odd, for the road is the former main runway, but a few brick building are still standing and the village hall at Weston looks incredibly like the old NAAFI canteen.

Memory may play false on such a pilgrimage; it was, after all, more than sixty years ago. But the welcome to erstwhile defenders and allies is always warm, and if the exact picnic spot cannot be found, it will not really matter. The cutlery left behind at High Ham has probably been written off by now.

SELECT INDEX

Abingdon, Berks,
    abbot, 35
Adams, Elizabeth, 90;
    Henry, John, Joseph,
    and Robert, 141
Addington, Henry, 162
Adelard of Bath, 50-1
Aisholt, 88
Alford, 155
Alfred, prince, 9
Allen, Benjamin, 122-3;
    Thomas, 18; Mr, 166-7
Ames, John and
    William, 140
Ammerdown, 14
Anthony, 'a Tawny
    Moore', 90
Arnold, Richard, 100
Ashburton, Devon, 35
Ashcott, 113, 147-8, 174;
    Pedwell, 147
Ashton, Long, 89, 142;
    Court, 14-15
Ashwick, 111
Athelney, abbey, 72;
    monks, 24
Avebury, Wilts, 118
Axbridge, 86
Axminster, Devon, 16
Babcary, 128
Backwell, 116-17
Bacwell, John, 87
Bailey, Ellen, Frances,
    and Jane, 168
Banwell, Richard, 113
Banwell, 50, 129, 164

Barrington, 16, 44
Barrow Gurney, 144
Bartlett, Bartholomew,
    81
Barton St David, 141
Basing, Hants, 22
Baskerville, Thomas, 73
Batcombe, 98, 140
Bath, Richard of see
    Ilchester, Richard of
Bath, 12, 16-17, 33, 45,
    50, 100, 120, 129, 133,
    146-7, 149, 154, 162-3,
    165, 171, 180; abbey,
    8, 30, 50; Charmy
    Down, 179-80; inns,
    73, 78, 146; Red book,
    41
Bathampton, 32
Bawdrip, Crandon
    Bridge, 113
Beaton, Humphrey, 64-
    5; Nathaniel, 65;
    Robert, 65
Beaufort, Cardinal, 33;
    family, 10-11
Beaulieu, abbey, 45
Becket, Thomas, archbp
    of Canterbury, 27-8
Beckington, 35
Bedwyn, Great, Wilts,
    35-6
Bekynton, Thomas, bp
    of Bath and Wells, 34-
    6
Bere, Richard, abbot of

Glastonbury, 48, 52-4
Berkeley, Charles,
    Viscount
    FitzHardinge, 13;
    Henry, 139; Maurice,
    Viscount
    FitzHardinge, 18, 106-
    7; Thomas, 40;
    Colonel, 107
Berkley, 90, 110
Bernard, Canon John,
    35; Masckiell, 140
Berrow, 64, 66, 78
Biddesham, 29
Binegar, 169
Bird, George, 64
Bishop's Lydeard, 112,
    128
Bisse, Alice, 62
Bivern, John, 110
Blackford, 13, 125
Bleadon, 89
Bobart, Jacob, 119
Bodmin, Cornw, 45;
    friary, 87
Bohun, Lady Mary, 48
Boswell, Mr, 67
Bothamley, C H, 170
Botreaux, William de, 33
Bourchier, John, earl of
    Bath, 12
Bovett, Col Richard, 118
Bowet, Henry, bp of
    Bath and Wells, 105
Bradley, North, Emma
    of, 32

181

Bradley, North, Wilts,
32
Bratton, 140
Bratton, Thomas son of
Peter, 85
Brent, South, 64, 66
Brewham, South, 107
Breynton, John, abbot
of Glastonbury, 96
Bridges, Edward, 90
Bridgwater, Bridgwater,
16, 25, 41-3, 45, 77-8,
81, 90-3, 100, 118, 122-
3, 128-9, 134, 148, 150,
165, 169; Carnival,
170; castle, 42;
church, 100; Dock,
130-1; friary, 87;
Hamp, 24, 26; Horsey,
96; inns, 72, 78, 91,
128
Bridport, Dors, 128-9
Bristol, Lord, 107
Bristol, 16, 25, 31, 33,
100, 123, 132, 136,
146, 149, 152, 159,
180; castle, 38;
Clifton, 129-30, 163;
corporation, 24;
grocer, 81; mayor, 25;
men of, 39, 44, 116;
sheriff, 41; St Mark's
hospital, 96
Brown, Thomas, 100
Bruton, Richard, 39-41
Bruton, 14, 39, 53, 78,
107-8, 128, 140, 150;
Abbey, 106; canons,
72; Cole, 148;
hundred, 139; inns,
73; Redlynch, 13-16,

18; West End, 18
Bruyn, John, 85
Bryan, Charles, 123
Brympton d'Evercy, 16
Bubwith, Nicholas, bp
of Bath and Wells, 41
Burnett, G J, 80; J D, 80-
1
Burnham (on Sea), 64-6,
132, 148-50, 168
Burrowbridge, 147;
Burrow Mump, 173
Burtle, 113
Butleigh, 121, 141;
Court. 14
Byam, John, 91
Cadbury, South, 116-17
Caddebury, Nicholas,
85
Cameley, 38-39; Temple
Cloud, 38
Camerton, 88, 116, 153-
4
Cammell, Gilbert, 33
Campbell, Lieut, 106
Caner, Henry, 142-4
Cannington, Court, 62;
nunnery, 62-63
Cannon, John, 128
Canute, king, 8
Carr, Robert, earl of
Somerset, 12
Carter, John, 116-17
Carver, Richard, 124
Castle Cary, 56, 58, 86,
128, 134, 139, 150, 155
Castro, Peter de, 74
Catcott, 113
Catsash, hundred, 139
Cerdic, king of Wessex,
8

Chaffin, Richard, 107
Chandee, Philibert de,
earl of Bath, 12
Chapman, Henry, 91
Chappell, Elizabeth
and John, 91
Chapple, Mr, 124
Chard, 16, 78
Charlinch, 169
Charlton Adam, 24
Charlton Horethorne,
99, 179-80
Charlton Mackrell, 24,
141, 155
Charlton Musgrove, 69,
140; Holbrook, 116
Charmy Down, nr
Bath, 179-80
Chastelayne, Joan and
Thomas, 85
Cheddar, 100
Chedzoy, 11, 24, 53
Cheeke, Edward, 18;
Mr, 107
Chewton Mendip, 147
Chilmark, Wilts, 107
Chilton Polden 169-72
Chinnock, East, 69, 98
Chudleigh, Devon, 35
Chudleigh, Colonel,
108
Churchey, Mr, 107
Churchstanton, 179-80
Cirencester, Glos, 43
Clarke, 'Painter', 56, 58;
Robert, 56-8; William,
168
Cleeve, abbot of, 33
Cleeve, Old, Chapel
Cleeve, 166
Clement, Thomas, 127

Clevedon, 132
Clifford, Lord, 63; Thomas, 63
Clifton Maybank, Dorset, 16
Cloutesham, William, 85
Coker, 20; Coker Hill, 69; East, 97, 167
Collingbourne, Wilts, 36
Collingridge, Bishop, 63
Columjohn, Devon, 35
Combe Florey, 151
Combwich, 128
Compson, Henry Edward, 168-9
Compton Dando, 100
Compton Dundon, 24, 137
Compton Pauncefoot, 13
Congresbury, 46
Coombe, Bartholomew and Joan, 62
Corfe Castle, Dors, 10
Corpe, John, 140
Corston, 128
Cossington, 112
Cothelstone, 117-18
Courtenay, Henry, 41
Coventry, earl of, 119
Coward, Capt, 107
Crabb, Thomas, 168
Crandon Bridge, Bawdrip, 113
Creech, 21
Crewkerne, 11, 21, 32, 36, 78, 107, 128, 134, 142; school, 96-7

Cricket St Thomas, 121
Crocker, Thomas, 138
Croscombe, 100
Cruse, Jeremiah, 89
Cucklington, 139-40
Cuff, Robert, 90
Curci, Robert de, 62
Curry Mallet, 24
Curry Rivel, 10-11, 128-9; Burton Pynsent, 120-1; Moreton (Moortown), 121
Curry, North, 24, 150
Curteys, a friar, 116
Custard, Mr, 130
Dane, John the, 29; Strang the, 29; Turchil the, 29
Daubeney, Giles, Lord Daubeney, 44-45
Davidge, Robert, 89
Defoe, Daniel, 100
Deneys, Richard le, see Ilchester, Richard of; William le, 29
Denning, Michael, 25
Devenish, Major, 107
Devizes, Wilts, 35, 44
Dinnington, 85, 98
Ditcheat, 98
Dodington, 81
Donyatt, park, 85
Dorchester, Dors, 44, 129
Dows, Fanny, 168
Drake, Sir Francis, 15; Richard, 91
Drayton, 121
Dulcote, 31
Dulverton, 112; Northmoor, 13

Dunkerton, 153-4; Tunley, 100
Dunstan, St, abbot of Glastonbury, 52-53
Dunster, 12, 78, 85, 100, 165; castle, 87; vicar, 88
Durborough, Sir John, 96
Durleigh, 127
Dyke, R A, 149-50
Eadgyth, queen, 9
Earith, Charles, 161
Earle, Colonel, 107
Eburne, Richard, 140
Edgar, king, 8
Edington, 169-72
Edmund Ironside, king, 8
Edward the Confessor, 9, 20; the Martyr, king, 8; earl of Wessex, 7
Egmont, earl of, 13
Ellis, Welbore, Baron Mendip, 13
Emma, queen, 8-9
Enmore, 13, 35, 42
Esland, Richard de, 74
Ethelred the Unready, king, 8-9
Evans, Owen, 137
Evercreech, 99, 149
Ewens, Matthew, 139
Ewley, John, 116
Exeter, 16, 35-6, 44-6, 109-10, 147; cathedral, 74
Fairfax, Sir Thomas, 22
Fane, Frederick, 129
Farewell, James, 139

Farleigh Hungerford, 48, 115-17; rector, 116
Farmborough, 32, 113
Fastrad, 50
Felton, Winford, 177
Felyps, William, 33
Fiddington, 127
Fisher, George, 174; Mr and Mrs, 168
Fisico, Roger, 97
FitzHardinge, Capt, 107; see Berkeley
FitzJames, family, 15
FitzRoy, Charles, duke of Southampton, 17-18; Henry, duke of Grafton, 17; Henry, duke of Somerset, 10
Flamank, Thomas, 44-5
Fontaine, James, 78-80
Forde Abbey, Dors, 16
Fox, Richard, bp of Bath and Wells, 52; Sir Stephen, 18, 107; Stephen, earl of Ilchester, 13; Major, 107
Frances, Josiah, 89
Frome, 77, 100, 110-11; Keyford, 44
Fussell, James and John, 111
Gambier, Lord, 66-7
Garland, William, 98
Gawayne, Thomas, 139
Gerrard, Lady Mary, 18; Philip, 91
Gibbes, Robert (or Sherborne, or Whitlocke), prior of Montacute, 98-9

Gibbons, George, 100
Gibson, Alexander, 151
Gimblett, Capt William, 67
Giso, bp of Wells, 50
Glasney college, Cornw, 45
Glasse, Mrs, 161
Glastonbury, 11, 14, 16, 45, 77, 98, 100, 109-10, 113, 148-50; abbey, 22, 24, 30, 43, 45, 48, 52-3, 97, 147; abbot, 35, 43; Bere Lane, 52; inns, 72, 78, 128; St Benignus's church, 53; Tor, 147; Twelve Hides, 53
Gloucester, 92; Humphrey, duke of, 34
Godwin, earl of Wessex, 8-9
Goldsmyth, Thomas, 116
Goodland, Henry, 93
Gorges, Helena, see Snakenborg; Sir Robert, 15; Sir Thomas, 15-16
Gough, Dr Francis, 127
Gould, William, 65
Granville, John, earl of Bath, 12
Greinton, 24
Grenville, James, Baron Glastonbury, 14; family, 121
Gytha, Countess, 21
Haberfield, Thomas, 123

Haddon, John, 92
Hallatrow, 116, 153
Halliday, George, John, and William, 166; Mrs, 166
Ham, High, 24, 39-40, 52, 58, 137, 179; Beer, 138; Low Ham, 118, 138
Hamelyn, William, 85
Hamme, Henry, 85
Hancock, T, 129
Harbord, family, 55
Hardidge, John, 64
Harding, Sir John, Baron Harding, 13; family, 100
Hardington, 110
Harleston, William and his wife Elizabeth (Luttrell), 87
Harold Harold, earl, king, 9; Harefoot, king, 8-9
Harptree, 13
Harris, Simon, 168; parish clerk, 88
Harthacnut, 8-9
Haselbury Plucknett, 126
Haselschawe, Thomas de, 72
Haskell, Mark, Roger, and William, 140
Hawley, Capt, 17
Heightre, church, 116
Hemington, 110-11
Henstridge, 140, 179
Herbert, William, earl of Pembroke, 42
Heron, John, 11-12

Hervy, John, 46
Hewys, Thomas, 82
Hext, Sir Edward, 138
Highbridge, 80, 131, 134-5, 148-50
Highmore, James, 161
Hill, Thomas, 35
Hindon, Wilts, 69, 107
Hinton, James, 142
Hinton Charterhouse, priory, 47-8
Hinton St George, 16, 75-6, 99, 128
Hobbs, Anne Elizabeth, 168
Hockelin see Ilchester, Richard of
Hogges, John, 116
Holbrook, Charlton Musgrove, 116
Holcombe, 111
Holland, William, 88
Honiton, Devon, 36
Hood, Capt Alexander, 121; Capt Samuel, 121
Hooper, George, bp of Bath and Wells, 159; Nicholas, 91
Hopkins, Nicholas, 47
Horethorne, hundred, 138
Horsington, 139, 162
House, Joseph, 1112
How, Harry, 174
Howard, Sir Algar, 48
Howell, Ralph, 64-5
Huish, Oliver, 85
Huish Champflower, 88
Hull, Sir Edward, 35-36
Hungerford, Berks, 117
Hungerford, Robert,

Baron Hungerford, 117; Sir Thomas, 115; Thomas, 41; Walter, Baron, 35, 115-17
Huntingford, George Isaac, 160-2
Huntspill, 38-9, 63-5, 80-1; Alstone, 38
Hurford, John, 65; Thomas, 65
Hurman, Thomas, 65
Hutchings, Miss, 161
Huwyssh, John, 85
Ilchester, Richard of, bp of Winchester, 27-9; earls of, 18
Ilchester, 16, 29, 40, 75, 78; courts, 73; inns, 73; Mead, 69; Sock Dennis, 29; St Michael's church, 39; Whitehall, 29
Ilminster, 16, 75, 78, 128, 152, 165, 167
Ilton, Merryfield, 179
Irving, Sir Henry (John Henry Brodribb), 155
Jacob, John, 58-60; Revd S.L., 58
Janyn, John, 116
Jenkin, Mr, 67
John, chaplain, 116; clerk of Keynsham, 116; Little, 35
Jolliffe, William, 13-14
Jones, Alexander, 90; Richard and William, 91
Joseph, Michael, an Gof, 44-5
Jossey, Thomas, 113

Keball, Thomas, 65
Keinton Mandeville, 155-6
Ken, Thomas, bp of Bath and Wells, 157-9
Kendall, John, 43-4
Kenton, Devon, 91
Kerk, Capt, 106
Keynsham, Thomas of, 98
Keynsham, 16, 77-8, 116, 146; abbey, 48; Somerdale, 133
Kidder, Richard, bp of Bath and Wells, 158-9
Killigrew, Henry, 91
Kilmersdon, 110-11
Kilmington, Wilts, 18, 107
King, John, 113; Oliver, bp of Bath and Wells, 52
Kinge, James, 139
Kinglake, Farmer, 100
Kingsdon, 24, 126
Kingston Seymour, 73
Kingston St Mary, Nailsbourne, 100
Kingweston, 141
Kitto, James, 98
Knight, Edward and Mary, 72; Robert, 122-3; Robert his son, 123
L, Mr J, 66-7
Labouchere, Henry, Baron Taunton, 13
Lanfranc, archbp of Canterbury, 20
Langford, Court, 162-3
Langport, 13, 25, 110, 112, 150, 155;

Eastover, 10-11
Langton, Stephen,
  archbp of Canterbury,
  30-1
Laud, William, archp of
  Canterbury, 32
Leaker, John, 65;
  Thomas, 64
Lechlade, Robert of, 40
Leddred, John, 85
Lee, Thomas atte, 40
Leech, Joseph, 89
Leversedge, W E, 99
Lewes, Robert of, bp of
  Bath, 51, 86
Limington, 75
Liskeard, Cornw, 36
Littleton, High, 113
Longford Castle, Wilts,
  15
Longleat, Wilts, 12, 16
Lopen, 74-5
Lostwithiel, Cornw, 36
Loughnan, Revd J E,
  174-5
Love, Robert, 139
Lovell, James, 113
Luccombe, East, 85
Lulsgate, Wrington, 179
Lundy Island, 37-9
Luttrell, Sir Hugh, 46,
  87-8; family, 100
Lydeard, Robert of, 97-
  8
Lydford, East, 155
Lyme (Regis), Dors, 91
Lympsham, 93
Lyng, 147
Lyte, John, 64
Maiden Bradley, Wilts,
  12

Malecomb, Geoffrey de,
  72
Malet, Elizabeth, 122;
  John, 122; William,
  123
Manchip, Mr, 130
Maperton, 116-17
Mare, Sir Peter de la, 22
Marisco, family, 38-9
Mark, 66, 91
Marksbury, 100
Marshall, Richard, 38
Marten, Christopher,
  139
Martin, William, 64
Martock, 10-11, 100,
  128-9; Ash, 69; Milton
  Falconbridge, 10-11
Mason, Sir William,
  Baron Blackford, 13
Masson, John, 116
Matthews, Charles, 72;
  George and Dina, 89;
  Rezia, 89
Meare, 98, 100, 169;
  Godney, 98
Medlycott, Lady, 161
Mells, 111, 165
Mere, Wilts, 69
Meriet, family, 74
Merriott, 74, 84
Merryfield, Ilton, 179
Mews, Peter, bp of Bath
  and Wells, 105, 158
Michael, William, 138
Middlezoy, 25, 96
Midsomer Norton, 55,
  133; Welton, 54
Milborne Port, 69, 78,
  128, 139, 160-1; inn,
  73

Mildmay, family, 119
Miles, T, 129
Mills, R B, 129
Milverton, 22, 58
Minehead, 39-40, 45,
  66-8, 78, 134; church,
  85-6
Mohun, William, earl of
  Somerset, 12
Molland, Devon, 111-12
Monkton, West, 22, 97
Monmouth, James,
  duke of, 16-17, 64, 77,
  118; rebellion, 64, 65,
  77, 81, 136, 158
Montacute, 14-15, 69,
  75, 128; monks, 21;
  prior, 98
Moone, Robert, 90
More, Hannah, 162-3
Morris, William, 64
Mosier, Hugh, 140
Mostyn, 93
Motcombe, Dors, 69
Muchelney, 127
Mulford, John the
  younger, 64
Nailsbourne, Kingston
  St Mary, 100
Nailsea, 16, 129
Newbolt, Revd W R,
  130
Newborough, Squire,
  90
Newport, John, 90
Nicholas, 'one that died
  in Matthew's Field',
  90
Normandy, Robert,
  duke of, 20-21
North, Frederick, Lord

North, 13, 120
Northampton, marquess and marchioness, 14
Northlode, Alice, 62
Norton, John, 174
Norton Ferris, hundred, 139
Norton Fitzwarren, 177-9
Norton St Philip, 17, 77
Norton sub Hamdon, 84
Norwich, friary, 87
Nunney, 22; castle, 21-22
Oby, John, 45
Odcombe, 69
Olaf, Saint, 29
Oldham, Bernard, 11
Olum (Olym), Hugh , John, and William, 40
Othery, 96, 137-8, 180
Ottery St Mary, Devon, 96
Owen, William, 161
Pacy, Thomas, 881
Padstow, Cornw, 92
Page, Edith, 142
Palmer, John, 129; William, 107
Parker, John, 22-3; Matthew, archbp of Canterbury, 23
Parr, Queen Katharine, 14; William, marquess of Northampton, 14-15
Patten, William, 91
Paul, Charles Kegan, 166-7

Paulet, William, 22; William, marquess of Winchester, 22
Paulton, 113, 147
Pawlett, 96; Stretcholt, 112
Peniston, John, 63
Pennard, West, 54, 99, 128
Penryn, Cornw, 36
Penselwood, 69, 89, 140
Pensford, 78
Petherton, Petherton, North, 24, 26, 48, 100, 128; battle, 91; forest, 42; Melcombe Poulett, 22
Petherton, South, 13, 16, 44, 75, 128-9, 130-1
Phelips, Joan, 107
Picke, David, 89
Pickrell, Mr, chaplain, 63
Pikebon, 97
Pilton, 98
Pinney, Colonel, 114
Pitminster, Poundisford, 100
Pitney, 24
Pitt, Hester, wife of William, 121-2; William, earl of Chatham, 120-2
Plymouth, 35, 110, 112-13, 179
Plympton, Devon, prior, 35
Pole, Anne de la, 84; John de la, 11; William de la, earl of Suffolk, 33

Poore, Herbert and Richard, 29
Popley, Robert, 139
Porlock, 9, 78, 88; Weir, 66
Portishead, 134
Poulett, Sir Amias, 75; Lord, 99
Prater, Colonel, 22; Richard, 22
Preston Plucknett, 69
Prewe, Francis, 137-8
Price, David, 90; William, 111
Priest, Joseph, 65
Prowse, John, 65
Pulham, Matilda, 62
Pulteney, William, earl of Bath, Viscount Pulteney, 12
Pynsent, Leonora, 120; Sir William, 120
Quantoxhead, West, 111
Quarle, John, 91
Queen Camel, 11, 126-7; Hazlegrove, 119
Radstock, Baron, 13
Rainsborough, Colonel, 22
Rathbone, Hannah Mary and William, 122; family, 122-3
Read, William, 140
Reynolds, Richard, 122-3; family, 123
Richard, 40
Rimpton, 28, 97
Rison, Amy, 91
Robert, nephew of Robert Gibbes, 98
Roberts, John, 91;

Ensign, 107
Roddaway, William, 89
Rodden, 90
Rode, 89, 110-11; Rode Hill, 89
Roger, Martin, 74
Rogers, Edward, 63
Rolle, Denys, 57; John, 57
Romane, Bartholomew, 72
Roode, Thomas, 64
Roper, Hugh, 65
Rosser, Mrs, 168
Rosseter, William, 91
Russell, Ernest Albert, 168; Thomas, 40
Ruthven, William, 108-10; family, 108-9
Ryall, John, 89
Ryvers, John, 85
Salisbury, Wilts, 36, 107, 160; cathedral, 15, 35, 116
Salmon, Mr, 130
Saltford, 117
Sanders, Sir Robert, Baron Bayford, 13
Sandhull, John, 86
Sarsfield, Patrick, 106
Saunders, Thomas, 81
Savaric, bp of Bath, 30
Schellinks, William, 146-8
Schulenberg, Ermengarde, Baroness of Glastonbury, 14
Scrope, Sir Thomas, 41
Searl, Richard, 66-7
Seavington Dennis, 29;

St Michael, 29
Sedgemoor, battle, 105-6
Semley, Wilts, 69
Sewell, Dr, 130
Seymour, Edward, duke of Somerset, 10, 12; William, marquess of Hertford, duke of Somerset, 12
Shaftesbury, Dors, 36, 116; abbey, 62
Shapwick, 58, 98, 112-13, 148
Shepard, John, 141
Shepton Beauchamp, 127-8
Shepton Mallet, 78, 113
Sherborne, Dors, 36, 69, 129; castle, 107
Skinner, John, 88
Skynner, William, 81-2
Slake, Nicholas, 40
Smith, Revd G C, 68
Smith, Revd Sydney, 151
Snakenborg, Helena von, marchioness of Northampton, 14-16
Somer, John, 87
Somers, Benjamin, 164; family, 164
Somerton, 13, 24, 75, 108-10, 112, 118, 126, 129-31
Sompnour, Richard, 62
Southwick, Wilts, 33
Spanyerd, John, 48
Sparkford, 119
Speke, Sir John, 46; family, 16

Spencer, father and son, 65
Spring, Howard, 156
Squire, Francis, 162; family, 141
St Austell, Cornw, 36
St John, Henry, 85
Stafford, Edward, duke of Buckingham, 46-48; Humphrey, earl of Devon, 41-44; John, archbp of Canterbury, 32-34, 100; Stafford, Sir Henry, 11; Sir Humphrey, 32;
Stagg, William, 124
Stancomb, Joseph and family, 167
Stanley, Thomas, Lord, 11
Stapledon, Thomas, 20
Stavordale, 13
Stawell, George, 117-19; John, Baron Stawell, 118; Sir John, 117; Ralph, Baron, 13, 118-19; Ursula, 119; family, 117
Stawell, 117, 123
Steele, Mrs, 161
Steepholm, 73
Stert Point, 73
Stogumber, 81
Stogursey, 99; Fairfield, 62
Stoke Lane, 113
Stoke sub Hamdon, 10-11, 69, 128-9
Stoke Trister, 13, 69, 89; Bayford, 13, 69
Stone, Thomas, 90

Stowey, Nether, 44; inn, 73, 128
Stowey, Over, 72, 88; Aley, 72
Strangways, Henry Bull, 112-13
Stratton, Thomas, 85
Street, 147, 150
Strete, Joan, 91
Stuart, Arabella, 12
Sturminster Marshall, Dors, 167
Summers, William, 175
Sutton Mallet, 122-4
Sutton Veny, Wilts, 175
Sutton, Long, 24, 126-7
Sweete, Thomas, 98
Sweeting, Hugh, 81
Sweyn, earl, 9
Sweyn, king of Denmark, 8
Swynford, Catherine, 10
Talbott, Mr, 130
Tapscott, Mr, 130
Taunton, John of, abbot of Glastonbury, 97
Taunton, 28, 35, 79-80, 87, 113-14, 149-52, 165, 178; borough, 13; castle, 147; cinema, 133-4; club, 101-3; cricketers, 129-30; inns, 78, 147; market, 100; priory, 45; rebels at, 16, 44-5; Rowbarton, 151-2; St Mary's, 127
Taylor, John, 45; John (another), 73
Temple, family, 121
Templecombe, 40, 96, 148, 150
Thierry, Jacobi, 146-8
Thornbury, Glos, castle, 47-8
Thorpe, Swithun, 22
Thynne, Thomas, earl of Bath, Viscount Weymouth, 12
Tilley, John, 64; Radigund, 62
Timsbury, 101, 113
Tintinhull, 69
Tiverton, Devon, 35, 114, 151
Toclyve, see Ilchester, Richard of
Tose, John, 46
Tours, John of, bp of Bath, 50
Towse, Joan, 62
Trelawney, Colonel, 108
Trimelet, Joan, 62
Troteman, Edward, 30
Truro, 36
Tuchet, James, Lord Audley, 44-45
Tucker, Jeremiah, 64; Samuel, 111
Tudor, Edmund, 11
Tuttle, Henry, 90
Twerton, 116
Twogood, George, 113
Twynyho, Roger, 44
Tynte, Sir Halswell, 78; John, 54
Ullathorne, Bernard, bp, 63
Underhay, Thomas, 91
Urchfont, Wilts, 121
Urswick, Christopher, 11
Varman, Thomas, 64
Vaughan, John and Malet, 122
Verney, Cecily, 62; John, 44
Verries, Joseph, 91
Villiers, Barbara, 17
Vincent, Capt. John, 17; William, 151-2
Vine, family, 131-3
Waldegrave, Lord, 118
Wall, George, 113
Walrond, Mr, 127
Walter, Lucy, 17
Walton, 147, 174
Warbeck, Perkin, 44-5
Ward, Dr Samuel, 127
Wardropere, William, 116
Warham, William, archbp of Canterbury, 53
Warman, Hugh and Margaret, 90
Warminster, Wilts, 161
Warre, Richard, 46; Thomas, 90
Warren, W, 66-7; William, 168-9
Watchet, 66-7, 134
Watts, John, 138; Nicholas, 139
Way, Charles, 168
Wedlake, James, 175-7
Wedmore, 101, 113
Weekes, James, 140
Welde, William, 85
Welles, Tobias, 92
Wellesley (Wesley), Arthur, duke of Wellington, 12-13;

Richard, earl of Mornington, Baron Wellesley, 12
Wellington, 147, 152, 165
Wellow, 115-16
Wells, Hugh of, bp of Lincoln, 30-31, 97; Jocelin of, bp of Bath, 30-32, 97; John, friar, 87
Wells, 30-2, 35, 42, 44, 50, 100, 133, 148, 150, 159; cathedral, 31, 33, 35, 39, 50, 53, 72, 125, 147, 159, 162; courts, 41; Dean and Chapter, 11; Deanery, 45; hospital, 31; inns, 72-3, 78; Palace, 32, 48, 147, 157; prison, 11; St Cuthbert's, 77; Theological College, 169; Wellesley, 12
Wescombe, Henry, 91
West, Francis, 121; Thomas, 64; family, 121-2
Weston, 146
Weston super Mare, 13, 131-3, 150, 178-9
Westonzoyland, 25, 53, 77, 96, 138, 179-80
Westover, Hugh de, 74

Whalley, Thomas Sedgwick, 162-4; family, 162
Wharton, Humphrey, 91
Wheeler, Mr, 135
Whitchurch, 179
Whitelackington, 16, 46
Whitelaw, 174
Whitley, hundred, 137
Wickham, Joseph, 65
Willcox, Richard, 127
William the cobbler, 72
Williams, John, 41; Robert, 68
Williton, 128; Doniford, 179-80
Willoughby, Lord, 45
Wills, H. O., Baron Dulverton, 13
Willynge, Hugh, 62
Wilmot, John, earl of Rochester, 122-3; family, 122
Wilton, Wilts, 10
Wimborne, Dors, 10
Wincanton, 78, 100, 107, 132, 140, 150
Winchester, 8-9, 44, 158; bp of, 97, 100; college, 160; gaol, 38; monks, 28
Windsor, Berks, 34-5, 146; castle, 47

Winford, Felton, 177
Winsham, 30
Witcombe, John, 100
Witham Friary, 12
Wiveliscombe, 112
Wolsey, Thomas, cardinal, 46, 48, 74-6
Woode, Peter and Mary, 90
Woodforde, Parson, 128
Woodlands, East, 110-11; West, 110-11
Wookey, 58; Wookey Hole, 147
Woolavington, 58, 165
Woolverton, 89, 110-11
Wootton Courtenay, 116-17
Worthy, William, 85
Wotton, George, 91; Joseph, 91
Wraxall, 16, 54-5, 129-30; Charlton, 15
Wrington, 12, 128; Lulsgate, 179
Writhlington, 166
Wryde, Stephen, 64; William, 64
Wylmotte, boatman, 25
Yarlington, 140
Yatton, 50
Yeovil, 13, 69, 100, 129-30, 133, 155, 167, 179
Younge, Nicholas, 40